Klaus Ernst, born in 1936, was a student of the doyen of Marxist African studies in the German Democratic Republic, Walter Markov. Employed since 1962 by the Africa and Middle East Department at Karl Marx University Leipzig, he made a considerable contribution to founding and developing a sociology of the developing countries in the GDR. After several field studies, he received his doctor's degree on the sociological problems involved in transforming agriculture in Mali. At present he is working on social classes in Africa, heads the research group on "Sociology in Developing Countries" attached to the Africa and Middle East Department of Leipzig University and is vice-president of the research committee into "Imperialism and the National Movements" at the International Sociological Society.

His main works so far are: „**Tradition und Fortschritt im afrikanischen Dorf**" (1973) and „**Soziale Prozesse und Strukturen im gegenwärtigen Afrika**" (a collection of essays of which he was the editor, published in 1975).

Klaus Ernst

Tradition and Progress in the African Village

Tradition and Progress in the African Village:
Non-Capitalist Transformation of Rural Communities in Mali

Klaus Ernst

ST. MARTIN'S PRESS · NEW YORK

English translation © C. Hurst & Co. (Publishers) Ltd., 1976
First published in 1973 by Akademie-Verlag, Berlin, as Tradition und Fortschritt im afrikanischen Dorf, in: Studies of Asia, Africa and Latin America, vol. 6, edited by the Central Council of Asian, African and Latin American Sciences in the GDR under the direction of Lothar Rathmann.
Translated from the original German by Salomea Genin, edited by Jürgen Herzog.

All rights reserved. For information, write:
St. Martin's Press, Inc., 175 Fifth Avenue, New York, N. Y. 10010
Library of Congress Catalog Card Number: 74 — 22292
First published in the United States of America in 1976
Printed in the German Democratic Republic.

Contents

Foreword to the English edition

Introduction
- The African village and non-capitalist development 9
- Prerequisites and essence of non-capitalist development 10
- Why is transformation of the village on non-capitalist lines necessary? 15

1. The conception of non-capitalist transformation of the traditional community in Mali 27
1.1. The Sudanese Union and its „*option socialiste*" 27
1.2. The „*action rurale*" 33
1.2.1. Basic orientation: development of the productive forces plus cooperatives 33
1.2.2. Traditionalist illusions and the danger of left-wing radicalism ... 38

2. The traditional community in pre-colonial Malinese society 58

3. The traditional community today and its significance for non-capitalist transformation 69
3.1. Colonial exploitation and the persistency of traditional economic and social structures 69
3.2. Traditional structures — an obstacle for economic and social progress 79
3.3. The traditional community and the political foundations for non-capitalist development 91

4. Spontaneous decay of traditional structures and the problems of non-capitalist transformation 117
4.1. Foundations, phenomena and causes of decay in traditional structures 117
4.2. New conditions for economic and social progress 133
4.3. The struggle for non-capitalist agrarian market relations 141

5. The gradual development of capitalist production 172
5.1. Veiled forms of exploitation through traditional conditions 172
5.2. Navétanes, landlords, planters and „bureaucratic" agrarian bourgeoisie 185

6.	Striking a balance	200
6.1.	Positive results and lagging behind the given tasks	200
6.2.	Objective and subjective obstacles for non-capitalist transformation	202

Conclusions

From the traditional community to social progress in the African village	205
Basic social, economic and political problems of non-capitalist transformation in the village	205
Elimination of colonial structures	205
Non-capitalist transformation of traditional community structures	209
Spontaneous development of capitalism in agriculture	216
The role of the state and peasantry in the non-capitalist transformation of agriculture	217
Appendix	225
Glossary of Bambara words	243
Bibliography	245

Foreword to the English edition

It is doubtless very satisfying for any author when his book is published in a foreign language shortly after it has appeared in his native tongue. In this case, I am particularly glad that it is coming out in English, not only because the readership is enlarged, but also because the book is now accessible to those to whom the German version was dedicated and whose assessment I especially value: namely, those African friends, colleagues and comrades who have devoted themselves to the complicated and difficult struggle for social progress in the African village.

This study is based on the conception that after political independence has been gained, the peoples of Africa are faced with two main and closely inter-linked tasks: on the one hand, the struggle against neo-colonial dependence and exploitation and, on the other, overcoming colonial economic and social backwardness which is connected with corresponding colonially deformed structures. In this connection, the economic and social transformation of agriculture is of particular significance. This is emphasized also by the tragic drought and resulting starvation in recent years in the Sahel areas, of which a decisive cause is that it has not yet been possible to overcome the colonial heritage in the African village.

One specific feature of the agrarian question in large parts of sub-Saharan Africa is that colonialism undermined the traditional pre-capitalist mode of production based on undeveloped productive forces, the subsistence economy and common ownership (in the form of the village communities) by integrating it into its system of colonial and neo-colonial exploitation and adapting it to the needs of this system. However, the inherent laws of this system (above all the development of commodity-money relations) led only to the traditional forms being undermined, without actually transforming them. Thus the traditional mode of production was largely preserved on the basis of a stagnation caused by colonial and neo-colonial exploitation, and the productive forces were simply mutilated and pauperized to be reproduced in an increasingly crippled form.

One of the basic problems for a solution of the agrarian question in Africa is to overcome the preserved, deformed and mutilated community relations which have arisen from the effects of the laws of social development at work through colonial and neo-colonial exploitation and dependence. A progressive development cannot consist in growing capitalist relations, not only because this is in contradiction to the interests of the broad mass of the peasants, but mainly because it is a law of social development that within a world capitalist market controlled by the super-monopolies, it is impossible to overcome backwardness. As a result of this law of imperialist exploitation, the solution to the agrarian question in Africa can be found only on the basis of a socialist orientation made possible by changed international relations of power.

This book seeks to analyse the multifarious and complicated problems involved in overcoming the preserved and deformed community relations resulting from colonialism in the spirit of a socialist orientation, through the example of the experiences of the Republic of Mali during the years 1960–1968. The phenomena, tendencies, problems and contradictions which come to light are in my opinion (even though this attempt to revolutionise society could not be successfully concluded) very valuable, because this experience can be used to solve the agrarian question in Africa in a spirit of social progress.

The material for this book was mainly collected in the course of several journeys to Mali, where I received every possible help from a large number of institutions, officials and authorities to whom I would here like to express my sincere gratitude. Many colleagues at home and abroad gave me valuable aid in assessing the material. To them too, particularly to Walter Markov (Leipzig) and Jean Suret-Canale (Paris), I say: thank you.

The character of the book – a case study limited in time and area – made it possible to translate unchanged the German edition of 1973. Only in some places were formulations made more exact, the statistics in the introduction brought up to date and the latest literature added.

I am particularly obliged to Jürgen Herzog (Berlin) for his great care in preparing the English manuscript, for which he applied his well-founded knowledge of both the subject-matter and the English language.

Klaus Ernst

Introduction

The African village and non-capitalist development

After achieving political independence, the struggle of Africa's nations entered a new stage. It is now directed against neo-colonial dependence and exploitation within the framework of the world capitalist economic system and towards overcoming colonial backwardness and deformation of the economy and social relations as a whole. Both aspects are very closely inter-woven because, on the one hand, elimination of dependence on imperialism and exploitation are inseparable from overcoming colonial backwardness and, on the other, backwardness and under-development are continually reproduced through neo-colonial dependency and imperialist exploitation, or as the documents of the 4th Summit Conference of the Non-Aligned Countries state, imperialism has proved to be the biggest obstacle to progress in the developing countries.[1]

The struggle of the peoples in the so-called Third World against neo-colonial exploitation, dependence and backwardness cannot be seen in isolation. It is an integral part of a world-wide revolutionary process of transition from capitalist exploitation to socialism, for which the decisive strength lies in the world socialist system.[2] As one of the current main anti-imperialist forces, those people fighting against neo-colonial dependence and exploitation are making an outstanding contribution to changing the international relations of power and to breaking down imperialist rule. This becomes visible particularly in the present stage of the general crisis of capitalism. At the same time, through the successful struggle of other departments of the world-wide anti-imperialist movement – especially through the growing strength of the socialist world and the significant result of its policy of peace and detente, but also through the upsurge of the proletarian movement in the main imperialist countries – more favourable conditions arise for the solution of the problems of those people in the „Third World" fighting for economic independence and social progress. Above all, the change in the international relations of power opens up the prospect for a gradual but definite breakthrough of the vicious circle: dependence – backwardness – dependence, on the road of a non-capitalist development.[3]

Prerequisites and essence of non-capitalist development

The Marxist-Leninist theory of non-capitalist development to socialism is based on the conception that our epoch is one of world transition from capitalism to socialism, a transition begun with the 1917 Socialist October Revolution in Russia. It is historically possible and also necessary for nations to build socialism even during this epoch of struggle between the two antagonistic social systems.

Lenin understood the victory of the October Revolution as being the beginning of a worldwide revolutionary change, taking place as a complex process over a whole epoch in which various elements link together and in which what has happened in one place gains international recognition or will be repeated with historical inevitability on an international scale.[4] He proved that socialism would not make a detour around the colonially oppressed countries, but that the historical place and function of the national liberation movement is determined by the character of our epoch – worldwide transition from capitalism to socialism – and that the national liberation struggle will, of historical necessity, become a struggle for social progress.[5]

In further development of the ideas of Marx and Engels[6], after an analysis of the character of our epoch, Lenin came to the conclusion in 1920 that with the help of the proletariat from the more progressive countries, the colonially oppressed nations would be able to achieve socialism in future "without having to pass through the capitalist stage of development"[7].

With the establishment and consolidation of the world socialist system, the international conditions arose both for the collapse of the imperialist colonial system and for the solution of the burning issues in the Asian and African countries on the road to social progress. "The establishment and consolidation of the world socialist system have strongly accelerated the historical progress begun with the October Revolution. New prospects have opened up for the triumph of socialism."[8] The existence and growing strength of the world socialist system and its successes in the struggle between the two systems increasingly limit the possibilities of imperialist pressure and strengthen the positions of the developing countries in the struggle against neo-colonialism; they also create the prerequisites for the developing countries gradually to free themselves from the system of neo-colonial dependence and exploitation and deepen their economic, political, cultural and other relations with the socialist states, with the prospect "that some developing countries, even before the transition to socialism, take part in the international socialist division of labour"[9]. At the same time, the experiences gained by other socialist countries in the application of Lenin's revolutionary theory — in particular in the Central Asian Soviet Republics and the Mongolian People's Republic[10] — are an indispensable signpost for the revolutionary forces of the developing countries in their struggle. Further strengthening of the socialist states and steady consolidation of the alliance between the socialist states and the progressive young states which have liberated themselves from the colonial yoke are an important prerequisite for social progress in the developing countries, and the struggle for strengthening the alliance with the Soviet Union and the other socialist states is an integral part of the struggle by the revolutionary forces in these countries for social progress.

The necessity for a transitional period within the developing countries on the road to social progress results from the inner contradictions and laws of the world imperialist economic system to which they are still attached. The relations of non-equality, dependence and exploitation between the imperialist countries and the developing countries, which have resulted for the former colonies within the world capitalist economy, are not removed after political independence is achieved, but are simply modified and further reproduced,[11] so that the economic and social gap between them is widened. This becomes very clear when comparing the development of the gross social product from 1950 to 1972.

Gross Social Product per capita (in dollars)[12]

	1950	1960	1972
Developed capitalist countries	1,080	1,417	2,775
Developing countries	105	132	210
of these: Africa	93	105	160
Gap between developed capitalist countries and the developing countries	10 times	11 times	13 times
Africa	11 times	13 times	17 times

Under imperialist conditions, the technological revolution does not overcome this gap, but leads to a new, neo-colonial division of labour on the basis of which neo-colonial exploitation is further increased because the main imperialist powers monopolise the latest technology, scientific research, etc.[13]

Thus the capitalist road of development proved inadequate for overcoming colonial backwardness in the developing countries and for solving their economic and social problems; this was because it necessitates the developing countries remaining part of the world capitalist economic system and thus subject to the social laws inherent in this system. Elimination of the cause of colonial backwardness and social progress can be achieved only through socialist orientation.

It is a new element in the class struggles of the developing countries at present "that the struggle for national liberation in many countries is becoming a struggle against exploitation – both feudal and capitalist"[14]. In view of the necessity – and the possibility – of achieving social and economic progress without passing through capitalism, the revolutionary forces are now more urgently faced with the question of how to take which concrete measures necessary for their countries on the road to socialism. In the majority of developing countries (particularly those in sub-Saharan Africa), their colonial past has prevented the prerequisites for an immediate transition to socialism from arising. Here, the level of the productive forces and labour productivity are extremely low, and pre-capitalist – sometimes even pre-feudal – production conditions determine social and economic relations (this is an objective factor independent of human consciousness). But what is missing above all is the political and ideological pre-condition for a socialist revolution (this is the subjective factor resulting from the human will): a well-organised working class and a strong Marxist-Leninist party which is capable of mobilizing the masses for socialism.[15]

These facts have caused imperialist ideologists, who realise that open propaganda for capitalism does not meet with much response in the developing countries, to present the theory of a so-called third path, because the capitalist and socialist roads – both of "western origin" – are allegedly unsuitable for them. However, in the final analysis, their "third" road ends in capitalism.

For example, Richard F. Behrendt writes: "Both [socialism and capitalism, K. E.] are of western origin and offer models of development on western patterns which are equally unsuitable for the present developing countries ..." Therefore, the developing countries should take the road of an "*active-syncretic acculturation*". In the process "... they would also realise that they will have to take over the essential renewals of capitalism which are valid for every development in our sense, if they want to pursue an effective policy of development."[16]

The aim of splitting the anti-imperialist front and separating the national liberation movement from its natural allies – the world socialist system and the international working class movement – is pursued both by the bourgeois conception of a so-called third path and the Maoist ideology of "struggle of the small countries against the big", the "poor against the rich countries", etc.[17] The policy of the Maoist group serves imperialism, whose neo-colonialist policy is to prevent the national democratic revolution from making progress and a revolutionary bloc of states taking the non-capitalist road in firm alliance to the socialist camp.[18] The conceptions of bourgeois or petty-bourgeois ideologists in the developing countries, who present one or the other variant of a "specific" socialism with a national or regional stamp, also serve either as a conscious cover-up for the capitalist road or objectively encourage it.[19]

The historically realistic alternative to capitalism in the developing countries is the non-capitalist road of development, which "makes it possible to overcome the backwardness left from the colonial past and to create conditions for transition to a socialist development."[20] For the developing countries it is the realistic path to social progress − taking into consideration their actual internal conditions − and to realising the main content of our epoch.

In its essence, the non-capitalist road is a transitional period − both as regards the relations of power and its historical function − whose duration and concrete phenomena depend largely on the conditions of each country, in particular on the social and economic level of development, the degree of class differentiation and the character of its driving forces.

In those countries taking the non-capitalist road, state power is exercised not by the working class in alliance with other working strata, owing to local historical conditions, but by a broad bloc led by progressive − generally revolutionary and democratic − intellectuals. This bloc embraces the growing proletariat as well as the petty-bourgeois stratum in the city and countryside, up to elements of the national bourgeoisie who advocate a progressive social development on an anti-imperialist basis.[21]

The function of the non-capitalist road is to create the material, technical, social, economic, political, ideological and cultural prerequisites for the transition to socialism through conscious re-organisation of society. That means: in the developing countries it prepares the objective and subjective factors for socialism − while by-passing or breaking off capitalist developments − which in the developed capitalist countries constituted the historic mission of the capitalist system.

In line with its function, the main tasks[22] of non-capitalist development are

(1) speedy development of the productive forces and overcoming the colonially deformed economic structure;

(2) far-reaching re-organisation of social and economic conditions with the aim of creating a strong state and co-operative sector, displacement of foreign monopolies in the national economy, speedy overcoming of pre-capitalist structures and setting limitations for national capital to develop privately;

(3) stabilisation of national-democratic state power by consolidating the alliance of the working people under the leadership of the democratic revo-

lutionary forces; strengthening the role of the working class in this alliance and consciously preparing it organisationally, politically and ideologically for its leading role in completing the national-democratic revolution and in the transition to socialist revolution [23]; solving the problems of a close alliance with the peasants; removing the bourgeoisie from a monopoly of power and further gradual limitation of its political influence as well as persistent fending-off of counter-revolutionary forces at home and abroad;
(4) raising living standards and improving the health of the working people, and increasing their general political and ideological maturity as well as their cultural level.

These are general, long-term tasks which cannot be carried out at one blow. Events in sub-Saharan Africa and in other parts of the so-called Third World have shown clearly that hasty measures, showing petty-bourgeois impatience, are a danger to non-capitalist development. Therefore, the communist and workers' parties have given clear warnings against voluntarism and left-wing radicalism in the national liberation movement.[24]

The non-capitalist road is a polymorphous and complicated process of development over several stages. Here we see the validity of Lenin's words that "in a country where the overwhelming majority of the population consist of small agricultural producers a socialist revolution can be carried out only through the implementation of a whole series of special transitional measures"[25], and in the practice of class struggle it is necessary to find those links which will drive society in a socialist direction.

The measures taken in the process of non-capitalist development are a complex of anti-imperialist, anti-feudal and increasingly anti-capitalist changes brought about by revolutionary and democratic or already socialist methods. This means that where revolutionary persistency is maintained, the non-capitalist path leads to socialism without directly mastering the tasks of socialism. The dominating factor is the generally democratic social program in the struggle against imperialism, pre-capitalist forces of exploitation and the reactionary upper strata of the local bourgeoisie and their social and political allies.

The tasks which the revolutionary forces must fulfill today on the non-capitalist path were formulated by Lenin in a talk to the communist organisations of the peoples of the east as follows: "Relying upon the general theory and practice of communism, you must adapt yourselves to specific conditions such as do not exist in the European countries: you must be able to apply that theory and practice to conditions in which the bulk of the population are peasants, and in which the task is to wage a struggle against medieval survivals and not against capitalism. That is a difficult and specific task, but a very thankful one, because masses that have taken no part in the struggle up to now are being drawn into it ..."[26] Successful non-capitalist development is unthinkable without the creative application of the connections between the struggle for democracy and that for socialism – under the specific social, economic and class conditions of the liberated countries of Asia and Africa.

Why is transformation of the village on non-capitalist lines necessary?

One of the basic tasks of the national democratic revolution in the countries of sub-Saharan Africa is re-organisation and development of agriculture. It is the most important social field because its economic, social and political development determines the whole social process.

Agriculture is of great economic significance for the non-capitalist development of the African countries as a whole, but particularly in the initial phase. As a result of the economic policy it is the largest and at the same time most backward sector of the African countries' economies.[27] When French West Africa achieved independence, some 92% of the population belonged to this sector.[28] By 1970 only about 13% of the population in this sector lived in settlements with over 5,000 inhabitants.[29]

Percentage of rural population in some countries of sub-Saharan Africa (1970)[30]

Angola	90	Mali	92
Ivory Coast	81	Nigeria	85
Upper Volta	96	Senegal	72
Zaire	85	Somalia	88
Zambia	75	Tanzania	94
Kenya	92	Uganda	93
Congo	70	Ethiopia	95

In a large number of African countries, particularly in sub-Saharan Africa, most of the Gross National Product (GNP) is produced in agriculture.[31] This applies particularly to the national income obtained from exports. A survey of the most important countries of sub-Saharan Africa shows that – so long as they do not expressly export wood or have a strong extractive industry[32] – the largest number of exported products are agricultural.

Percentage of agricultural products compared to total export of countries in sub-Saharan Africa (end of 1960 s)[33]

Ethiopia	99	Ivory Coast	70
Mali	97	Ghana	69
Chad	95	Nigeria	65
Somalia	90	Togo	53
Uganda	89	CAR	44
Senegal	87	Liberia	43
Tanzania	78	Congo	6
Kenya	75	Zambia	2

Agriculture is important for the solution of economic problems in African countries in the spirit of social progress from at least three viewpoints:
(1) Because it constitutes such a large part of the economy in the sub-Saharan African countries as a whole, it is their main source of national accumulation.[34] Thus it has great significance in attempts to overcome quickly the colonially deformed structure of the whole economy and in particular for the construction of a national industry. Only by fully exploiting the agricultural resources will it be possible to gain the necessary investments for economic and social development, and to limit debts to countries abroad. Therefore, the under-estimation of the role of agriculture in the development process by some bourgeois industrialisation theoreticians does not lie in the interests of the developing countries, but aims further to deepen their dependence on the main imperialist powers and ensure favourable conditions for export of capital.[35]
(2) Speedy agricultural development is needed from a second viewpoint to overcome colonial backwardness and economic deformation, and particularly for a fast construction of industry. To a steadily growing degree, industrialisation demands: first, an active home market, and with the given structure of the population – especially during the initial stage – the basis will be mainly agriculture; secondly, a continual supply of high-quality agrarian raw materials for industry. If both are not guaranteed, the capacity of the factories will not be sufficiently used with a resulting lack of profit and a growing dependence on imports.[36]
(3) The need for food production for the non-agrarian population in the African countries is growing. As in Asia and Latin America, a large increase of population can be observed in Africa, particularly among city inhabitants whose number is now growing, on an average, two to three times more quickly than the total population.[37]

Population growth in Africa 1950–1971 (in 1,000)[38]

1950	1960	1965	1971	1965–71 (annual growth in %)
217	270	303	354	2.6

To avoid an increasing amount of state finances and particularly hard currency being used up for food imports instead of for economic and social development, the growing need for food must be met by homegrown produce.[39]

This shows the great importance of agricultural development in the African countries as a part of the general economic processes. On this will largely depend whether and how quickly the young states succeed in eliminating the economic basis for dependence on imperialism and setting the material prerequisites for victory of the non-capitalist road.

Solution of the agrarian problem in Africa is also of fundamental significance for building up the political foundations for non-capitalist development. The establishment and consolidation of an alliance between the leading democratic-revolutionary (and in future proletarian) forces with the peasants, who are the vast majority of the working people, is an important prerequisite for consolidating democratic national state power. At the Moscow Meeting of Communist and Workers' Parties in 1969, Leonid Brezhnev said: "Today the main issue of the revolutionary process in Asia and Africa is the position of the peasants, who are the majority of the population there."[40]

However, the agrarian and peasant question is decisive not only for demographic reasons. A special feature of this revolution is that its anti-imperialist content — the struggle to overcome economic and social backwardness — cannot be separated from the struggle of the peasants for democracy and against the remnants of pre-capitalist production relations conserved by colonialism. The democratic national revolution is largely an agrarian revolution; it cannot fulfill its tasks without social liberation of the peasant masses from pre-capitalist and imperialist exploitation and oppression.[41] Sometimes, the peasantry is not only the mass basis, but also an important driving force of the revolution. Thus the peasant masses have played an outstanding role in all phases of the anti-colonial struggle.[42] The speed and direction of developments and the guarantees for the non-capitalist path depend largely on the breadth and depth of the peasant movement, its social effectiveness and the consolidation of the alliance between the leading revolutionary forces and the peasantry.

Effective utilisation of African agricultural resources for economic and social development, and political mobilisation of the peasants is at present being hindered by a number of obstacles. This applies particularly to the technical and economic aspects. In most African agricultural areas, the level of the productive forces is very low, largely due to use of the hand hoe, land clearance, a rhythm of production dictated by ancient rites, and the lack of a productive link between farming and cattle-breeding.[43] This results in low labour productivity, which is expressed in the small amount of arable land per head of population and low yields per acre. According to UN statistics, ten labourers in African agriculture are able to produce food for only 10–15 people.[44] This very low labour productivity causes a high degree of subsistence economy. The producer is forced to use most of his labour power for production of his own means of subsistence. This means low commodity production, a very modest income and very small buying power for the peasants.

Percentage of subsistence economy in agrarian production of some African countries[45]

Burundi	84	Chad	64
Ethiopia	79	Kenya	60
Mali	78	Tanzania	55
Malawi	75	Ivory Coast	50
CAR	70	Senegal	40
Zambia	67	Rhodesia	27

This low level of economic development in traditional African agriculture means that a significant sector of the African economy is still not able to meet the economic demands placed on it by national development. So it is now a question of developing the productive forces and increasing labour productivity, overcoming the subsistence economy and diversifying the structure of production — which means developing the production of industrial plant and animal raw material (for export and the national industry) with a proper relationship between production of food for national requirements and for export.[46]

Colonial economic and social backwardness and exploitation condemns the peasant masses to a life of poverty, self-supporting isolation and dispersion, religious superstitution, and illiteracy, thus preventing all political mobilisation. The theoreticians of the national liberation movement — in line with the anti-Marxist Maoist "revolution strategy"[47] — contradict objective historical facts when they claim a leading role in the national liberation movements for the peasants and declare them to be the only revolutionary force. For example, Frantz Fanon writes in his book *Les damnés de la terre*: "... Only the peasantry in the colonial countries is revolutionary. It has nothing to lose and everything to gain ..."[48]

However, the history of the national liberation movement confirms clearly the thesis of Marx, Engels and Lenin resulting from the investigation of class struggle in their own and earlier times, that the peasant masses can be the main partners of both a rising bourgeoisie and a revolutionary proletariat, and no contemporary revolutionary movement can triumph without establishing an alliance with them. Engels writes: "... The agricultural population ... never can attempt a successful independent movement; they require the initiatory impulse of the more concentrated, more enlightened, more easily moved people of the towns"[49]. This more flexible city population in Africa today is the democratic revolutionary intelligentsia and, to an increasing extent, will become the working class.

But it is not only the low level of the productive forces and the isolation and narrowness resulting from a subsistence economy which is an obstacle to economic growth and consolidation of the alliance with the peasantry, but it is to at least an equal degree, the social and political structures of the village left behind by the colonial period.

As the result of colonial rule, the African peasant masses are subjected to a system of multifold exploitation by foreign monopoly trade capital, a national trade and usury capital which arose in the shadow of the former, a rich semi-feudal and semi-capitalist peasantry and a developing parasitic bureaucratic bourgeoisie.[50] These forces – particularly foreign monopoly capital – acquire their modest surplus product through non-equivalent exchange – forced on them under colonial rule by non-economic means – and by sheer robbery. This particularly reactionary variation of the unfolding of capital conditions – control of production by trade capital – means withdrawal of a large part of the national income by foreign and local firms which have no interest in developing the national economy. It also means stagnation of the productive forces and economic and social processes as well as political oppression of the peasants.

So a solution to agrarian problems in sub-Saharan Africa necessitates far-reaching social and economic changes. It requires above all that the peasant producers be no longer subjected to foreign monopoly capital and local parasitic bureaucratic, trade and usury capital; that pre-capitalist conditions of exploitation be liquidated; and that the possibilities for capitalist development be curbed.

However, no matter how important and basic such measures may be, the agrarian revolution in the countries of sub-Saharan Africa cannot be limited to such measures alone. Their specific nature is largely dictated by the existence and part-domination of socalled traditional[51], pre-capitalist community structures in the agrarian sector. These structures were preserved and deformed by colonialism and were then adapted to imperialist exploitation. They are a micro-system of social relations which have developed on the basis of a low degree of control over nature by man, and contain at a low level all essential prerequisites for ensuring subsistence and for reproduction of the communal structure. The structure lacks any driving force to develop the productive forces and make social or economic changes; this is due to its isolation, its simple production organism and its primitive system of production and distribution. The traditional communities have the tendency to reproduce themselves economically and socially at the same level. Thus they become a decisive obstacle to the speedy economic development of African agriculture. And their economic and social isolation and narrowness, their fossilised social and political structures – plus the ideology of the traditional community directed at the reproduction of what already exists – also greatly impede an alliance with the mass of peasants and the penetration of revolutionary ideology into the village.

Thus overcoming traditional structures becomes a central task for the solution of the agrarian question in sub-Saharan Africa. As in all decisive questions of development, the attitude of the different social forces to the traditional structures and how to overcome them depends on the various class interests.

Under colonialism, the imperial powers were interested in conserving the traditional community in West and Central Africa, because it seemed the form best suited to the economic exploitation and political oppression of the peasant masses.[52] Today there are many bourgeois conceptions of tradition, but in the final analysis they add up to nothing more than the establishment of capitalism in agriculture.[53] This aim is generally veiled by a seemingly class-indifferent question of "Tradition-Modernisation". And by modernisation they always mean on the western pattern – "occidentalisation"[54]. "In this sense I believe that modernisation ultimately produces libertarian systems", writes the American political scientist David Apter.[55] The bourgeois theoreticians' fears of possible revolutionary developments leads them to seek starting-points for a gradual evolutionary transformation to capitalism in the traditional societies.[56]

The concepts of pro-capitalist African leaders differ little in ideological content from their West European or American models. For them tradition serves simply to "cover up existing social conditions, the developing social differentiation and subordination of general interests to individual reactionary interests of the local bourgeoisie, of whom many are closely linked with imperialism"[57].

The program set up by the revolutionary democrats in a number of African states differs fundamentally from such views.[58] It aims at a non-capitalist – often declared as a socialist – path via agricultural co-operatives.[59] It is here that they see the possibilities of a transition from the traditional community to social progress. However, their conceptions are often linked with illusions about the village community similar to those held by the Narodny movement in Tsarist Russia, or with radical views about the co-operative road.[60]

The Marxist-Leninist theory of a non-capitalist development considers the traditional structures to be of great importance. While taking into account the general laws of social development and the character of our epoch, this theory states that traditional, pre-capitalist community conditions must be overcome because of their backward social and political character in order to open up the road to social progress, but that today it is not inevitable for capitalism to follow. The Marxist-Leninists are of the opinion that at present it is possible, within the framework of general non-capitalist social changes, to overcome traditional village conditions in the direction of a co-operative via various intermediate stages and thus create the prerequisites for socialism without the African peasant of necessity having to experience the tortuous road of capitalist development.[61]

In this process it is possible to use certain elements of the traditional structures, not in order to conserve them[62], but to direct them into the non-capitalist path, with the aim of overcoming them at a higher level of economic development.

The real possibility of non-capitalist development out of traditional community conditions is one of the results of the triumphant forward march of socialism on a world scale. It is a phenomenon of our epoch, unique in the development of mankind. All the more valuable are the experiences, both positive and negative, gained by various nations in trying to take the non-capitalist path. One of these – the Malinese experience – is the subject of the following examination.

REFERENCES

1. 4th Summit Conference of the Non-Aligned Countries, Algiers, September 1973, Economic Declaration.
2. See *Internationale Beratung der kommunistischen und Arbeiterparteien* (Moscow 1969), Berlin 1969, p. 25; *Rechenschaftsbericht des Zentralkomitees der KPdSU an den XXIV. Parteitag der Kommunistischen Partei der Sowjetunion.* Speaker: L. I. Brezhnev, Moscow/Berlin 1971, pp. 9ff; *VIII. Parteitag der Sozialistischen Einheitspartei Deutschlands* (Berlin 1971), Bericht des Zentralkomitees an den VIII. Parteitag der Sozialistischen Einheitspartei Deutschlands. Speaker: Genosse E. Honecker, Berlin 1971, pp. 11–12.
   For the role of the national liberation movement during the revolutionary world process see L. Rathmann et al., *Grundfragen des antiimperialistischen Kampfes der Völker Asiens, Afrikas und Lateinamerikas in der Gegenwart*, part 1, Berlin 1974, pp. 1–211.
3. Comprehensive Marxist-Leninist literature exists on the problem of non-capitalist development. The following can give only a brief sketch. For further details, see L. Rathmann et al., op. cit., pp. 457–792; A. A. Iskenderov, *Die nationale Befreiungsbewegung. Probleme, Gesetzmäßigkeiten, Perspektiven*, Berlin 1972; Nichtkapitalistischer Entwicklungsweg. Aktuelle Probleme in Theorie und Praxis, Berlin 1972; *Non-Capitalist Way of Development in the Third World*, Warsaw 1971; V. G. Solodovnikov, *Nekotorye voprosy teorii i praktiki nekapitalističeskogo puti razvitija*, Moscow 1971; R. A. Ulyanovski, *Der Sozialismus und die befreiten Länder*, Berlin 1973; *Razvivajuščiesja strany: zakonomernosti, tendencii, perspektivy*, Moscow 1974.
4. V. I. Lenin, *"Left-Wing" Communism – an Infantile Disorder*, in: Collected Works, vol. 31, Moscow 1966, p. 21.
5. V. I. Lenin, Third Congress of the Communist International, *Report on the Tactics of the R. C. P.*, in: Collected Works, vol. 32, Moscow 1965, p. 482.

6 In their dispute with the Russian Narodniki, Marx and Engels deal in particular with the transition from pre-capitalist conditions to socialism. They reached the conclusion that the old Russian village community of the nineteenth century can be spared the capitalist path only if the Russian (bourgeois) revolution becomes the signal for the proletarian revolution in western Europe and if both supplement each other. (See: K. Marx, *First Draft of the Reply to V. I. Zasulich's Letter*, in: K. Marx/F. Engels, *Selected Works*, vol. 3, Progress Publishers, Moscow 1973, p. 152, and F. Engels, "On Social Relations in Russia" (article V from *Flüchtlingsliteratur*), in: ibid., vol. 2, p. 395).
7 V. I. Lenin, The Second Congress of the Communist International. *Report of the Commission on the National and Colonial Questions*, in: *Collected Works*, vol. 31, Moscow 1966, p. 244.
8 *Rechenschaftsbericht des Zentralkomitees der KPdSU an den XXIV. Parteitag der Kommunistischen Partei der Sowjetunion*, loc. cit., p. 9.
9 V. G. Solodovnikov, "Die gegenwärtige Entwicklung der afrikanischen Staaten und ihre aktuellen Probleme", in: *Asien, Afrika, Lateinamerika*, Berlin, 3/1073, p. 99.
10 See Th. Büttner/B. Brentjes/R. Felber, "Revolution und Tradition in den Ländern Afrikas und Asiens", in: *Revolution und Tradition. Zur Rolle der Tradition im anti-imperialistischen Kampf der Völker Afrikas und Asiens*, Leipzig 1971, pp. 44—51.
11 See *Razvivajuščiesja strany*, loc. cit., pp. 20ff.
12 Compiled from A. Oresz, *Einige wichtige Probleme der Erzeugung des gesellschaftlichen Bruttoproduktes, des Wachstums der industriellen und landwirtschaftlichen Produktion der Entwicklungsländer*, Budapest 1966, p. 14; *Afrika. Ekonomičeskij spravočnik*, Moscow 1974, p. 35.
13 See *Razvivajuščiesja strany*, loc. cit., pp. 79ff.
14 *Rechenschaftsbericht des Zentralkomitees der KPdSU an den XXIV. Parteitag der Kommunistischen Partei der Sowjetunion*, loc. cit., p. 25.
15 See R. A. Ulyanovski, "Besonderheiten und Schwierigkeiten der nationaldemokratischen Revolution auf dem nichtkapitalistischen Entwicklungsweg", in: *Einheit*, Berlin, 6/70, pp. 786—9.
16 R. F. Behrendt, *Soziale Strategie für Entwicklungsländer*, Frankfurt am Main 1968, p. 637 and p. 209. For critical polemics with other West German bourgeois conceptions of development see: K. Hutschenreuter, "New Disciplines of Science in the System of West German Neo-colonialist Policy", in: *Theories on Africa and Neo-Colonialism*, Leipzig 1971, pp. 39—62.
17 See K. Hager, *Die entwickelte sozialistische Gesellschaft. Aufgaben der Gesellschaftswissenschaften nach dem VIII. Parteitag der SED. Referat auf der Tagung der Gesellschaftswissenschaftler am 14. Oktober 1971 in Berlin*, Berlin 1971, pp. 66—7.
18 See M. Kossok, "Die nationale Befreiungsbewegung im weltrevolutionären Prozess der Gegenwart", in: *Zeitschrift für Geschichtswissenschaft*, Berlin, 1 and 2/1969, p. 156.

19 See Y. Bénot, *Idéologies des indépendances africaines*, Paris 1969, pp. 169—92; I. Cox, *Socialist Ideas in Africa*, London 1966.
20 *Internationale Beratung der kommunistischen und Arbeiterparteien*, loc. cit., p. 33.
21 See R. A. Ulyanovski, "Besonderheiten und Schwierigkeiten der national-demokratischen Revolution auf dem nichtkapitalistischen Entwicklungsweg", loc. cit., pp. 794—5.
22 See A. Sobolev, „Einige Probleme des sozialen Fortschritts in Afrika", in: G. Liebig, *Nationale und soziale Revolution in Afrika*, Berlin 1967. pp. 108—9; *Klassen und Klassenkampf in den Entwicklungsländern*, vol. 3, Berlin 1970 pp. 289—324.
23 Developments in Ghana have shown that an under-estimation of the role of the working class not only places doubts on a socialist future, but can have very negative effects for the revolution already in the non-capitalist phase. (See T. Otegbeye, "Leninism and the Problems of Revolution in Africa", in: *World Marxist Review*, 8/1970).
24 *Internationale Beratung der kommunistischen und Arbeiterparteien*, loc. cit., pp. 232ff.; U. Bagdache, "V. I. Lenin and the Struggle against Opportunism and Revisionism in the National Liberation Movement"', in: *World Marxist Review*, 4/1970.
25 V. I. Lenin, Tenth Congress of the R. C. P. (B). *Report on the Substitution of a Tax in Kind for the Surplus-Grain Appropriation System*, in: *Collected Works*, vol. 32, Moscow 1965, p. 214.
26 V. I. Lenin, *Address to the 2nd All-Russia Congress of Communist Organisations of the Peoples of the East*, in: *Collected Works*, vol. 30, Moscow 1965, p. 161.
27 On the significance and development of African agriculture in general, see I. A. Svanidze, *Sel'skoe chozjajstvo tropičestkoj Afriki*, Moscow 1972; S. Münch, "Grundfragen des Aufbaus einer progressiven Landwirtschaft in den Ländern Asiens, Afrikas und Lateinamerikas", in: *Probleme des Aufbaus einer progressiven Landwirtschaft in den Entwicklungsländern*, Leipzig 1970.
28 See P. Viguier, *L'Afrique de l'Ouest vue par un agriculteur*, Paris 1961, p. 9.
29 See S. Amin, *L'Afrique de l'Ouest bloqués*, Paris 1971, p. 305.
30 See UN, ECA. *Statistical Yearbook 1973*, Addis Ababa 1974, part 1—4.
31 Altogether, almost 40% of the Gross National Product of the African development countries was produced in agriculture at the end of the 1960s. (See UN, ECA. *Survey of Economic Conditions in Africa*, (part I), New York 1971, p. 26). In countries whose economic structure is not stamped by a large amount of extractive and wood industry, over 50% and sometimes even more than 70% (Burundi) of the gross product was produced in agriculture. (See ibid., pp. 225—9).
32 These countries are not taken into account for the rest of this chapter.
33 FAO. *Trade Yearbook 1969*, vol. 23, Rome 1970, pp. 411—26.
34 See K.-J. Michalski, *Landwirtschaftliche Genossenschaften in afroasiatischen Entwicklungsländern*, Berlin 1974.
35 See A. Kress, "On the Function of Neo-Colonialist Industrialisation Models", in: *Theories on Africa and Neo-Colonialism*, Leipzig 1971, pp. 79—102.

36 See *Afrika. Kleines Nachschlagewerk*, Berlin 1970, pp. 86 ff.
37 From 1950 to 1970, the average urbanisation rate in sub-Saharan Africa was around 6—7%. (See S. I. Kuznecova, *Social'naja struktura afrikanskogo goroda*, Moscow 1972, pp. 166—7). However, the big cities like Dacar, Abijan, Lagos, Nairobi, etc. have growth rates of over 10%. (See M. Petit-Pont, *Structures traditionelles et développement*, Paris 1968, p. 44 and p. 288; *Employment, Incomes and Equality. A Strategy for Increasing Productive Employment in Kenya*, ILO Geneva 1972, p. 49).
38 See UN. Statistical Yearbook 1972, New York 1973. The annual increase of 2.6% is higher than in other regions of the "Third World" (Asia 2.3% and Latin America 2.4%). See ibid.
39 At present, the countries of sub-Saharan Africa as a whole — in contrast to those of the Middle and Far East — do not import food, but the food export decreased by 20% from the mid-fifties to mid-1960s because of rising demand and stagnating production, and this resulted in less hard currency being made available. (See J. Guiffan, *Surpopulation et malnutrition*, Paris 1969, p. 73). This tendency is continuing in most countries of sub-Saharan Africa. Compared to 1961—5, the per capita production of food in 1972 sank in Nigeria to 88%, in Upper Volta to 89%, in Mali to 67% and in Senegal to 54%. (See UN, ECA. *Statistical Yearbook. West Africa 1973*, Addis Ababa 1974).
40 *Internationale Beratung der kommunistischen und Arbeiterparteien*, loc. cit., p. 191.
41 See *Agrarno-krestjanskij vopros v stranach Azii, Afriki i Latinskoj Ameriki*, Moscow 1965, p. 3.
42 For details see *Klassen und Klassenkampf in den Entwicklungsländern*, vol. 3, loc. cit., pp. 70—4.
43 See J. C. Wilde, *Expériences de développement agricole en Afrique tropicale*, Paris 1967, pp. 27—40.
44 See *Afrika. Kleines Nachschlagewerk*, loc. cit., p. 86.
45 According to M. Petit-Pont, op. cit., p. 267; UN, ECA. *Survey of Economic Conditions in Africa*, loc. cit., p. 33.
46 For details see S. Münch, op. cit., and R. Dumont, *Développement agricole africain*, Paris 1965.
47 According to Mao Tse-Tung, the peasantry play the leading role in the democratic revolution: "That is to say, the Chinese revolution is virtually the peasants' revolution, and the resistance to Japan now going on is virtually the peasants' resistance to Japan. New democratic politics is virtually the granting of power to the peasants." (Mao Tse-Tung, "On New Democracy", in: *Selected Works*, vol. 3, International Publishers, New York 1955, p. 137 f.).
48 F. Fanon, *Les damnés de la terre*, Paris 1968, p. 25.
49 K. Marx/F. Engels, *Selected Works*, vol. 1, Progress Publishers, Moscow 1973, p. 307.
50 See R. Barbé, *Les classes sociales en Afrique Noire*, Paris 1964, pp. 12—54 and I. I. Potechin, "Land Relations in African Countries", in: *The Journal of Modern African Studies*, 1/1963.

51 The term "traditional" is not exact as it does not express the social and economic character of these structures. Therefore, we are using it in the sense of J. Suret-Canale as an operational term "to describe everything which belongs to the pre-colonial and pre-capitalist heritage in the economic, social, cultural and ideological fields". (J. Suret-Canale, "Die Bedeutung der Tradition in den westafrikanischen Gesellschaftsordnungen", in: *Tradition und nichtkapitalistischer Entwicklungsweg in Afrika*, Berlin 1971, p. 107).
I try to find socio-economic definitions on pages 53 to 68. On the discussion about the use of this term see H. Mardek/I. Sellnow/G. Friede, in: *Tradition und nichtkapitalistischer Entwicklungsweg in Afrika*, loc. cit., pp. 12—13 and Th. Büttner/B. Brentjes/R. Felber. loc. cit., pp. 15—20.

52 See J. Suret-Canale, "La communauté villageoise en Afrique tropicale et sa signification sociale", in: *Etudes Africains*, Leipzig 1967, p. 173.

53 See H. Mardek/I. Sellnow/G. Friede, op. cit., pp. 15—21.

54 See J. Maquet, *Africanité traditionelle et moderne*, Paris 1967, pp. 121—2.

55 D. E. Apter, *The Politics of Modernization*, Chicago 1965, p. 38.

56 This becomes very clear in the works of the West German sociologist Trappe. See also H. Mardek/I. Sellnow/G. Friede, op. cit., p. 20.

57 Ibid., p. 26.

58 For details on the agrarian conception of the revolutionary-democratic leaders in Africa, see *Klassen und Klassenkampf in den Entwicklungsländern*, vol. 3, loc. cit. pp. 108—11.

59 See K.-J. Michalski, op. cit.

60 The Narodniki arose in the second half of the 19th century in Russia. They were a peasant version of utopian socialism and did not understand the laws of development under capitalism. They denied the leading role of the proletariat in the transition to socialism and considered the village community to be the germ of socialism and the peasantry the main revolutionary force. These ideas were opposed particularly by Lenin in his writings: *What the "Friends of the People" Are and how they Fight the Social-Democrats*, in: *Collected Works*, vol. 1, Moscow 1960; *The Economic Content of Narodism and the Criticism of it in Mr. Struve's Book*, in: *Collected Works*, vol. 1, Moscow 1960, pp. 395—423; *On Narodism*, in: *Collected Works*, vol. 18, Moscow 1963, pp. 524—8; *Narodism and the Class of Wage-Workers*, in: *Collected Works*, vol. 20, Moscow, 1964, pp. 105—8.
In *Socialist Ideas in Africa*, loc. cit., pp. 47—49, Idris Cox also deals with questions of the communal land system in Tsarist Russia.

61 See A. D. Kuršakov, *Sozdanie gosudarstvenno-kooperativnogo sektora chozjajstva v uslovijach nekapitalističeskogo razvitija*, Leningrad 1969, pp. 128—38.

62 Marx, Engels and Lenin expressly warned against this (see Th. Büttner/B. Brentjes/R. Felber, op. cit., pp. 25—7).

1. The conception of non-capitalist transformation of the traditional community in Mali

The conception of the Sudanese Union for changing the traditional village economically, socially and politically was an integral part of its total conception for social development of Mali and cannot be separated from the Union's social character and its leadership.

1.1. The Sudanese Union and its "option socialiste" [1]

The Sudanese Union (S. U.)[2] was a national-democratic mass party which had grown out of the struggle to achieve political independence. The basis of this cohesion of all the national social forces, with the exception of the *Chefferie*[3] and a small part of the tradesmen[4], into one political organisation was their common opposition to imperialist colonial rule and their joint interest in eliminating national and social oppression exercised by French monopoly capital.

The social contradictions within Malinese society were neither very deep nor very sharp, because of the embryonic character of capitalist conditions on the one hand, and because they were overshadowed by the larger contradictions caused by foreign oppression on the other.[5]

The historical process of the Sudanese Union developing into a national-democratic mass party embraced the whole period from the end of the Second World War until the eve of political independence. It can be dealt with only briefly here.[6]

The Sudanese Union originated in 1946[7] and – as a territorial section of the Rassemblement Démocratique Africain (R. D. A.)[8] – acted as the consistently anti-colonial wing of the Malinese national liberation movement.
At the beginning, the S. U. concentrated largely on the cities[9] while the flat land was mainly controlled by the Parti Soudanaise Progressiste (P. S. P.)[10] and the so-called administrative dwarf parties.[11] At the end of the forties and beginning of 1950, the S. U. extended its influence to the peasants and in the second half of the sixties became the strongest party.[12] After the P. S. P.[13]

was dissolved, the administrative dwarf parties [14] were banned, and the S. U. and the Parti Africain de l'Indépendence - Soudan (P. A. I.) [15] merged (in 1959) to became the only political organisation in the country.

As a unity party with the character of a national front, the S. U. embraced practically the whole adult population of Mali during the first half of the 1960s.[16]

The peasants were its mass basis and made up the vast majority (90%) of its members. The working class was very weak with a corresponding representation in the S. U. While it had very small political influence in the party, the working class made itself felt through the trade union (Union Nationale des Travailleurs du Mali – U. N. T. M.) which worked closely together with the S. U.[17]

The leading social force within the alliance of classes and strata in Mali was the mainly petty-bourgeois intelligentsia largely employed in the public service (teachers, doctors, civil service employees). Most of its leading and middle cadres in the party came of this strata.[18] The majority of them made up the revolutionary-democratic wing of the intelligentsia. It was they who drew up the Sudanese Union's conception for establishing a socialist society in Mali both on the eve of achieving political independence and in the first years after 1960.

Apart from the leading democratic revolutionaries, there was also a small group of Marxists [19] in the party who did not set up their own political platform, but fought for development of the revolutionary aspects in the official concept and worked to have them made reality.

In addition, there existed a relatively strong right wing in the leadership [20], which – while it did not openly oppose the non-capitalist path – began more and more to represent the rising bourgeoisie.[21] They used above all the bureaucratic, bourgeois sections of the party and state apparatus [22] which, through corruption, nepotism and "administrative feudalism" (Modibo Keita) became a growing hindrance for the aims of the revolutionary-democratic forces.

In the second half of the 1960s growing economic difficulties [23] and greater social differentiation [24] led to a sharpened dispute within the party and state leadership about the path to be taken. The right-wing forces went on the offensive when the French-Malinese finance agreement [25] was signed and tried to push Mali off the non-capitalist path.[26] This process was the concrete expression of a general tendency in the developing countries which was described by the Moscow Meeting of Communist and Workers' Parties as follows: "In those countries which have liberated themselves, social differentiation is progressing. There is a growing conflict of the working class, peasantry and other democratic forces including democratic-minded strata of the petty-bourgeoisie, with imperialism and the forces of local reaction, with those elements of the national bourgeoisie who are collaborating with imperialism."[27]

In this sharpened class struggle, the revolutionary leadership took measures which aimed to overcome the objective difficulties and to weaken the opponents of the non-capitalist path. They tried to strengthen their political power by removing many of the right-wing forces from party leadership[28] and parliament[29], by curbing them in the government[30], purging the party and state apparatus of bureaucratic–bourgeois elements[31] by measures to strengthen ideological work,[32] to increase industrial[33] and agricultural production[34] and the efficiency of state co-operative trade.[35]

This made it possible to temporarily beat back the attacks by the right-wing and consolidate the political power of the revolutionary-democratic forces for the time being. Further, the struggle against the opponents of the non-capitalist path was accompanied by ideological clarification among the revolutionary forces so that greater attention was paid to scientific socialism.[36] There was also progress in the economic field.[37] However, many of the huge economic problems could not be solved, so that the continued bad social situation of the working people, combined with a political[38] and ideological[39] left-wing radicalism during the *"révolution active"*[40] led to increased isolation of the revolutionary democrats from the masses. Thus, the overthrow of the Modibo Keita government by a military coup in November 1968 did not meet with any serious resistance from the people.

The Sudanese Union's conception of socialism was by no means a cohesive ideological system, but, due to the social and ideological heterogeneity of the party and its leadership, contained elements from varying social backgrounds and differing ideologies.[41] The significance of this conception was that it orientated towards historical progress, towards the establishment of a socialist society in Mali and thus correctly reflected the basic direction of the world revolutionary process. It corresponded to Lenin's forecast that "in the impending decisive battles in the world revolution, the movement of the majority of the population of the globe, initially directed towards national liberation, will turn against capitalism and imperialism".[42]

Apart from a formal acceptance of an "African" socialism during the existence of the Parti de la Fédération Africain (P. F. A.)[43], the Sudanese Union for the first time openly stood up as a party for a path which would lead to a socialist society at its Extraordinary Congress on 22 September 1960[44]. Based on this decision, in which several important theoretical positions of the leading revolutionary forces became visible, the party leaders worked out their conception for the construction of socialism in Mali. It was explicitly formulated in the documents of the 6th Party Congress (1962)[45] and found concrete expression in the Five-Year Plan (1961–6).[46]

The Sudanese Union's conception of socialism contained important elements of scientific socialism; it did not reject scientific socialism on sight, but considered a gradual approach to such positions possible. The revolutionary-democratic forces in Mali set themselves the task of building a society "in which the social ownership of the means of production corresponds to the social character of production"[47] and in which the exploitation of man by man would thus be completely eliminated.[48] They considered the construction of such a society – socialism – to be a world-wide historical necessity.[49] They were convinced that there is only one type of socialism in the world[50] and their basic aims differed in no way from scientific socialism[51], a knowledge of which they considered indispensable for every cadre in the S. U.[52] They also expressly disassociated themselves from the demagogical character of so-called African socialism[53], which claims to be an *African* counter-model to European scientific socialism.[54] Differences, caused by the concrete conditions, can exist only – they say – in the methods and means used to build socialist society.[55] And finally – although it has not been possible to give a comprehensive picture – the significance of the S. U.'s conception is that it objectively orientated the practical tasks to a non-capitalist path, to the material and ideological preparation for building socialism in Mali, despite some serious theoretical weaknesses. This applies particularly to the planning of the first stage for the gradual construction of a new society.

The documents of the 6th Congress spoke of two main phases: the phase of "socialist re-organisation" of existing conditions, to be followed by the phase of "socialist construction"[56]; in Cairo, Diarra added a third phase: that of "consolidating socialist society" which was to be followed by "the construction of communism"[57].

During the first phase, which was dealt with in greater detail at the 6th Congress than the second, two main tasks were set: "socialist re-organisation of existing production conditions" and "creation of new means of production"[58].

According to the details described in the 6th Congress documents and in the plan of development[59], "socialist re-organisation of existing conditions of production" were to include above all nationalisation of those branches of the economy through which the foreign monopolies were mainly able to practise exploitation, i. e. decisive sections of export and wholesale trade, financing and banking plus the state-owned colonial companies and private monopoly firms in the transport system, electricity supply, in agriculture and building. The main sector of the economy – agriculture – was to be made cooperative as well as the handicrafts and important sections of home trade.

"Creation of new means of production" referred mainly to technical modernisation of traditional farming, improvement of the economic infrastructure, construction of a state-owned (or mixed) industry for processing farm products plus prospecting the ground to prepare for the heavy industry which it was planned to build in the second phase. The revolutionary democrats in Mali were convinced that an indispensable prerequisite for successfully realising these tasks is continual organisational and ideological strengthening of the national-democratic party and state power.[60]

The material of the Congress stressed that the stage of "socialist construction"[61] was to follow "socialist re-organisation".

Apart from these positive elements which corresponded to objective needs, the S.U.'s conception also contained petty-bourgeois ideas which were an objective ideological obstacle to non-capitalist development.

During the first period, these tendencies were expressed in traditionalist-utopian views of socialism[62], in a non-historical approach to socialism as a social system. Certain structures and norms of socialism were identified with similar structures and norms of the pre-colonial community, but the former had developed on a completely different social level, so that the construction of socialism was seen as a "duty, to give rebirth to our ancient heritage, to develop and rehabilitate certain of our own values'[63]. On this basis, Mali's revolutionary leaders tended to see in the basic structures of the traditional community a type of micro-model of socialist society. This became very obvious when S. B. Kouyaté described how socialist society functions. One could have thought that he was describing the traditional community, but transposing the whole process to the level of the whole society.[64]

Petty-bourgeois Narodnik ideas[65] based on the abstraction of socialism from its historical roots and prerequisites, played an important role in the S. U.'s conception of the path to socialism. They were expressed particularly in the negation of the historical role of the working class and communist party in building socialism and the over-estimation of the strength of a national-democratic mass party with its petty-bourgeois leadership. Kouyaté (S. Badian), as official representative of the party leadership declared in Dakar in 1962:

"In summarising, we can say that the socialist path which we have chosen is based on two fundamental factors: (1) a socialism which is constructed by a movement that is not led by mainly proletarian forces . . .; (2) and, as a logical conclusion from the first factor, we are of the opinion that socialism can be made reality without a communist party. We think that the political organisation of the people, seen as the motor of the nation, can lead the country to socialism. It is not any longer a question of a communist party made up of selected proletarian elements, but of the whole people who are forming themselves into a political force in order to master their own fate."[66]

The overestimation of the political unity of the people led to the under-estimation of the process of social differentiation and class struggle. While certain contradictions within Malinese society were recognised, their cause was not sought in the social and economic roots, but more or less considered as solely ideological phenomena and the class struggle was reduced to education within the party: "There certainly exist elements who dream of taking the place of the foreign bourgeoisie; others do not understand the necessity of certain sacrifices demanded of them and dream of special privileges. But these contradictions will be overcome through education and the cohesion of the party."[67] Caught up in these concepts, the S. U.'s revolutionary-democrats were not able to avoid the dangers of identifying the non-capitalist path with the socialist revolution described at the Moscow Meeting of Communist and Workers' Parties.[68] They theoretically rejected the non-capitalist stage of development [69] – as a historically necessary stage to prepare the objective and subjective prerequistites for the transition to a socialist revolution – and Idrissa Diarra declared at the Cairo Seminar on behalf of the S. U. Political Bureau: "On this question we are of the opinion that there is no qualitative difference between the noncapitalist and the socialist path of development."[70] Thus, developments in Mali are a very obvious example of Simoniya's claim that traditionalist and utopian ideas of socialism are a big obstacle for the necessary process of ideological clarification.[71]

In the process of putting their conception of development into action and in the dispute with the right-wing forces, the ideological differentiation within the party leadership grew and in the course of this they freed themselves to some extent from their traditionalist illusions. They came nearer to scientific socialism through new insight into questions of class and class struggle, the historical role of the working class and the necessity of a vanguard party.[72] At the same time greater left-wing radicalism in the identification of the non-capitalist path with the construction of socialism came to the fore. This found its most concentrated expression during the *"révolution active"* when the socialist revolution was factually proclaimed [73] and led to isolation of the revolutionary-democrats from the masses and to socialism being discredited in Mali. The statement by Ulyanovski applies, on the whole, to the ideological situation in Mali in 1967–8: "Representatives of radical nationalism are turning more strongly to several principles of scientific socialism where they not seldom find a suitable ideological basis for their political platform. However, the petty-bourgeois nationalist background to their conceptions is often a serious obstacle for a consistent and all-round acquisition of scientific socialist theory."[74]

1.2. The "*action rurale*"

The Sudanese Union's conception was re-organisation of agriculture and this became one of the main tasks during the so-called "*action rurale*". Modibo Keita described it as "the key for our economic development and for the success of our revolution ..."; at the 6th Congress it was called "the fundamental problem ... on which rests, in reality, our whole action for economic liberation and creation of socialist structures,"[75] and it played a central role in the development plan.[76]

1.2.1. Basic orientation: development of the productive forces plus cooperatives

The "*action rurale*" — apart from the "socialist re-organisation" of the state Office du Niger[77], which is not relevant here — was to contain two main elements[78]:
(1) the socialist organisation of peasants in a co-operative system, and
(2) the modernisation of agriculture with the help of a state system to teach the peasants how to use the new machines and apply modern methods of production.

The co-operative system[79] was to embrace four different levels: At the village level the Groupement Rural de Production et de Secours Mutuel (G. R. P. S. M.); at the level of several villages the Groupement Rural Associé (G. R. A.); at the *Arrondissement* level the Fédération Primaire (F. P.)[80]; at district level the Société Mutuelle de Développement Rural (S. M. D. R.).

Structure of the agricultural co-operatives and the state development service in Mali (within a district):

Administrative Level	Co-operative Body	State Development Service (*encadrement rural*)
District	Société Mutuelle de Développement Rural (S. M. D. R.)	Secteur de Développement Rural (S. D. R.)
Arrondissement	Fédération Primaire (F. P.)	Zone d'Expansion Rurale (Z. E. R.)
8–12 villages	Groupement Rural Associé (G. R. A.)	Secteur de Base (S. B.)
Village	Groupement Rural de Production et de Secours Mutuel (G. R. P. S. M.)	

The *Groupement Rural de Production et de Secours Mutuel* was conceived as the basic unit of the Malinese co-operative system. It was to embrace all the inhabitants and be presided over by an administrative council chaired by the village head. This administrative council was to be composed of members of the village council[81] plus the village delegates in the *Arrondissement* council[82]. A special office, to be set up by the administrative council, was to organise the day-to-day work.[83]

The general assembly, composed of the whole village population over 18, had the task of deciding on "the proposals made by the Council for Economic Organisation of the Village and the program of social activities"[84]. The G. R. P. S. M. had economic, social and cultural tasks.

The economic tasks were:

(1) Co-operative organisation of the *"circuit commercial"*. This meant co-operative marketing of individual production at state prices, supplying the peasants with means of production, seeds and fertilisers plus food and industrial goods, also at prices fixed, this time, by the G. R. P. S. M.

(2) Joint work for collective interests outside of actual agricultural production the so-called *"investissement humain"*[85].

(3) Credits for members of the co-operative and guarantees for credits granted by state or co-operative institutions. As the G. R. P. S. M. would probably not have sufficient capital[86] in the first few years to grant credits to its members, it was to act first of all as guarantor for credits granted by the state-run Caisse Centrale du Credit Agricole (C. C. C. A.) to the G. R. P. S. M. as a whole or to its individual members (to buy seed, fertiliser or means of production, or for marketing)[87].

(4) Joint cultivation of the collective G. R. P. S. M. field, which would serve as the example for new agricultural methods (fertilising, crop rotation, ploughing, etc.), be the main source of income for the G. R. P. S. M. and become the "embryo for strong collectivisation of agricultural production"[88]. The social and cultural tasks were to be: help for the needy, old and sick, improvement of hygiene and of living conditions in the village and organisation of folklore.

The *Groupement Rural Associé* (G. R. A.) was to be the umbrella organisation for the G. R. P. S. M. and consisted of 8–12 villages. It was to be administered by a council composed of two delegates from each G. R. P. S. M. and with obligatory leadership from the head of the arrondissement. The general assembly of the G. R. A. embraces all council members of the village co-operatives which belong to the G. R. A. It was to meet at least twice a year and decide on the "work programs, the budgets, the loans and distribution of credits"[89]. The G. R. A. were also to organise the further sale of production from their G. R. P. S. M. and to supply these with industrial goods, etc. In addition, they also had transport and small workshops at their disposal, which were to be made available to the G. R. P. S. M. The G. R. A. were also conceived as a link in the credit system. Its capital was the membership dues and the profits made from commercialisation. Several G. R. A. were to be joined at the *Arrondissement* level into the *Féderation Primaire* (F. P.), with an administrative council and a general assembly constituted on the same principle – on a higher level – and with the same functions (now at *Arrondissement* level) as the G. R. A.

The top co-operative institution on a district level was to be the *Société Mutuelle de Développement Rural* (S. M. D. R.). It was to co-ordinate the work of the co-operative organs under it, in particular to register the stream of commercialised agricultural products and pass them on to the state buying organs; and it was to be the co-operative starting point for supplying the G. R. P. S. M. and its members with tools, fertilisers, insecticides and consumer goods. At the same time, the S. M. D. R. administered the *Caisses Locales du Crédit Agricole*.[90] According to the development plan, the construction of this co-operative system was to be completed by the end of 1965–6.

Parallel to the co-operative system, there was conceived a system of state agricultural development service (*encadrement rural*)[91] which was mainly to make the peasants acquainted with modern tools and methods of agricultural production. In order to fulfill this task as effectively as possible, the *encadrement* system had its decisive operative organs below district level, but it was also closely interwoven with the whole co-operative system.

The *Basic Sector* (secteur de base – S. B.) was intended to be the primary cell of the system. The territory was to be of a size which would enable the development agents to maintain direct contact to the producers, i. e. to 2,000 to 3,000 inhabitants, and in Mali this meant 150 to 200 family farms with 1,000 to 1,500 hectares of cultivated land.[92] In general, a basic sector had eight to twelve villages which also made up a G. R. A.

The basic sector was to be managed by an agricultural technician who was to work hand in hand with so-called "*animateurs ruraux*" in the individual villages. An animateur was not a paid official, but an advanced farmer ("*cultivateur-pilote*") who was chosen from among the villagers for "his dynamic attitudes, his progressive spirit and his influence on the people"[93], and who had the task of demonstrating modern methods of production and planting under the guidance of the basic sector head. The aim was for the whole village population to gradually acquire his level of skill, which he received at a seasonal school (*Ecole saisonnière*) or in the *Service Civique*. He was to receive certain advantages "in respect to the supply of tools, fertiliser and seed"[94].

The G. R. P. S. M. and the G. R. A. were to be the actual field of activity for the heads of the basic sectors. Their main task was the economic development of these co-operative institutions. Therefore, their development work was not in direct contact with the producer, but indirect contact via the G. R. P. S. M. and the G. R. A. In order to make this influence as effective as possible, a far-reaching inter-linking of personnel in both systems on the village and on the G. R. A. level was intended, so that in the management of the G. R. P. S. M. and the G. R. A., the *animateur rural* and the head of the basic sector took over the role of *"gestion journalière"* representing the administrative council.

So the theoretical conception of the tasks of the basic sector head and his animateurs was that they were not only to explain how to use the modern methods and tools, but also that they take over certain functions in the economic management of the co-operative. In other words, the state wanted to take a direct influence on the development of the co-operatives via the development service.

The basic sectors of an *Arrondissement* were regrouped into a *Zone d'Expansion Rurale* (Z. E. R.). It was managed by a *Conducteur d'Agriculture* who was at the same time technical adviser for the *Arrondissement*. His main function was to give leadership to the heads of the basic sectors and exert a direct influence upon the work of the *Fédération Primaire*. In addition, the head of the Z. E. R. was to have two specific instruments of development at his disposal: the *Centre Coöpératif d'Education et de Modernisation Agricole* (C.C.E. M. A.) and the seasonal schools. The C. C. E. M. A. was to be established in the area with the most favourable conditions for development and become a demonstration centre for the whole Z. E. R. For this reason it was to be equipped with a co-operative shop, a store-room, and means of transport and production, and be given a field of some 20 hectares for demonstration purposes. It was also intended to provide it with a literacy and medical centre, in order to enable it to play a leading role also in the social field. In the season schools – which, according to the original conception were also to be placed directly under the Z. E. R.[95] – the best young peasants received an exclusively practical training[96] during the course of one season in modern methods of production and then returned to their village, equipped with a pair of oxen, a plough and an ox-cart – for which they received the necessary credit from the *Crédit Agricole* – in order then to become the *"animateurs"*. At district level, the development service had its organ in the *Secteur de Développement Rural* (S. D. R.), whose head was also the technical adviser to the district commandant and responsible for working out and putting into action the agricultural development program for the district. The S. D. R. was subordinated on the regional level to the technical adviser of the governor. On the regional level, the development service had a state farm and a *"centre d'apprentissage"* in which the *moniteurs d'agriculture* were trained.

On the national level, the whole system was completed by the *Service de l'Action Rurale* – subordinated to the Ministry of Development – with its two main departments (*Division du Développement Rural* and *Centre National de la Coöpération*) which made up the state administrative summit for both the development service and the co-operatives.

It was planned to establish 150 Z. E. R. s., the same number of season schools and C.C.E.M.A. and 400 basic sectors by 1965/6. By the end of the planning period it was intended that 7,000 youths should have passed through the seasonal schools.

Apart from the development service, another instrument was conceived on the initiative of the youth organisation[97] and became a part of the *"action rurale"*: the *Service Civique*[98]. Its task was to gradually train all the youth of Mali and awaken in them a national consciousness and sense of responsibility for the "socialist" change in Mali.[99]

The young people of the *Service Civique* – at least 75% of them came from the traditional village environment – were to receive this training during a two-year stay in camps organised on semi-military lines. These camps were also to give practical and theoretical training on the fundamentals of modern field work and animal husbandry, and in important trades (above all building) plus political, ideological, military and general knowledge (reading and writing, basic hygiene, first aid, etc.). After these two years of service, the young people were to be obliged to return to their villages – with ox and plough acquired through state credits from the C. C. C. A. in order to work there as an *"animateur rural"*. Altogether 4,000 youths were intended to pass through the *Service Civique* camps by the end of the planning period.

In accordance with their conception of the leading role of the national democratic mass party in building socialism in general, the Malinese revolutionary democrats saw in this party the decisive instrument for socialist change in agriculture: "Of all the means at our disposal for this work of creation, education and de-mystification, political organisation is the most certain and most effective."[100] Therefore, the S. U.'s conception was to have party branches even in the smallest villages and to ensure the leading role of the party on all levels.

The lowest organisational level was the village committee composed of all adult village inhabitants and guided from a local office.[101] Its role was ". . . above all to mobilize the masses and educate them".[102] The Committee was to popularise party policy in the village and see to it that it was carried out, politically prepare and control[103] the activities of the administrative bodies (village council, village head), found the G. R. P. S. M. and ensure its proper functioning, and to mobilize the people for voluntary labour (the *"investissement humain"*) etc.[104]

At the next lowest administrative level, the *Arrondissement*, the organisation of the S.U. was the sub-section, guided from a Political Bureau. Its highest organ was the sub-section conference.[105] The sub-section either had a direct influence on "socialist" changes or worked through the head of the *Arrondissement*, who administered it as a representative of state power, and who was "above all politically responsible" and "urged to work closely with the highest political body of the arrondissement, the sub-section". The sub-section had the task of "popularising the party slogans, seeing to it that they were made reality, controlling and supporting the work of the head of the *Arrondissement*, so that it never deviates from the line set down by the party and government".[106]

At the district level – several *Arrondissements* joined together – the section had basically the same function and structure.[107] In the region, the administrative level between district and state, the party had no special institution. Its functions were carried out by the delegates of the Political Bureaux of the sections in the regional cadre conferences held quarterly and by the political commissars[108], who were also members of the National Political Bureau.[109]

By its orientation on co-operatives and technical and methodical progress in agriculture to be carried through by a revolutionary democratic state leadership and a national democratic mass party, this conception corresponded in principle to the objective requirements and possibilities of non-capitalist development in Mali. In this respect it served the revolutionary democrats as a signpost for overcoming the backwardness of the productive forces and the largely subsistence economy in the agrarian sector,[110] for liberating the peasant masses from servitude to the foreign monopolies and local trade and usury capital[111], and to prevent widespread, spontaneous development of capitalist relations of production in agriculture. And yet it also contained a number of important ideological elements which were strong obstacles to putting its positive aspects into practice and, in the final analysis contributed to its failure.

1.2.2. Traditionalist illusions and the danger of left-wing radicalism

The traditionalist ideological elements in the S. U.'s conception were particularly strong in the agrarian sphere, because it was here that there appeared to be a particularly strong link to pre-colonial structures. In their conception of how to reorganise the village on socialist lines, the revolutionary democratic ideologists in Mali based themselves on the traditional community in its fundamental social relations and the norms regulating it, which, when abstracted from their economic conditions, were seen as the original African style of living, as the structural model for the "socialist organisation" of the village. After describing conditions in the pre-colonial African village,

Kouyaté writes: "This organisation is in fact general in Black Africa, it is the *original reality* . . ." and he speaks elsewhere of "the community which has existed at all times . . ." and of "the African mutual aid which is one of the best heritages that we have received from the past. . .".[112]

In the same spirit, Modibo Keita stressed when making public the five-year plan. "Long before the colonial period, the community spirit dominated our villages and was the foundation and root of our society. For us, the village is the basic cell, and the vitality of this cell will become the source of the vitality of the whole nation . . ."[113] In the official documents on "co-operation", the "old and traditional way of life" was proclaimed as "one of the forms of human values in African civilisation"[114]. Logically enough, those who held this view considered all traditional forms of dependence and exploitation (aristocracy, slaves, etc.) and the social and structural changes during the colonial period as deformation of the original community, as something imposed from outside and foreign to their system.[115] Kouyaté speaks of the village community as "the original reality which had other structures forced onto it through the play of outside forces which – like the *Chefferie* and the state – are no more than peripheral phenomena".[116]

During the course of the "socialist change", the basic relations of the traditional community are to be re-established in the form of co-operatives: "The community which has existed at all times – despite the destructive elements the colonial regime was able to introduce – *must once again be put on its feet*, and on the village level the co-operative will interest those who live and work together and who are linked by strong and ancient bonds. Thus the village will be the production and marketing cell; in addition, the African mutual aid will have to be laid down by law. The village co-operative will be so conceived that the peasants sell their products together, buy the products they need together and help each other in all fields. The old and sick will be cared for by the community when they need help as used to be the case in the old times."[117]

This revival of the traditional community implies the necessity of liberating the community from all pre-colonial and colonial alterations and degeneration. This means, first, structural changes such as "the liquidation of feudal and colonial structures",[118] i. e. elimination of the colonial administrative *Chefferie* and the traditional aristocratic elements integrated into it through colonial rule, including the degeneration of internal family relations,[119] liberation of the peasant from exploitation through the trade monopolies and the "African and Asian intermediary traders"[120] who have grown up in their shadow. It also means the rehabilitation of traditional values and norms "so that every Sudanese will rediscover the meaning of the soil and the community through collective work".[121] In particular, "work on the field" and the position of the peasant must find their old place in the value system of the country: "Therefore, a moral upheaval is necessary in order to rehabilitate the soil and its tillers . . . Through joint effort we must rediscover what was the foundation of our community of yesterday. For us it is a sort of return to ourselves . . ."[122]

The reborn community, freed from its deformations must finally undergo a "psychological revolution" through which "the inner will to progress" must be born in the peasant to adapt to the demands of a modern economy: "Our peasantry lives in a subsistence economy, a self-supplying economy in which the human being produces above all to feed himself, in which he tries to hold a sort of balance of poverty between the minimum and what he produces . . . The inner need for progress, the striving for a better life, in other words, the will to get out [of the balance of poverty — K. E.] must be born . . ."[123]

Thus, in their desire to develop the agricultural productive forces and at the same time prevent further social differentiation and establishment of capitalist production relations in the village, Mali's revolutionary democrats wanted to preserve and revive the traditional community — in which they "discovered" socialist patterns of society and behaviour — and then, after liberation from the "degeneration", adapt it to modern economic requirements through education and enlightenment of the peasants in a "psychological revolution".

This conception is in many respects similar to the Narodniks — in that it is a peasant-petty-bourgeois conception — and like these, it is based on an unscientific approach to the problems of development, of structure and the functioning of society as a system of social relations. It is also similar in the abstraction of certain social structural elements from the concrete conditions of the system in general, leading to the idealisation of traditional relations in the peasant community in particular.

From the mid-1960s, a process of re-assessment and modification of the agrarian conception took place (similar to reconsiderations being made in society as a whole) in which the revolutionary democrats recognised just how complicated it is to put agriculture on the non-capitalist road [124] and gradually freed themselves from Narodnik-like views.[125] Madeira Keita stated as early as 1964 that "socialist co-operative work differs in many respects from the traditional forms of collectivism on the [African — K. E.] continent . . ."[126] and Modibo Keita spoke in a New Year message in 1966 of the necessity for "urgent change in the extremely backward agrarian structure"[127].

This process of disillusionment found its ideological climax at the co-operative seminar in May 1968.[128] Here it was stated: "It is necessary to recognise that a certain number of contradictions are hidden in our society, whose negative aspects we have not yet paid sufficient attention to up to now ..." By this was meant the patriarchal gerontocracy, the traditional and theocratic feudal elements and the newly rich who arose in the village after independence. At the same time it was admitted that (as a result of the traditionalist illusions about the "socialist character" of the village community) the oppressed social strata and groups in the village – the poor peasants, the youth and women – had up to then been insufficiently recognised or used as revolutionary potential for the non-capitalist re-organisation.[129] Upon recognising the class character of the changes necessary for the countryside, tasks were set at the seminar which were suitable to strengthen the non-capitalist elements of the Malinese agrarian conception, like alterations in the political conditions of the village and in the relations of power among the managements of the co-operatives in favour of the progressive forces, like strengthening the role of the state, consolidating the relations of exchange between the co-operative and the state, or the intensified political, ideological education and vocational training of the peasants. At the same time a number of radically left-wing slogans were raised at the seminar – a general tendency of the *"révolution active"* – which strongly limited the effectiveness of the valuable new orientation. For example, in line with the slogan "for a socialist revolution", socialist collectivisation was, in fact, put on the agenda, although – as will be shown later – the most elementary objective conditions let alone the subjective prerequisites did not exist even for agricultural co-operatives.

The mainly traditionalist Narodnik elements at the beginning as well as the left-wing opportunist tendencies during the *"révolution active"* – both an ideological expression of the generally petty-bourgeois character of the revolutionary democratic movement in Mali – were a strong ideological obstacle for pushing through a non-capitalist development.

From 1960 to 1968, the revolutionary democratic leaders in Mali tried to put into practice their – gradually modified – conception of a non-capitalist re-organisation of traditional sectors of agriculture. During this process they had to gain clarity about many complex problems of development of both an objective and a subjective nature. In order to be able to place this into its proper perspective, it appears necessary to define the social, economic and historic place of the pre-colonial African community.

REFERENCES

1 Under this term, the leadership of the Sudanese Union summarised everything that made up the transformation of Malinese society.
2 French: *Union Soudanaise*. Until the military coup in November 1968 it was the leading political force in Mali. Since then, it has been suspended.

3 Under colonialism, the *Chefferie* were a strata of village and canton chiefs who were imposed by the colonial powers on the lowest levels of administration — village and canton — as an instrument of their power. I prefer to use the French word "*Chefferie*" because the word "chief", often used in this connection, really signifies the tribal chiefs, and can be misleading.

4 Most of the merchants were suitable for an alliance, as they had an objective interest to eliminate monopoly rule because this inhibited their own development. That is why they also subjectively supported the anti-colonial struggle (see Union Soudanaise — R. D. A. Bureau Politique National, Circulaire No. 11, juillet 1961, pp. 2—8).

5 As I cannot go into this further, see the paper by A. B. Letnev, "Social'naja differencija v Mali i sopredel'nych raionach Zapadnoi Afriki", in: *Narody Azii i Afriki*, 1/1963, pp. 74—84 and K. V. Vladimirova/V. V. Zalnin, *Respublika Mali — Social'no-ekonomiče skieproblemy*, Moscow 1970. According to the figures given by the *Enquête démographique* in 1960 structure in the classes and strata became visible as follows (the *Chefferie* are not included as these were already liquidated in 1960):

Peasants, fishers and animal keepers of the pre-capitalist type	90.5%
Independent (city) merchants and craftsmen	4.7%
Bourgeois elements (above all wholesalers, jobmasters, embryonal village bourgeoisie)	0.5%
Wage labourers (city and country together)	2.8%
Employees (mainly public servants)	1.5%
	100.0%

(see *Annuaire statistique 1966 du Mali*, Bamako 1967, pp. 33f.)

6 For details see G. S. Kontratyev, *Put' Mali k nezavisimosti, 1945—1960*, Moscow 1970.

7 The Sudanese Union was founded on 22 October 1946 through the merger of political organisations founded the previous year, the Bloc Soudanais and Parti Démocratique Soudanais (see "Souvenez-vous, Camarades", in: *Mali-Magazine*, 3/1964, pp. 10—11; „L'U. S.—RDA", Ms., pp. 1—2; Th. Hodgkin/ R. Schachter-Morgenthau, "Mali", in: *Political Parties and National Integration in Tropical Africa*, ed. by James S. Coleman and Carl G. Rosberg, Berkeley/Los Angeles 1964, pp. 230—2).

8 Up to its betrayal by the right-wing leaders around F. Houphouet-Boigny (1950—1), the supraterritorial R. D. A. — founded in October 1946 in Bamako — was the centre for the persistently anti-colonial forces in the former French colonies of West and Central Africa (for details see *Le Rassemblement Démocratique Africain dans la lutte antiimpérialiste*, s. l. 1950; D. A. Olderogge and I. I. Potechin, *Die Völker Afrikas*, vol. 1, Berlin 1961, pp. 424—8; F. Ansprenger, *Politik im Schwarzen Afrika*, Köln and Opladen 1961, pp. 126—44 and E. Milcent, *L'A. O. F. entre en scène*, Paris 1958, pp. 35—54).

9 Lower employees of the colonial administration, teachers, employees of trad-

ing companies, workers, some merchants. In 1946/7 the S. U. had some 10,000 members.
10 See pages 91—93 of this book for details about this party.
11 Local "parties" created by the colonial power in order to control the local "representative bodies". See pp. 91 ff.
12 See details on p. 92 f.
13 The reason given for dissolving the P. S. P. was the merger of the parties in the Mali Federation, formed in January 1959 by Mali and Senegal. The resulting party was the Parti de la Fédération Africaine (P. F. A.). In fact, it was the logical conclusion of political developments inside Mali. On the origins and development of the Mali Federation see *Chronique de Politique Etrangère*, 1—3/1961, pp. 109—47. On several concrete aspects of the dissolution of the P. S. P. in Mali and its merger with the S. U., see *L'Essor*, 3/4/1959; Th. Hodgkin/R. Schachter-Morgenthau, op. cit., p. 242 and *Journal Officiel de la République Soudanaise*, 29/1959, p. 685.
14 See page 93.
15 From the foundation of the supra-territorial Parti Africain de l'Independence (P. A. I.) in 1957 by left-wing intellectuals and Marxists, a branch of it existed in Mali. In 1959 it joined the S. U. On the general aims of the P. A. I. see M. Diop, *Contribution à l'étude des problèmes politiques en Afrique Noire*, Paris 1959, pp. 149—241.
16 Of 1.7 million adults (over 19 years of age, *Annuaire statistique 1966*, loc. cit., p. 32) some 1.5 million were members of the S. U. at the beginning of the 1960s (see *Jeune Afrique*, 222/1965, supplement, p. 6).
17 On the political role of the trade unions in Mali, see W. Wilke, "Zu einigen Fragen des Verhältnisses der nationaldemokratischen Parteien und der Gewerkschaften in Guinea und Mali", in: *Protokoll der wissenschaftlichen Beratung der Fakultät für Ausländerstudium* 11 and 12 June 1965 on the subject "Theoretische Probleme und praktische Erfahrungen des gewerkschaftlichen Kampfes bei der Interessenvertretung und der Durchsetzung des sozialistischen Entwicklungsweges in Afrika", part 2, Bernau 1965, pp. 41—51; G. Julis, "L'action des masses populaires au Mali", in: *Les Cahiers du C. E. R. M.*, 54/1967 and the documents of the 1st U. N. T. M. Congress (24—28 July 1963).
18 Typical for the social and political background of the S. U. leaders is Mamadou Konaté, the founder and leader of the S. U. for many years. He did a teaching course at the Ecole Normale de Gorée and worked as teacher from 1919 to 1946 in Bamako, Diafarabé and Kolokani. During the period of the first people's front government in France, he founded the first teachers' trade union (1937) of which he was head until 1946. From 1946 until his death (1956) he was president of the S. U. But also after 1960, most of the leaders were teachers or administration officials. The leading role of this stratum is also expressed in the composition of the party congresses. At the 6th Congress. 64.2% of the delegates were of this stratum. (see *L'Essor*, 11. 9. 1962).
19 Most of these leaders had begun to study Marxism-Leninism after the Second World War in the Groupes d'Etudes Communistes (G. E. C.) created by the

French Communist Party, or they came out of the P. A. I. or the trade unions. After independence, younger people came up into the leadership of the S. U. who had worked mainly in the youth organisation and were not free of left-wing sectarian tendencies.

20 Up to 1967, this wing made up almost half the members of the National Political Bureau (Bureau Politique National — B. P. N.), and temporarily controlled such important fields at the State Ministry, Home Affairs, Technical Assistance, Trade, Foreign Affairs and Education (see M. Keita in *L'Essor*, 17. 11. 1967, pp. 5—6).

21 After independence, a spontaneous process of social differentiation took place in Mali during the course of which a national bourgeoisie grew. Their main groups were the merchants and money-lenders (above all cattle and fish traders), transport and building contractors, an agrarian bourgeoisie and the bureaucratic bourgeoisie, and often they were closely interwoven.

22 After independence, the state and party apparatus grew enormously. Apart from the positive aspects of this largely necessary process, there grew the strata of those who found themselves with certain privileges compared to other classes and strata through the statute on officials passed in the 1950s. Despite a number of measures taken by the revolutionary-democratic leaders, petty-bourgeois tendencies became stronger which was expressed by the fact that many of the officials used their positions to enrich themselves. For details see G. Julis, op. cit., pp. 7—10.

23 The economic situation became very complicated in the mid-sixties because the economy was not growing quickly enough (the annual growth rate of 2.25% was a little below the rate in the growth of population). There was a growing deficit in foreign trade (1965/66: 9.7 billion) and the balance of payment (1967/68: 8.4 billion). Increasing difficulties arose in supplying the people with basic foods. (For details on economic developments in the second half of the 1960s see: *Comptes économiques du Mali 1964—65*, Paris 1967; *Comptes économiques du Mali du 1er juillet 1964 au 30 juin 1967*, Bamako 1969; *Evolution de la situation économique au Mali depuis la dévaluation de mai 1967*, Bamako 1968).

24 The main expression of this process was in the stronger development of a national bourgeoisie on the one hand and the worsening in the situation of the city workers on the other (in 1962—8 the average prices rose by 90%. See *Annuaire statistique 1968 de la République du Mali*, Bamako 1969, p. 198).

25 After long negotiations with France, economic and financial agreements were signed in February 1967 which laid down that Mali return into the Franc zone in several stages (see *L'Essor*, 20. 2. 1967, 8. 5. 1967, 26. 12. 1967).

26 They tried to accelerate the return into the Franc zone and achieve closer economic inter-lacing with France by pointing to the objective economic difficulties. At the same time through well-aimed slander they tried to isolate the revolutionary forces, who saw the financial agreements as a necessary compromise and not as subordination under French monopoly capital (see M. Keita in: *L'Essor*, 27. 11. 1967).

The conception of non-capitalist transformation 45

27 *Internationale Beratung der kommunistischen und Arbeiterparteien*, loc. cit., pp. 32ff.
28 This was achieved by dissolving the B. P. N. on 22 August 1967 and transferring its functions to the Comité National de Défense de la Révolution (C. N. D. R.) created in March 1966. *L'Essor*, 28. 8. 1967. *L'Essor* 25. 9. 1967 gives the details of its composition and concrete powers. The whole stage after 22 August 1967 was described as the *"révolution active"*. A collection of the most important documents of this phase can be found in: *1967. An I de la révolution*, Bamako n. d.
29 The National Assembly dissolved itself on 16 January 1968 (see *L'Essor*, 22. 1. 1968). It was replaced — up to the intended new elections — by a Délégation Législative appointed by President Keita which was composed mainly of left-wing forces (L'Essor, 29. 1. 1968).
30 Through changes in the government in September 1966 and February 1968, right-wing forces were partly eliminated and partly curbed in influence (by cutting down their authority). See *L'Essor*, 12. 2. 1968.
31 On 22 August, a whole number of leading functionaries were released from their position in the state apparatus on a national and a local level. The local Political Bureau were also dissolved and replaced by *Comités Locaux de Défense de la Révolution* (C. L. D. R.). Additionally, an *"Action Taxi"* was carried out in which officials who ran more than one taxi were listed and reprimanded. A check on those who rented out houses and owned real estate was being prepared (see *L'Essor*, 27. 11. 1967 and the following issues).
32 Stronger ideological work had already begun in 1965/6 with the extension of the system of party schools to the *Arrondissement* level. In autumn 1967 it was intensified. The C. L. D. R. was given the task of dealing in mass meetings with ideological subjects which were laid down by the C. N. D. R. (see *L'Essor*, 25. 9. 1967).
33 As early as 1965/6, the struggle to raise productivity — above all led by the trade unions — began in the state factories. Some of the methods used were emulation, awarding titles of "socialist brigade" etc. (see *Le Mali*, 4/1965, pp. 23—5). In 1967/8 these efforts were increased.
34 See pp. 152ff.
35 See "Une nouvelle phase du mouvement coopératif au Mali", in: *Le Mali*, 1/1966, pp. 6—19.
36 See further down.
37 In the field of production, there was progress made in the industrial sector which increased its production volume by putting new units into operation. In agriculture, commercialisation of food cultures was raised which resulted in a better supply for the city population (see details on page 154). The annual foreign trade deficit could be gradually decreased by rigorous import limitations from 1966/7. (For details see *Comptes économiques*, op. cit., 1964/7 and *Evolution de la situation*, op. cit.).
38 With the measures that had become necessary against the right-wing in the party and the developing bourgeoisie, the principles of a flexible policy of

alliances were often violated and transgressions against the working people (particularly by the people's militia) occurred, so that important social forces were driven into the arms of the gathering counter-revolutionary elements.

39 See further down.
40 See page 40f.
41 It is impossible to depict, analyse and assess the whole of this conception here. Here I can include only the main ideas which are necessary to understand the S. U.'s conception for a "socialist transformation" of traditional agriculture.
42 V. I. Lenin, Third Congress of the Communist International. *Report on the Tactics of the R. C. P.*, in: *Collected Works*, vol. 32, Moscow 1965, p. 482.
43 The doctrine and program of the P. F. A. were largely stamped by "African" socialism (see Congrès constitutif du P. F. A., Dakar 1.–3. 7. 1959).
44 See Congrès extraordinaire de l'U. S.–R. D. A. 22. 9. 1960. Le Mali continue, s. l., n. d., In his report to the Congress, Modibo Keita said: "From now on, the issue is to find the ways and means for introducing a planned socialist economy. And we shall not cling to alogans and existing formulas, but work creatively, based on Malinese reality and taking into consideration the experiences of other countries." (ibid., p. 16) The decision was also formulated in the Congress's economic resolution (see ibid., p. 42).
45 The documents of the 6th Congress (10 to 12 September 1962) and the seminar preparing the Congress (5 to 7 September 1962) were published in two pamphlets: "VIe Congrès de l'Union Soudanaise-R. D. A., Bamako les 10–11–12 septembre 1962"; "2e Séminaire de l'Union Soudanaise-R. D. A., Bamako les 5–6–7–septembre 1962".
46 République du Mali. "Rapport sur le Plan Quinquennal de Développement Economique et Social de la République du Mali, 1961–65", s. l., n. d.
47 Modibo Keita speaking to trade union cadres. See *L'Essor* of 8. 1. 1963. This criterion is implied in all official documents on the essence of the "*option socialiste*". In many places it is also explicitly formulated. For example, at the independence celebrations in 1963, Modibo Keita declared: "Deciding in favour of socialism means, making the working person the owner of the means of production, the controller of production" (see *L'Essor*, 30. 9. 1963).
48 S. Badian (Kouyaté), *Les dirigeants africains face à leur peuple*, Paris 1965, p. 58.
49 Ibid. p. 57.
50 See *L'Essor*, 8. 9. 1962. This thesis was formulated in many other places, e. g. in the political resolution passed at the 6th Congress it is stated: ". . . based on the fact that our fundamental and irrevocable decision is socialism, which is indivisible in its aims . . ." (VIe Congrès, loc. cit., p. 171).
51 S. B. Kouyaté declared in this spirit at the 2nd seminar: ". . . Our aim (social ownership of the means of production to satisfy collective needs) is the aim of scientific socialism . . ." (2e Séminaire, loc. cit. p. 73).
52 The organisational resolution of the 6th Congress states: "The Congress . . . decides, that cadre schools will be founded . . . It proposes to the party that the program [for the cadre schools – K. E.] include the historical, economic,

cultural and social events in the Republic of Mali, Africa and the world, the history and principles of the party *plus the principles of scientific socialism without a knowledge of which a responsible functionary cannot successfully cope with the problems involved in building socialism in our country*" (VIe Congrès, loc. cit., p. 182; my emphasis − K. E.). Extension of the party scholls to a national, regional and district level was begun from 1963/4 against the resistance of the right-wing forces in the party leadership. For details of their curricular − which basically corresponded to the demands of the 6th Congress − see *Programme de l'Ecole Supérieure du Parti*, Bamako n. d. (Ms.) and *Programme des Ecoles Régionales du Parti*, Bamako n. d. (Ms.). From the mid-1960s, Marxism-Leninism was not only taught at the party schools, but included in the philosophy lessons of the schools for general education.

53 S. B. Kouyaté characterised the representatives of this ideology very well in his book (see S. Badian, op. cit., pp. 55ff.).
54 See Yves Bénot, *Idéologies des indépendences africaines*, Paris 1969, pp. 169−81.
55 See 2e Séminaire, loc. cit., p. 73. In this spirit, the 6th Congress documents also state: ". . . The ways and means we shall apply will differ to the same extent as the starting conditions differ in those countries (which have built or are still building socialism) where they have already been applied" (VIe Congrès, loc. cit., p. 91).
56 See VIe Congrès, loc. cit. pp. 105−6.
57 I. Diarra, "Mass Party and the Construction of Socialism", in: *World Marxist Review*, 1/1967.
58 VIe Congrès, loc. cit., p. 91.
59 See ibid. pp. 91−109 and *Plan Quinquennal*, loc. cit., pp. 12−32. For details of the development plan and its problems generally, see G. Thole, "Die Republik Mali", in: *Geographische Berichte*, 4/1967, pp. 257−84.
60 See VIe Congrès, loc. cit., pp. 169−73.
61 This stage was described at the 6th Congress in the following way: "On the basis created by socialist transformation, i. e. on the basis of a semi-socialism, which will be a feature of agricultural, handicraft and industrial production, and as a result of the industry that arises through utilisation of the hydro-electrical resources and perhaps the mineral resources, an accelerated development to socialism will be necessary" (ibid., p. 106).
62 Ulyanovski states that traditional utopian elements are generally a part of socialist thinking in the developing countries (see R. Ulyanovski, "Der Einfluß des wissenschaftlichen Sozialismus auf die nationale Befreiungsbewegung", in: *Aus der Internationalen Arbeiterbewegung*, Berlin, 14/1968, p. 25).
63 2e Séminaire, loc. cit., p. 77.
64 "On a national level, the wealth is created by all for the use of all. The state is the instrument which creates the wealth with the help of those means that the nation has given it, and then distributes this wealth in the interest of the community. Here the development is in the direction, not of encouraging a few rich, but of satisfying the needs of the whole national community. In this way, the cohesion of the economic fate with all its demands is made

reality. Under these circumstances — and only under these — will Africa find back to itself, by experiencing the deep spirit of humanity and contributing the best from its heritage into modern life." (See Badian, op. cit., pp. 58ff.).

65 For literature on the Narodny movement, see footnote 60 of the Introduction in this book.
66 *Colloque sur les politiques de développement*, loc. cit., p. 179. See also I Diarra, op. cit., pp. 25—8.
 At the 2nd Seminar, Kouyaté tried to substantiate the leading role of the national-democratic mass party and its petty bourgeois intellectual leaders by describing the relationship between the colonial power and the colonised people as a specific variation of the labour-capital relationship and thus concluding that the national liberation movement is comparable with the proletarian movement in the industrial countries and the leading social force — the intellectual officialdom — is homologous with the proletariat (see 2ᵉ Séminaire, loc. cit., pp. 74—6). He also expressed this opinion in his book published in 1965 (see especially pp. 157—64 and I. Diarra, op. cit., pp. 26—8).
67 2ᵉ Séminaire, loc. cit., p. 76.
68 In Moscow, the head of the Tunisian delegation, M. Harmel, declared: "Both [non-capitalist path and socialist stage — K. E.] may not be separated by a Chinese wall and are even linked logically and historically, so that the non-capitalist path can develop into socialism. However, there is a difference between them and it would be wrong to identify them and to claim that the non-capitalist path leads almost automatically to socialism. Not all material and subjective prerequisites exist for this. It is a stage which can take a long time and in which sharp struggles can be necessary and possibilities of set-backs, retrograde movements and stagnation . . . exist" (*Internationale Beratung der kommunistischen und Arbeiterparteien*, loc. cit., pp. 232—3).
69 In practice, the Sudanese Union definitely took steps to solve the problems of this stage, however, it saw them as part of an already existing socialist transformation.
70 I. Diarra, op. cit., p. 26.
71 See N. S. Simoniya, *Ob osobennostach nacional'no — osvoboditel'nych revolucij*, Moscow 1968, p. 88.
72 See speech by M. M. Keita in Moscow for the 50th anniversary of the October revolution (*L'Essor*, 15. 1. 1968), speech by M. Keita for 1 May 1968 (*L'Essor*, 6. 5. 1968) and a number of articles on ideological questions printed in *L'Essor* after 22 August 1967.
73 See *1967. An I de la révolution*, Bamako n. d.
74 R. A. Ulyanovski, "Besonderheiten und Schwierigkeiten der national-demokratischen Revolution auf dem nichtkapitalistischen Entwicklungsweg", in: *Einheit*, Berlin, 6/1970, pp. 788—9.
75 *L'Essor*, 3. 1. 1966 and VIᵉ Congrès, loc. cit., p. 96.
76 The five-year plan intended to raise national gross production from 52.4 billion Fr.-CFA (1959) to 84.8 billion Fr.-CFA (1965) which would have corresponded to an annual increase of 8%, particularly through increasing plant (by 70%)

and animal (by 87%) production. This increased production (linked with a diversification of production structure) was to make Mali independent of food imports and it was intended to increase the export of agricultural products (some part-processed) by 40% in order to help finance industrial and infrastructural projects (see *Rapport sur le Plan Quinquennal* loc. cit., pp. 7—18).

77 See the corresponding section of the plan (ibid., pp. 22—4), especially: S. L. Traoré, "Activités de l'Office du Niger", in: *Economie et Politique*, 123/1964, pp. 109—19.

78 See *Rapport sur le Plan Quinquennal*, loc. cit., pp. 21—2.

79 The description of the co-operative system is on the basis of the most important documents of this conception: *Action rurale. Edition spéciale. Conférence territorial de l'Union Soudanaise*, 17/18/19/10/1958, s. l., n. d.; "Collectivités rurales et action", in: *Le Mali*, 12/1959, pp. 37—41; Loi No. 60—8 du 9 juin 1960 portant statuts des Sociétés mutuelles de Développement rural dans la République Soudanaise. *Journal Officiel de la République Soudanaise*, 57/1960, pp. I—V; Loi No. 60—9 portant statuts des Groupements ruraux de production et de secours mutuel et des Groupements ruraux associés dans la République Soudanaise, ibid., pp. V—VIII; *Action rurale. Edition spéciale. Organisation du Monde Rural en République du Mali*, s. l., n. d.; "Action rurale. Edition spéciale. Encadrement Rural en République du Mali", s. l., n. d., pp. 96—8 and "Le Développement de notre monde rural", in: *Le Mali*, 3/9/1965, pp. 13—18. In the following I will only give the sources with actual quotations or allude to documents not mentioned here.

80 In the 1959/60 conception (including Loi 60—9) the F. P. stage was not yet included. At this time, the G. R. A. was intended for the *Arrondissement* level.

81 This was based on the democratisation of the local administrative organs carried out in 1958/9, to which I shall return.

82 On Mali's administrative structure, see supplement.

83 It is composed as follows: *Vice-président, Secrétaire, Trésorier, Délégué à la production, Délégué à la commercialisation, Délégué à l'approvisionnement, Délégué aux affaires sociales*.

84 See Loi No. 60—9, art. 7, loc. cit., p. VI.

85 In 1963, this term was replaced by *"chantier d'honneur"* without the content being changed.

86 The G. R. P. S. M.'s capital was to be composed as follows:
1. members' dues which were to be paid by the family head for each taxpayer (*parts sociales*). Its amount was to be laid down by the *conseil d'administration* and approved by the *assemblée générale* and they ". . . are of the same obligatory nature as taxes" (Loi No. 60—9, art. 12, loc. cit., p. VI);
2. a sum to be taken from the "cotisations spéciales", to be used for certain expenditure which exceeded the finances of the G. R. P. S. M. It was to be laid down and collected in the same way;
3. gifts and donations;   4. profits made by collectively produced goods;
5. interest for credits, loans, etc.;
6. assests and real estate of the G. R. P. S. M.

87 Certain prerequisites for a credit had to be fulfilled which are laid down in art. 11 Loi No. 60—9 (loc. cit., p. VI).
88 VIe Congrès, loc. cit., p. 97. The use to be made of the income from the co-operative field is laid down in detail there.
89 Loi No. 60—9, art. 19, loc. cit., p. VII.
90 On the S. M. D. R. administrative system and other details see Loi No. 60—8, loc. cit., pp. I—V.
91 Here, the same applies for the sources as for the section on the co-operatives. This section is based on the following documents: *Collectivités rurales et action*, loc. cit., pp. 37—41; Salah Niaré, "Evolution de l'économie rurale au Soudan", s. l., n. d. (photostat); "Note sur l'encadrement rural", s. l., n. d. (photostat). *Encadrement rural en République du Mali*, loc. cit., *Report sur le Quinquennal*, loc. cit., p. 22; VIe Congrès, loc. cit., pp. 31—8.
92 These figures, taken from the "Encadrement Rural en République du Mali" (p. 5) contradict somewhat those from the Enquête agricole 1960, which (p. 6) ascertained 10.3 persons for the medium farms so that 2,000—3,000 inhabitants are divided among 200—300 farms.
93 *Encadrement Rurale*, loc. cit., p. 6.
94 See ibid.
95 In 1966, the season schools became a part of the Service Civique.
96 It says: "This training is purely practical, all theoretical instruction is excluded; therefore, it is suitable for illiterates" (see *Encadrement Rurale*, loc. cit., p. 9).
97 The idea of a *Service Civique* was born at the 1959 foundation congress of the S. U.
98 The *Service Civique* was first called *Service Civique Rural* and in 1966 was renamed *Centre d'Animation Rurale*. The description of the structure and tasks of the *Service Civique* given here is based in particular on "Décret Nr. 300 portant organisation du Service Civique rural du 29 octobre 1960", *Journal Officiel de la République du Mali*, 3rd year, No. 75, 17. 1. 1961 and the "Décret Nr. 247 portant organisation, mode de Recrutement et statut du Service Civique du Mali du 21 décembre 1963", *Journal Officiel de la République du Mali*, 6th year, No. 161, 15. 1. 1964, pp. 48—50.
99 See "Décret No. 247", loc. cit., p. 48.
100 *Colloque sur les politiques*, loc. cit., p. 174. The Five-Year Plan states: "As our party Congress decided in October 1958, the organization of the village will be based on the co-operative. Creation of this new co-operative organization will require a campaign of education and training which must be led by the state and the whole of the political organizations (party, trade unions, youth organisation, the women's organisations, etc.) (*Report sur le Plan Quinquennal*, loc. cit., p. 21).
101 Details of the S. U.'s organisational structure are contained in "Réglement intérieur de l'Union Soudanaise — R. D. A.," in: *VIe Congrès*, loc. cit., pp. 160—6.
102 M. M. Keita, "L'application des principes du parti dans l' organisation administrative", in: *2e Séminaire*, loc. cit., p. 31.

103 "They have now the right to control and advise the administrative organs so that the party and government decisions are correctly carried out" (M. M. Keita, op. cit., p. 32).
104 On further concrete tasks, see ibid., pp. 31—2.
105 The conference was composed of the Political Bureau members of the sub-section and delegates from the village committees.
106 M. M. Keita, op. cit., p. 34.
107 See ibid., pp. 35—6 and VIe Congrès, loc. cit., pp. 157—8.
108 See M. M. Keita, op. cit., pp. 36—8 and VIe Congrès, loc. cit., p. 164.
109 The Political Bureau was the highest executive body in the S. U. It was elected by the party congress which met every three years, in accordance with the constitution, and was also responsible to it.
110 See pages 71 ff.
111 On the system of exploitation by foreign monopoly capital and the role of trade and usury capital, see pages 69 ff.
112 S. Badian, op. cit., pp. 23—6 and p. 140, (my emphasis, — K. E.).
113 Modibo Keita, *Appel à la Nation*, Paris 1961.
114 The same sentence from which this is quoted appears in *Collectivités rurales et action*, loc. cit., pp. 38 and in *Organisation du Monde Rural*, loc. cit., p. 4.
115 See S. Badian, op. cit., p. 156.
116 Ibid., p. 26. He considered such outside structures in the precolonial period to be Islam and slave trade (see ibid., pp. 26—7).
117 Ibid., p. 140 (my emphasis — K. E.). The ideas developed here by Kouyaté appear in all documents of the S. U. and of the Malinese government in which an attitude is expressed towards its relationship to the traditional community-co-operative. "The issue is not . . . to oppose an old traditional way of life, but to adapt an already existing form of co-operation to the demands of today" (see *Collectivités rurales*, loc. cit., p. 38 and *Organisation du Monde Rurale*, loc. cit., p. 4). In the last document, it is stated on co-operative law: „Elle codifie les pratiques d'entraide et de solidarité qui ont toujours animé la vie villageoise et fait du village malien une cellule administrative et économique" (ibid., p. 6). Kouyaté used almost the same formulation in Dakar, (see *Colloque sur les politiques de développement*, loc. cit., p. 174). And M. Keita said in his appeal to the nation: "We created the country co-operatives on the village level *which perpetuate by law the bonds of solidarity which nature itself formed over centuries between the inhabitants*" (my emphasis — K. E.).
118 See S. Badian, op. cit. p. 136. By feudal structures, Kouyaté means mainly the pre-colonial aristocracy which he describes elsewhere as being "*pseudo-féodalité*" (ibid., p. 157).
119 On this question, Kouyaté takes an interesting position which, however, in the final analysis, would mean that it is necessary to regenerate decayedf innerfamily relations. He writes: „Together with the Chefferie, all forms o exploitation of man by man through personal dependence must die; e. g. the patriarchal structures on the family level which have now developed into a genuine system of exploitation of the young by the old, or the scandalous

subordination of woman under the absolute domination of man, the father over his daughter, the husband over his wife. Regenerating relations to protect the child, the young person and the woman is most important, because many of the social evils which our countries suffer from – such as flight from the village by youth, kidnapping of women, prostitution, etc. ... have their roots there" (ibid., pp. 137 ff.).

120 Ibid., pp. 139–41.
121 So says the resolution passed at the territorial conference in October 1959 (see *Conférence territoriale de l' Union Soudanaise*, loc. cit.,°p. 30). This thesis was directed in practise above all against the desertion from the countryside and was concretely expressed in the "back to the soil" movement.
122 Modibo Keita at the 1958 conference (ibid., p. 24). These views were obviously influenced, or at least confirmed, by his impressions of Israel. In a report on his journey, he says: "This economic upsurge is above all the work of loyalty to an ideal which consists in the rebirth of a country, in the rehabilitation of a persecuted and dispersed people who are re-establishing their unity, and who are doing this through a community which believes in that which binds them together, the soil ... For them, the Fatherland is above all the soil, and this attitude, which some consider sentimental, makes it possible for Israel today to be the only really socially balanced and truly independent country in the Middle East" (ibid., p. 8).
123 *Colloque sur les politiques*, loc. cit., p. 172. This largely reducing the development problems to psychological problems while not seeing that these are determined by the material conditions, clearly shows the influence of the late-colonial paternalistic agricultural doctrine which also concentrates on such problems. P. Viguier writes: „Nothing is possible so long as the ground is not psychologically prepared. Everything becomes possible from that moment on when this is the case" (P. Viguier. *L'Afrique de l'Ouest vue par un agriculteur. Problèmes de base en Afrique tropicale*, Paris 1961, p. 101).
124 In 1965, Modibo Keita declared: „The fact is that the socialist transformation of agriculture is an extremely difficult task" (*Le Mali*, 6/1965, p. 42).
125 This does not mean, that right up to the last, illusions about the traditional community did not exist to some extent. As late as 1968 it was stated: "The basic economic cell of our society is, despite everything, the extended patriarchal family in most cases, and the spirit inherited from the primitive community of solidarity and mutual aid has still not completely disappeared. In its struggle for collectivisation of agriculture, the party bases itself on this" (*Rapport de synthèse du Séminaire National sur la Coöpération en Milieu Rural*, s. l., n. d., pp. 12 ff.).
126 *L'Essor*, 24. 9. 1964, p. 6.
127 *L'Essor*, 3. 1. 1966.
128 The co-operative seminar took place in the frame of the *"révolution active"* from 27 to 30 May 1968 in Bamako. The main speech was published as a booklet (see *Rapport de synthèse*, loc. cit.).
129 Ibid., p. 13.

2. The traditional community in pre-colonial Malinese society

The social and economic relations in pre-colonial Mali were a pre-capitalist type of exploitation and dependency which had developed to differing degrees in various territories. However, there continued to exist common ownership of the land and of the most important means of production and the pre-capitalist production methods. Compared to primitive society there existed a higher level of the productive forces, leading to a greater division of labour which, in turn, made it possible to produce surplus products and exploit foreign labour.[1] But there was not enough surplus for a nuclear family to become self-sufficient and this made economic independence impossible for them.[2] The economic and social basis for the society which arose out of the existing productive forces was the village community.[3]

The economic basis for the system of social relations in the pre-colonial village community (DUGU)[4] was a short-handled hoe with an iron blade (*daba*) of various forms, used for extensive slash and burn agriculture.[5] The level of the productive forces was such that the human being saw the land as the objective natural conditions for work, but in isolation he was unable to ensure his subsistence through it. At the most, the human being could, as Marx wrote, "live off it as a substance, as the animals do"[6]. So his relationship to the soil as the natural prerequisite for his labour was the objective pre-condition for his existence as a member of the community. The low level of the productive forces demanded collective subsistence guaranteed by the community. Thus the decisive relationship in the traditional community is that of the individual as a member of the community – and only as such – to the naturally existing conditions for the realisation of his labour. What Marx said of the Asian community also applies in principle to these social and economic relations: "Property thus originally means no more than a human being's relation to his natural conditions of production as belonging to him, as his, as presupposed *along with his own being*; relations to them as *natural presuppositions* of his self, which only form, so to speak, his extended body. He actually does not relate to his conditions of production, but rather has a double existence, both subjectively as himself, and objectively in these natural nonorganic conditions of his existence. These *natural conditions* of production have two forms: (1) his existence as a member of a community ... (2) the relations to *land and soil* mediated by the community, as *its own,* as communal landed property ..."[7]

Under these conditions, the purpose of labour is to ensure the subsistence of the community and its members, i. e. to create products for use and not for exchange. This does not mean, however, that in the pre-colonial community the level of the productive forces made it impossible to produce a small amount of surplus, (and this gave rise to an exchange economy and exploitation) which made possible and necessary the division of labour, especially the separation of the most important trades (such as that of the smith) from field work.[8] However, the division of labour between handicrafts and agriculture did not develop between the various villages, but within the community itself through the direct exchange of products between farmers and craftsmen. Each member of the community had a specific, concrete contribution to make to ensure the subsistence of the whole community. The community knew only one use for those products which were not necessary for immediate subsistence or for fulfillment of duties towards a higher community in the social structure or for real or imagined powers dominating them: unproductive hoarding.[9]

Thus the traditional community was economically a far-reaching closed system of relations which lacked the driving power for development of the productive forces and for changes in its social and economic conditions, because it had almost no contact to a larger local market.[10]

These social and economic relations in the traditional African village community contain the basic elements of the small Indian community "... based on possession in common of the land, on the blending of culture and handicrafts, on an unalterable division of labour ..." and formed "... self-sufficient production units ..." in which "The chief part of the products is destined for direct use by the community itself ..."[11] As in the Indian communities, the simple productive organism delivers the key to the inner stability of these self-sufficient social systems.[12]

The traditional African village community was organised on a territorial basis and consisted of several extended families (Lu). The individual was not a direct member of the village community, but indirectly through the extended family, which was organised on lines of blood relationship. So the actual members or elements of the village community system were not isolated individuals (or nuclear families), but extended families with their own specific structural and functional relations.

The extended family consisted of nuclear families of several generations knit into one family union. Engels described this as the transitional stage "between the maternal family which evolved out of group marriage and the individual family known to the modern world"[13]. As a part of the territorial community, it had the permanent right to use a particular section of the land belonging to it. It was under these circumstances, i. e. as a part of the village community, that it acted as the basic economic cell of the village [14] and it was in this framework that the soil was effectively used as part of the production process.

The extended family owned communally [15] all the tools necessary for the subsistence of the community and its members, and also owned the products created. They formed the FOROBA of the extended family.

First, the FOROBA included above all the whole land placed at the extended family's disposal by the higher community and the tools necessary for its cultivation. The main part of the cultivated soil was the common field of the extended family where all the active family members worked in a definite natural division of labour [16] on a certain number of days in the week. The products they created also became part of the FOROBA. Because of its importance for the subsistence of the primary community, this common field was also called Foroba.[17]

A smaller part of the cultivated ground was DIONFORO, which was a field left to the nuclear families and unmarried adults for their individual use. The products created there were small compared to the total product and played a secondary role economically.[18]

To the FOROBA also belonged all secondary means of production necessary for field work (animals, tools, fishing ground, etc.) [19] and all the products gained, the weapons – above all those used for collective defence – and hunting booty as well as any slaves captured.[20]

The FOROBA ensured the subsistence of the family community. It fed and clothed the members, and all the acquisitions necessary for subsistence and production were made through it.[21] All the tributes to the higher community (the village – DUGU) and real or imagined powers over the community and also the FURU-NA-FOLO (the symbolic price for a bride [22]), were taken out of the FOROBA in the form of taxes, contributions or sacrifices.

The head of the extended family or the FAKOROBA [23] played an eminent role in the LU's social system. In general, he was the oldest man from the oldest generation. The position of the FAKOROBA corresponded to the role he played in ensuring the subsistence of each individual member of the community. He was the incarnation of this community, administered its FOROBA, and managed and organised the whole production and reproduction process of the extended family. He received support from a type of family council, the KOROU (the elders). He was the only representative of the extended family for the other primary or higher communities and for the forefathers and spirits of the Lu.

The social relations between the extended families within a village were determined by the low level of the productive forces, which on the one hand, necessitated collective guarantee for subsistence on the village level expressed in common ownership of the soil and, on the other, enforced a specific division of labour.[24]

The mutual aid and collective responsibility for subsistence of the whole community was institutionalised in different ways in the various ethnic groups. The LAMA was one of the two main forms among the Bambara and Malinké.[25] Within the framework of the LAMA, two or more extended families helped each other in times of need or to do work which one family could not cope with. The TON[26] had basically the same function. As an institution it had simply a different organisational basis. It was a youth organisation to which all circumcised[27] unmarried youth of the village belonged. Its main task was to carry out quickly all difficult agricultural work in return for a symbolic present and food for the extended family members, to cultivate the fields of sick or needy members of the community and to do work necessary for the collective interest (road-building, etc.).[28]

Apart from these relations, based on the necessity to ensure collective subsistence, there also existed relations based on the division of labour within the village community. They were between the mass of the community members who, as farmers, were the actual respected community members (HORON) and the NYAMAKALAU[29], the craftsmen. These were divided up into various endogamous groups in accordance with their specialisation: the NUMU (smiths), LORO (coppersmiths), GARANKA (saddlers), KULE (woodcarvers), DONSO (hunters), DYELI (Griots – praise-singers and memorisers of history). Their labour-based isolation was, in fact, an institutionalisation of a specific form of labour division within the village community and was the social expression of its simple production mechanism.

The classification and separation of certain families as NUMU, LORO, etc., within the community, ensured for the community, the necessary economic supplementation for agriculture, guaranteed – independent of other economic entities – the self-sufficiency[30] of the total economic system and its continuous, unchanged reproduction. The NYAMAKALAU's economic function corresponded to their role in the non-economic field: they were isolated from the community members doing farming (HORON) and could, therefore, never become their representative, i. e. the village head; on the other hand, they were respected and often feared, because they fulfilled social functions which only they could carry out and which were necessary for the functioning of the whole system: making masks, circumcision, the work of the hangman and gravedigger, they passed on the words of the village head, kept oral traditions, etc.

Thus the traditional agricultural community was a system of social relations of co-operation and solidarity based on communal ownership of the land with specific organisation of the division of labour (organic connection between field-work and crafts within the community). The village head or DUGUTIGI played a decisive role to keep this system functioning.

The unity of the agricultural community existed through the DUGUTIGI. He managed this self-sufficient community and carried out all the functions to collectively guarantee subsistence on the village level which were necessary either in reality or only in the imagination of the community members. As the personification of the community he administered the land, distributed it to the community members, laid down the main stages of agricultural work, organised collective labour of general interest and, as priest, ensured the favours of the spirits.[31] He administered the village reserves[32], which were the collective security for the community. They were used to help distressed members, keep guests of the village, make sacrifices, pay taxes or tributes. And finally, the DUGUTIGI represented the community, organised its defence when necessary and arbitrated in cases of dispute. All the DUGUTIGI's decisions and measures were checked by the village council, composed of all FAKOROBA; and in the presence of the men of the village, it discussed and decided on all questions concerning the community, and the DUGUTIGI could not change them without agreement of the council.[33]

So one can say: the pre-colonial agricultural community was a social system whose economic and social (and on this basis, political and ideological) structure was completely directed at collectively guaranteeing the subsistence of the community and its members. It contained the necessary prerequisites for the reproduction of the community under conditions where man had very little control of nature. The individual was able to exist only to the same extent as the community was able to ensure subsistence. And this could only be ensured if the system functioned, i. e. – apart from unexpected events like war, natural catastrophes, etc. – if each member of the community adapted himself to the system. This meant no more and no less than that year in and year out each individual had to make a definite material or mental contribution of a certain quality and quantity for the reproduction of the community. And it also meant being unconditionally satisfied with the little that the community had to offer, i.e. developing no ambitions, it meant absolute subordination to the norms of the community and the instructions of its representatives. Only such behaviour of each community member enabled the system for collective subsistence to function. Thus, in the final analysis, the social behaviour of the traditional community peasant was economically determined, it was the expression of an inherent part of the system of social relations in the community. "During this stage", Arnauld wrote, "no one can survive outside the community; only the community could care for the needs of childhood and youth, and ease the want of the old and sick. The community is both the means for survival and the result of this necessity. Its 'democracy' is also a democracy for survival: it is a form of social organisation necessary for survival."[34]

In general, the farming communities in pre-colonial Mali[35] were integrated into a larger social system[36] which was ruled by an aristocracy that acquired the peasants' surplus products in the form of a product or labour rent.[37] The basis of this exploitation was not the ruling class's private ownership of the land. The genesis of this aristocracy and the exploitation it practised was *essentially* like the model of oriental despotism described by Engels in *Anti-Dühring*. This was that the originally higher organ, which formed a comprehensive entity in respect to the individual community with its bodies, began to lead a life of its own. Its original representatives began to subordinate the lower bodies.[38] Even if precolonial Mali did not have a predominating collective interest, such as irrigation in the ancient orient, to develop a comprehensive entity standing above all small communities[39], there did exist a federation of villages called KAFO, which represented an originally higher organisational form of the community.[40] They were based on collective economic (exchange of products, land clearance, water supply, labour power exchange, road-building, joint fishing and hunting grounds, etc.), military (defence in general and against slave-hunting from the 17th to 19th centuries in particular) and religious interests which arose objectively or subjectively out of the need for existence of each community (DUGU) and could be taken care of only by a higher, more complex entity. The KAFO, as this higher entity, thus became the pre-condition to ensure subsistence of each village community and its members. In other words: the common property of the particular village communities described above, could be realised and mediated only through the fact that it belonged to the KAFO. Thus the KAFO became the higher owner to whom belonged a part of the producers' surplus product, be it in the form of natural produce for the KAFO reserves, of labour for collective projects, be it in one or another form for the upkeep of the person – the KAFOTIGI[41] – through whom the higher community existed and for his functions for each community, or for homage to the KAFO spirits.[42]

These relations between the higher community, the village community and the individual correspond to those described by Marx in all Asian communities where "... the *comprehensive unity* standing above all these little communities appears as the higher *proprietor* or as the *sole* proprietor; the real communities hence only as hereditary possessors. Because the *unity* is the real proprietor and the real presupposition of communal property, it follows that this unity can appear as a *particular* entity above the many real particular communities, where the individual is then in fact propertyless, or property — i. e., the relation of the individual to the *natural* conditions of labour and of reproduction as belonging to him, as the objective, nature-given inorganic body of his subjectivity — appears mediated for him through a cession by the total unity . . . to the individual, through the mediation of the particular commune. The surplus product — which is, incidentally determined by law in consequence of the real appropriation through labour — thereby automatically belongs to this highest unity."[43]

Marx described this relationship in which the individual, in fact, owns nothing and to a certain degree is himself the property of the community, as "general slavery", but he carefully separates them from the socio-economic relations of slave society and feudal society (serfdom). He differentiates between this "general slavery" and the socio-economic relations of the slave and feudal societies (serfdom) ". . . where the worker himself appears among the natural conditions of production for a third individual or community (this is not the case, for example, with the general slavery of the orient, *only* from the European point of view) — i. e. property is no longer the relation of the working individual to the objective conditions of labour . . ."[44] This general slavery, i. e. the subordination of the individual to the communal structure, appeared as a social relation in pre-colonial Mali, not only in the relation of the individual to the higher organisation (KAFO), but also in his relation to the DUGU and to the LU, each time mediated through the lower community. On each level, this relationship made possible the acquisition of the producers' surplus product by that person through whom the community existed, enabling this person to become gradually independent of and to raise himself above it. Such possibilities were decisively limited in the lower community (LU, DUGU), because here, the original democracy had much stronger roots and the low level of the productive forces and the subsistence character of the economy stopped any attempts of the village and extended family heads to exploit its members. These factors were much weaker on the higher community level: The original democracy was less effective, the small surplus product of the individual was compensated for by the greater quantity and there were greater possibilities for sale on the market (such as through contact with interregional trade routes).[45] Thus, the leaders in the KAFO became an aristocracy which exploited the community peasants, by raising themselves above and acquiring for themselves the surplus product due to the higher community. Even though the function of the higher community official and of the exploiter were now interwoven into one person[46], it was still necessary to develop a special apparatus of oppression to safeguard the exploiter function. This became the state and continued to appear as the higher community into which further individual communities were incorporated through its official institutions.

In accordance with its genesis, the socio-economic basis of acquisition of the community peasant's surplus labour by the ruling aristocracy was not feudal private ownership of the land, but the higher property which was originally passed from the higher community structure to the developing state and which in no way threatens the continued existence of the common property – now mediated by the higher state property – in each village community. In precolonial Mali, as in the early Asiatic societies, "clan or communal property exists in fact as the foundation".[47]

This specific variant of land property is realised in a specific form of ground rent, which is the personal or collective acquisition of the surplus product of the particular communities, legally due to the higher communal body by the former representatives and officials of this higher structure who are now raising themselves to a ruling class. Therefore, Marx makes a fundamental difference between them and other forms of ground rent[48] through the example of early oriental societies and calls its characteristic feature a tribute relation as against slave or serf relationships.[49]

Ground rent was demanded in pre-colonial Mali in the form of a tax or through "work in the public interest", "labour-service on the chief's or king's field".[50] In accordance with the under-lying social relationship, it was not given directly, but mediated through the particular community.[51]

The contradiction between community property and higher state property, between the function of the official and the exploitative role of the ruling aristocracy, between original democracy and hierarchical subordination, which grew up in pre-colonial West African society at the beginning of the Middle Ages – at the earliest since the development of the Ghana Empire in the fourth century – became particularly strong during the slave trade period (sixteenth to nineteenth century) and elements of exploitation and oppression penetrated into the primary community.[52] They were expressed by a differentiation between the extended families, in tendencies by the older to exploit the younger, of the DUGUTIGI to exploit the community members, of the men to exploit the women and a strong subordination of the NYAMAKALAU under the HORON. However, these social contradictions could not destroy the basic relations of the village community before colonial rule; up to the end of the nineteenth century, the original community relations were stronger than the elements destroying it. One of the reasons for this was that slave trade, with its resulting stagnation of the productive forces, made it economically necessary for centuries, to maintain communal relations of solidarity.

Apart from the two main classes[53] – the aristocracy and the peasants – living at the time and on the territory here under consideration, there also existed the DYON (slave) class, a secondary factor in this socio-economic relationship.[54]

The DYON had been generally enslaved during wars of conquest.[55] No longer saleable after the first generation, they were generally freed after the third and fourth generation as DYONGORON.[56] If they were not sold, the DYON were either distributed or made soldiers,[57] settled on the territory of the state that enslaved them or were left on their own territory whose higher property was taken over by the ruler. In every case, the inner structure of the enslaved community was maintained or reproduced; the DYON were simply obliged to pay tributes and do forced labour for the ruler, so that their internal relationships were hardly modified compared to the free communities.

The DYON could also become the property of an extended family – but never an individual – through sale or in another way. He was then integrated into the extended family as a WOLOSO, took part in the production process and had the right to guaranteed subsistence within the extended family. His different socio-economic position to the other members of the extended family was that his surplus product belonged to the primary community, but he himself, not belonging to this (but to the FOROBA) had not even an indirect claim on this product and always lost it. However, where the aristocracy acquired most of the surplus product of *all* producers, his position differed very little from the other members of the family.[58] The production conditions of society in pre-colonial Mali made it impossible for slavery to become a mass phenomenon determining the social system. It modified, but did not eliminate, the decisive relationship. Thus, in most of pre-colonial Mali, the basic socioeconomic relations can be described as follows: under the conditions of relatively undeveloped productive forces, an aristocracy placed itself above the community which was based on common property (or mediated ownership) of the land, to which agriculture and handicrafts were directly connected. They (the aristocracy) acquired for themselves that surplus product of the community which was actually due to the comprehensive community unit, but which was now state property. Further, this aristocracy exploited slaves, but this exploitation relationship was not a determining factor from a socioeconomic viewpoint. The essential feature of these relations correspond to what Marx called the Asiatic mode of production[59] and about which he wrote in 1859 in the foreword to *A Critique of Political Economy* that it is the first of the four antagonistic economic social formations[60] — a view which "was never denied or corrected by Marx and Engels"[61]. If in pre-colonial Mali a number of phenomena and features of the Asiatic mode of production in its classical Asiatic form — such as the despotism or the strong economic function of the state, determined by the irrigation systems — do not exist, and instead we find the original democracy and the importance of the community (also the larger significance of its property as against the higher state property) carrying greater weight within the whole society, this cannot be considered a reason to grasp pre-colonial social relations in Mali as not being a form of the Asiatic mode of production. These facts show simply that in these areas (1) this was a specific *variant* of the Asiatic mode of production — Marx speaks in the plural in this foreword when naming each mode of production and in the *Foundations of the Critique of Political Economy* he emphasizes that, according to the concrete conditions, the relations described can take on a more despotic or more democratic form[62] — and (2) the process of its development was still at a *relatively early stage*.

REFERENCES

1. On the concrete stage of development of the productive forces, see J. Suret-Canale, *Schwarzafrika. Geschichte West- und Zentralafrikas*, Berlin 1966. pp. 70—7.
2. See V. V. Krylov, "Osnovnye tendencii razvitija agrarnych otnošenij v Tropičeskoj Afrike", in: *Narody Asii i Afriki*, 4/1965, pp. 2—5.
3. Whenever I speak of "the village community" here and in the following, I always mean the village community based on agriculture.
4. The words written in small capitals are taken from the Bambara. They are used by all Mandé groups to describe the various social institutions.
5. As it is not possible to deal here with the system of soil cultivation in detail in pre-colonial Mali, see H. Labouret, *Les paysans d'Afrique Noire*, Paris 1941, pp. 155—206 and P. Viguier, op. cit., pp. 17—32.
6. K. Marx, *Foundations of the Critique of Political Economy*, The Pelican Marx Library 1973, p. 485.
7. Ibid., p. 491.
8. The first social division of labour between agriculture and animal husbandry took place in West Africa on an ethnic basis. On the specialisation of the various ethnic groups in Mali, see J. Gallais, "Signification du groupe ethnique au Mali", in: *L'Homme*, 2/1962 and N'Diayé, *Groupes ethniques au Mali*, Bamako 1970.
9. Cattle, gold. This tendency is found generally in societies with undeveloped exchange relations, but is particularly strong in those based on the village community: "In the early stage of the circulation of commodities, it is the

surplus use-values alone that are converted into money. Gold and silver thus become of themselves social expressions for superfluity or wealth. This naive form of hoarding becomes perpetuated in those communities in which the traditional mode of production is carried on for the supply of a fixed and limited circle of home wants. It is thus with the people of Asia, and particularly of the East Indies." (K. Marx, *Capital*, vol. 1, Progress Publishers, Moscow n. d., p. 131).

10 A highly developed trade, which existed especially in West Sudan during the Middle Ages and on which the wealth and fame of Timbuctoo, Djenné and other cities was based, was less an expression of developed internal exchange relations, but far more of an interregional (foreign) trade between the Sudan and North Africa which was concentrated (up to monopolisation: gold, slaves) in the hands of the aristocracy and hardly touched the communities (see L. E. Koubbel, *Le problème de l'apparition des structures étatiques au Soudan occidental*, Moscow 1967). The developing slave trade of the sixteenth and seventeenth centuries decisively affected the life of the communities. However, its main affect was the stagnation and even partly retrogression of the productive forces and it can in no way be compared with the internal market which revolutionises the productive forces and production relations (see J. Suret-Canale, *Schwarzafrika*, loc. cit., pp. 191–205).

11 K. Marx, *Capital*, vol. 1, loc. cit., p. 337.

12 See Marx' comments on the causes of the unchangeability of Asian societies (ibid., p. 338).

13 F. Engels, "Origin of the Family, Private Property and State", in: K. Marx/ F. Engels, *Selected Works*, vol. 3, Moscow 1973, p. 234.

14 Over and above this, and on this basis, the extended family was, of course the basic social cell of the village community in the broadest sense (see J. Gallais, *Signification du groupe ethnique au Mali*, loc. cit., p. 116; E. Leynaud, *Les cadres sociaux de la vie rurale dans la Haute-vallée du Niger*, Paris 1961, vol. II, pp. 156–63; V. Paques, *Les Bambara*, Paris 1954, pp. 50–3; H. Labouret, *Les paysans d'Afrique Noire*, loc. cit., pp. 138–54 and *Les Manding et leur langue*, Paris 1934, pp. 53–62 and the comprehensive ethnological works of M. Delafosse, G. Dieterlen, Ch. Monteil, M. Palau Marti, D. Paulme and B. Holas which are listed in the bibliography).

15 Property in the defined sense, i. e. property mediated through belonging to the higher community (Dugu).

16 For details about division of labour in the extended family, see V. Paques, op. cit., pp. 64–7 and H. Labouret, "Le travail familial chez les Mandingues", in: *L'Anthropologie*, 43/1933, pp. 220–1.

17 To make the difference clear, I write this in small letters.

18 See S. E. R. E. S. A., *Etude sur l'économie agricole au Soudan*. juin-octobre 1959, Rapport Général, s. l., n. d., pp. 37–8. Among the Mande group the Dionforo already played a significant role, but it was still economically secondary: the product produced on it on two days a week (Ula-No means millet of the evening, because it was produced outside of the collective five-

day working time, and sometimes during the evening) served to provide food on these two days and to satisfy personal needs – additional clothing, perhaps animals (see H. Labouret, *Les Manding et leur langue*, loc. cit., pp. 61ff.).

19 For further details about the composition of the FOROBA see E. Leynaud, *Les cadres sociaux*, loc. cit., pp. 223ff. and H. Labouret, *Les Manding et leur langue*, loc. cit., pp. 50–64.

20 On this, see further down.

21 The main thing here is the exchange of products with the smithy, who produced the means of production (the *daba* and the cult objects, masks, etc.). Generally, only salt and cola-nuts were brought in from beyond the DUGU border or the border of a village federation.

22 The marriage and the "bride-price" were always negotiated between the FAKOROBA of the extended family concerned, i. e. only via the FAKOROBA and his approval was it possible for a young man to found his own family which was a necessary prerequisite for future economic independence. Thus the FURU-NA-FOLO helped to maintain the system. However, one must not make this function too absolute – as I. Diallo does by strongly following Cl. Meillassoux – because the decisive factor for maintaining the system was the necessity for the existence of a community to ensure mere subsistence and this was determined by the level of the productive forces and reflected in the property relations (see Ibrahim Diallo, *Les traditions, III. Les mécanismes fonctionnels de la société traditionelle*, in: *L'Essor*, 5. 2. 1971, p. 3 and Cl. Meillassoux, "Essai d'*interprétation* du phénomène économique dans les sociétés traditionelles d'autosubsistance", in: *Cahiers d'Etudes Africaines*, 4/1960, pp. 38–67).

23 On his position and function, see Ch. Monteil, *Une cité soudanaise – Djenné, métropole du delta central du Niger*, Paris 1932, pp. 159–60 and H. Labouret, op. cit., pp. 55–6.

24 Needless to say, apart from these economic factors, there also existed other causes for co-operation within the village community (common defence interests, common cult, etc.) which cannot be dealt with here (see J. Gallais, "La signification du village en Afrique de l'Ouest", in: *Cahiers de Sociologie économique*, 2/1965, pp. 128–62).

25 On the organisation for mutual aid among another important ethnic group of farmers, the Minyanka, see the very interesting and detailed study by R. P. D. Malgras, "La condition sociale du paysan minyanka dans le cercle de San", *Bulletin de l'I. F. A. N.*, series B, 1–2/1960, pp. 276–98, particularly the section: La vie du paysan minyanka au sein des communautés rurales.

26 The only sound sociological investigation of the TON which also exists among the Minyanka under another name (see Malgras, ibid.) has been undertaken by E. Leynaud ("Fraternités d'âge et sociétés de culture dans la Haute-Vallée du Niger", in: *Cahiers d'Etudes Africaines*, 21/1966, pp. 41–68). Even if his investigations were made in 1959–60 and after, he defined in detail the place of the TON in pre-colonial society in this work. Some economic aspects of the TON are also dealt with by S. de Ganay, "Les communautés d'entr'aide des

Bambaras du Soudan Français", in: *Actes du 5ᵉ Congrès International des Sciences Anthropologiques et Ethnologiques*, Philadelphia 1956, pp. 425–9. D. Zahan, *Sociétés d'initiation Bambara*, Paris 1960, deals especially with the relation between the initiation societies and the TON.

27 On the question of circumcision and age-groups see G. Dieterlen, *Essai sur la réligion Bambara*, Paris 1951.

28 The TON was also a type of village police which maintained order on behalf of the community (see S. de Ganay, op. cit., pp. 425–6). Further, it had an important function in the Bambara state army (see Ch. Monteil, *Les Bambara de Ségou et du Kaarta*, Paris 1924, p. 311).

29 The most comprehensive work on this problem is the book by Bokar N'Diayé, *Les castes au Mali*, Bamako 1970. An older work by Mamby Sidibé is also valuable ("Les gens de caste ou Nyamakala au Soudan Français", in: *Notes Africains*, 81/1959, pp. 13–17). J. Suret-Canale (*Schwarzafrika*, loc. cit., pp. 115–17) goes into the problem, but not in detail as corresponds to the character of his book.

30 As the NYAMAKALAU only produced handicraft products necessary for the community they had only few customers so that in regard to quantity of production they were more farmers than craftsmen. However, their function and position in the village community was determined exclusively by their handicraft work.

31 The DUGUTIGI or one of his forefathers – or so it is imagined by this ethnic group, concluded an agreement with the earth (DUGU) spirit (NYANA), the actual owner of the earth (NYANA DUGU-DA-SIRI) on the community's use of the soil and he is, therefore, looked upon as the high priest of the NYANA whose favours he asks for through sacrifices and rites on behalf of the community. For details of the religious aspects of the traditional farming community see G. Dieterlen, op. cit.

32 The village reserves were composed mainly of part of the spoils from hunting and fishing and the millet harvest. In its socio-economic essence it was part of the product of the primary community passed over to the village community to ensure collective subsistence. For other aspects of its composition and use see V. Paques, op. cit., p. 62.

33 H. Labouret, *Les Manding et leur langue*, loc. cit., p. 49.

34 J. Arnauld, *Du colonialisme au socialisme*, Paris 1966, p. 269.

35 This concerns at least the main ethnic groups being considered here.

36 On Malinese territory, this concerns, apart from the medieval empires, above all, the non-Islamic Bambara kingdom of Ségou (1600–1882) and Kaarta (1633–1854), the Islamic Fulbe kingdom of Massina (1810–62) and the kingdom of the Toucouleur El Hadj Omar Saidu Tall (1797–1864) and his son and successor Ahmadu which was destroyed in 1893 by French colonial conquerors. In the south, in the second half of the nineteenth century, the Kong kingdom (Sikasso) and the Samory state reached Malinese territory (see J. Suret-Canale, *Schwarzafrika*, loc. cit., pp. 210–19 and 256–67). The most important literature is also given there.

37 As I do not intend to analyse all the social relationships in precolonial West Africa in this book, I have limited myself to describing the most important inter-relationships in order to make myself understood. For details see J. Suret-Canale, *Schwarzafrika*, loc. cit.
38 See F. Engels, *Anti-Dühring*, Progress Publishers, Moscow 1969, pp. 214–15.
39 Marx and Engels have never limited the common interests that led to the development of the higher community to the need for irrigation only. (See ibid., p. 214; see also G. Lewin, "Zu einigen Problemen der 'asiatischen Produktionsweise' in der gesellschaftlichen Entwicklung Chinas", in: G. Lewin, *Die ersten fünfzig Jahre der Song-Dynastie in China*, Berlin 1973, p. 231).
40 This federation of villages, which has nothing in common with the character of the (colonial) cantons established later, existed among all the Mande people (see H. Labouret, *Les Manding et leur langue*, loc. cit., pp. 43–7); among the Bobo and Dogon, who never reached the stage of founding independent states, it became a very pronounced form of the highest social organization (see J. Gallais, *Signification du groupe ethnique au Mali*, op. cit., pp. 116–17; D. Paulme, *Organisation sociale des Dogon*, Paris 1940 (Diss.) and M. Palau Marti, *Les Dogons*, Paris 1957. See also Cl. Meillassoux, "Histoire et institutions du Kafo de Bamako, d'après la tradition des Niaré", in: *Cahiers d'Etudes Africaines*, 14/1963, pp. 186–22).
41 The position of KAFOTIGI, like the DUGUTIGI, was inherited by the younger brother from the older. It was controlled by an annual meeting of the DUGUTIGI (see H. Labouret, *Les Manding et leur langue*, loc. cit., pp. 45–6).
42 For details see, apart from the literature given in footnote 34, V. Paques, op. cit., pp. 58–60.
43 K. Marx, *Foundations of the Critique of Political Economy*, loc. cit., pp. 472–3.
44 Ibid., pp. 495–6, see also p. 493.
  In my opinion, this fundamental difference which Marx emphasized excludes from the beginning that one can — as several authors silently or explicitly do — identify the relations dealt with here with those of a feudal society. One example of this is H. Stöber, "Zum Problem des Feudalismus in Afrika vor der Kolonialherrschaft", in: *Ethnographisch-Archäologische Zeitschrift*, Berlin, 12/1971, pp. 80–1.
45 Particularly for this reason, control of the trade routes played such an important role for the medieval states (see J. Suret-Canale, *Schwarzafrika*, loc. cit., p. 122).
46 This double function is very clearly seen with the FAMA (king) of Ségou (see V. Paques, op. cit.).
47 K. Marx, *Foundations of the Critique of Political Economy*, loc. cit., p. 473.
48 K. Marx, *Capital*, vol. 3, Progress Publishers, Moscow n. d., p. 634 and pp. 790ff.
49 Ibid., p. 326. In this connection it appears to me incomprehensible also on the subject dealt with in footnote 44 in this chapter, that H. Stöber and other authors use those Marx quotations where Marx makes a special point of differentiating between tribute relations and the form of rent linked to them on the

one hand, and the feudal relations and feudal rent on the other, in order to describe social relations in pre-colonial Africa as feudal.
50 See for details D. T. Niane, *Recherches sur l'Empire du Mali au Moyen Age*, Conakry 1962, pp. 41–2; J. Bazin, "Recherches sur les formations sociopolitiques anciennes en pays Bambara", in: *Etudes Maliennes*, 1/1970, pp. 37–53.
51 J. Suret-Canale points out in this connection that the generalisation of the village community in the "societies with a state" is caused by the fact that under the given conditions, the village community is the most convenient form of organization for the ruling aristocracy to exploit the peasants (see J. Suret-Canale, "La communauté villageoise en Afrique tropicale et sa signification sociale", in: *Etudes Africaines*, Leipzig 1967, p. 173).
52 See J. Suret-Canale, "Die Tradition in westafrikanischen Gesellschaftsordnungen", in: *Tradition und nichtkapitalistischer Entwicklungsweg in Afrika*, Berlin 1971, pp. 116–17.
53 Both in reality and abstractly, it is very difficult to draw the line between the classes because the border between exploitation and public office are not distinct.
54 Here is meant only the use of slave labour within West Sudanese society and not exported mass slavery in the era of slave trade.
55 They were generally prisoners of war who were kept, distributed or sold by the "king" and general (FAMA among the Bambara). Slavery through debt was very rare. This occurred only in times of hunger when a FAKOROBA felt forced to sell a family member in order to buy food for the subsistence of the family. However, the FAKOROBA was obliged to buy back the enslaved family member as quickly as possible (see H. Ortoli, *Le gage des personnes au Soudan Français*, Bulletin de l'I. F. A. N., 1/1939, pp. 313–24).
56 According to H. Labouret (op. cit., pp. 107–08), the dissolution of the masterDYON relationship took place in stages over four generations.
57 At the time of Biton Mamari Koulibali, who ruled in 1712–55, the slaves as TON-DYON played an outstanding role in the Bambara kingdom (see L. Tauxier, *Histoire des Bambara*, Paris 1942, pp. 77–8).
58 The significance of the WOLOSO for the extended family was that it received one or more labourers. This was important due to the low degree of control of nature which in turn led to the greater danger of economic difficulties (if a labourer became unable to work through illness, etc.) for the whole family. Additional labour made the family more independent from support by others and gave it greater authority in the whole village.
59 The most important features of the Asiatic mode of production described by Marx are summarised by E. Engelberg as follows: "Common ownership of the land in the village community, to which corresponded the entity of agriculture and home handicrafts as a particular form of the productive forces; as against this, there existed the higher ownership of the land which was embodied through the economic and political system of despotism. The ground rent had the form of a tribute and was thus the main element of state taxes." (E. Engel-

berg, "Probleme der gesetzmäßigen Abfolge der Gesellschaftsformationen", in: *Zeitschrift für Geschichtswissenschaft*, Berlin, 2/1974, p. 1964). Comprehensive summaries of Marx' ideas on the Asiatic mode of production are given by F. Tökei, *Sur le mode de production asiatique*, Budapest 1966 and M. Godelier, *La notion de "mode production asiatique" et les schémas marxistes d'évolution des sociétés*, Paris 1964.

H. Mohr gives an instructive survey about the international discussion on problems of the Asiatic mode of production, with special emphasis on Soviet literature (see H. Mohr, "Vorkapitalistische Klassenformationen in der Diskussion", in: *Zeitschrift für Geschichtswissenschaft*, Berlin, 11/1972, pp. 1401ff.).

Up to now, J. Suret-Canale has given the most comprehensive assessment of pre-colonial African society on the basis of Marx' concepts of the Asiatic mode of production (see especially J. Suret-Canale, "Les sociétés traditionelles en Afrique tropicale et le concept de mode de production asiatique", in: *Sur le mode de production asiatique*, Paris 1969, pp. 101—133). A contrary opinion is expressed e. g. by H. Stöber and Th. Büttner (see H. Stöber, op. cit.; Th. Büttner, "Probleme des Feudalismus in Afrika in der vorkolonialen Periode", in: *Zeitschrift für Geschichtswissenschaft*, Berlin, 3/1964, pp. 460ff.).

60 K. Marx writes at this point: "In broad outlines Asiatic, ancient, feudal, and modern bourgeois modes of production, can be designated as progressive epochs in the exonomic formation of society." (Preface to the *Critique of Political Economy*, in: K. Marx/F. Engels, *Selected Works*, vol. 1, Progress Publishers, Moscow 1973, p. 504).

61 E. Engelberg, op. cit., p. 147.

Engelberg also stressed that "contrary to a widespread opinion held for a long time, it can be proved" that Marx and Engels "did not give up . . . the concept of the Asiatic mode of production". In the 1880s, they "did not cross out anything, but added something, namely they placed classless primitive society first in the order of the antagonistic social formations" (ibid., p. 150).

62 K. Marx, *Foundations of the Critique of Political Economy*, loc. cit., p. 473.

3. The traditional community today and its significance for noncapitalist transformation

During the course of more than seventy years of French colonial rule[1] changes took place in traditional Mali society which resulted in the integration of the Malinese economy into the world imperialist economic system[2] and into commodity-money relations penetrating into the community. This process took place under the concrete conditions of French monopoly rule in the West African colonies.[3]

3.1. Colonial exploitation and the strong persistency of traditional economic and social structures

Compared to other imperialist countries, French imperialism showed very little interest in exporting its capital to the African colonies, in particular to such areas as Mali which lie far from the coast.[4] It preferred to invest its capital in areas more promising for profit (Eastern Europe and, up to 1917, Russia) in the form of loan capital, which is the reason that Lenin called it usury imperialism.[5] In the territories of West Africa (Afrique Occidentale Française – A.O.F.), French monopoly capital operated almost exclusively in the circulation sphere. Investments outside of this sphere were rare and generally subordinated to the interests of trade.[6]

The economy of the French colonies in West Africa was controlled by some dozen monopoly trading companies[7] which limited their activities on the one hand to buying and exporting the African peasants' products – the cultivation of which was forced on him with economic and non-economic means – and to importing and selling European industrial consumer goods on the other. Its striving was to buy as little and as cheaply as possible, and to sell as little for as much as possible.

The rule of trade monopoly in French West Africa was a system of imperialist colonial exploitation, in which monopoly capital (adapting itself to imperialist conditions) used the methods of mercantile colonial trade (French: *"la traite"*), i.e. it acquired the surplus product of the African producers without itself penetrating into the production sphere, but through non-equivalent exchange with the help of a whole range of non-economic pressures. This system differed considerably from the methods used by monopoly capital in East and South Africa and in the Belgian Congo (the expropriated wage labourers were exploited in the extractive industry and on European plantations)[8] and was described by Jean Dresch with the now classic term *"économie de traite"* (trade-based economy)[9].

Peasant exploitation in Mali did not take place within a system of European plantations (with expropriation of the producers), but foreign monopoly capital (in the form of merchant capital) subordinated itself to the traditional community and acquired the surplus product of the peasant, without, at first, destroying the existing mode of production. Only several secondary elements of the pre-colonial system were eliminated by monopoly capital, such as "slavery"[10] and the traditional aristocracy, in order to be able to acquire the *whole* surplus product of *all* producers. The village community, however, was largely preserved[11] and *integrated* into a system of exchange which was controlled by monopoly capital and which". . . may offer more materialised labour *in kind* than it receives . . ."[12] because of its low level of economic development.

This tendency is very clearly reflected in the structure of the Malinese gross product (1959, in billion Fr.-CFA), divided up into the forms of ownership in which it was created.[13]

Form of Ownership	Farming Animal-breeding Fishing	Industry Crafts	Services Trade Transport	Total	Percent
traditional agriculture and crafts	34.4	5.8	—	40.2	66.9
state enterprises	1.3[14]	0.2	1.1	2.6	4.3
private European enterprises	—	0.9	8.3	9.2	15.3
private African enterprises	—	—	7.8	7.8	13.0
administration and private households	—	—	0.3	0.3	0.5
Total	35.7	6.9	17.5	60.1	
Percentage	59.4	11.5	29.1	100.0	100.0

In order to set up a system whereby monopoly capital could acquire the producers' labour, it was necessary to use large-scale non-economic and administrative means, because in its production mechanism, the traditional community was almost completely self-sufficient and not directed at production of exchange value. This meant that the traditional forms could not develop any internal economic necessities for integrating into a system of exchange relations. The main non-economic pressures used were forced labour, forced cultivation and delivery of products, and a poll tax.[15]

However, the non-economic pressure aimed not only at this integration — i.e. forced transformation of some of the products into commodities in order to create the prerequisites for a non-equivalent exchange — but it also served monopoly capital to acquire the labour power of the producer in its natural form (forced labour) and to make extra profits through sheer fraud. Thus, what Marx said about the rule of trade capital over the undeveloped community in the precapitalist era, also applies basically to the system of exploitation of the peasants by trade monopoly:

"So long as merchant's capital promotes the exchange of products between undeveloped societies, commercial profit appears not only as out-bargaining and cheating, but also largely originates from them . . . Merchant's capital, when it holds a position of dominance, stands everywhere for a system of robbery, so that its development among the trading nations of old and modern times is always directly connected with plundering, piracy, kidnapping slaves, and colonial conquest . . ."[16]

In addition, the peasants were subjected to further exploitation by the colonial-administrative *Chefferie* and the local merchant's and usury capital growing up in the shadow of the monopolies.

Under colonialism, the village and canton[17] chiefs acted as instruments of the colonial administration to carry out the tasks of authoritarian colonialism on the lowest level of administration.[18] They were placed into their positions by the colonial power and their social and political character could not be confused with the traditional DUGUTIGI and KAFOTIGI.[19] On the basis of their function in the system of direct colonial administration, the village and canton heads pressed additional natural tributes and unpaid labour out of the peasants.[20] Local merchant's and usury capital developed — excluded from the big trading business[21] — either in branches which appeared not profitable enough to the monopolies[22] or as agents, buyers, transporters, commissioners, on the lowest step of the *Traite-pyramide*.[23] Generally, they lent both natural products and money.[24] From the mid-fifties onward, the big trade monopolies concentrated their activities more and more on wholesale trade and their big stores in the capital cities, and left the retail and intermediary trade, particularly in the countryside, to Lebanese and African traders under their control through commission agreements, credits, etc.[25] Thus the peasants were subjected to double exploitation during the colonial period: by the colonial trade monopolies and colonial administration on the one hand, and local merchant's and usury capital and the *Chefferie* on the other.

Under conditions of the *économie de traite*, the natural economic basis of the traditional community was gradually undermined through penetration of commodity-money relations into the original community which caused changes in the socio-economic relations and structures. However, this process was very slow and dragging because, on the one hand, trade monopoly made no productive investments and the colonial administration only the absolute minimum [26], and on the other, the peasants themselves were unable to accumulate and invest because of the high degree of exploitation within the *économie de traite* system and the low level of production. So, generally — despite regional differences — the level of the productive forces remained low and the degree of commodity production small.

Characteristic for the low level of the productive forces in the village is that the main instrument of production continued to be the daba. In 1960, only 12.4% of all farms in the traditional sector of agriculture had a plough.[27] As maintenance and improvement of soil fertility were largely unknown [28], the traditional shifting cultivation with land clearance continued to be the main form of land cultivation. It was practised on 76.4% of the cultivated soil.[29]

The low level of the productive forces corresponded to a low labour productivity which had an intensive (low yields per hectare) and an extensive (small area per person) aspect. On an average, one producer was able to cultivate not quite one hectare (0.82 hectares) which meant half a hectare (0.43) per head of the population living off traditional agriculture.[30] With such low yields (500–600 kg for millet, 800–900 kg for rice, 200 kg for cotton and 650 kg for peanuts)[31] and average subsistence requirements of 200–250 kg of millet or rice per person, most of the cultivated area had to be used to grow food: in 1960 food was grown on 80.2% of the cultivated area [32], whereas only 8.4% and 3.3% was used for peanuts and cotton, respectively.[33] So at the end of the 1950s, traditional agriculture made up a large sector of the subsistence economy which was almost identical with production of food [34] and a far smaller sector was used for commodity production and to grow almost exclusively export crops.[35] The subsistence economy consisted of 80% to 85% [36] of the total values produced.

The low development of the commodity-money relations — characteristic for traditional agriculture — was very clearly reflected in the budgets of the village farms. The following figures apply to the Macina-Mopti-Djenné area, which represents the average level of development of traditional agrarian economy.

Average annual income and payments of a farming family per head (1957/58)[37]

	Income Fr.-CFA	%	Payments Fr.-CFA	%
self-sufficient production	4631	67	4631	68
Presents	510	7	366	5
Exchange of products	685	10	716	11
Monetary form	1131	16	1052	16
	6957	100	6765	100

The section "Presents" and "Exchange of products" consists mainly of traditional products (food, craft products[38]) which are exchanged directly between the producers and in no way interfered with the subsistence economy.

The monetary income[39] resulted mainly from the sale of products gained through agriculture[40] (60.3%), fishing[41], animal breeding, hunting (17.2%) and other products (14.7%, including the re-sale of cola nuts with 5.8%), and only 4.2% came from wage labour, transport, money-lending, etc.

Most of the money was spent on food[42] (43.5%) and of this only 8.3% was used for products not produced in the village itself or in the immediate vicinity like salt (5.9%) and sugar (0.9%); 13.2% was spent on clothes, 11.7% on pleasure (tobacco, cola), but only 6.4% and 5.4% were spent on means of production and household goods, respectively. Taxes made up 10.2% of the expenditure.

The budget analysis showed clearly that 84% of the peasant's production served his immediate subsistence and only 16% was turned into commodities on the market. The income gained through commodity production was almost completely used up to acquire means of subsistence (in commodity form), so that productive accumulation and extended reproduction was impossible for the majority of the producers. A plough with pair of oxen cost 30,000 Fr.-CFA[43]. Even in the developed areas, this meant years of saving or debt and usually both.

The traditional village crafts were produced even less for exchange than were the farmed products. They remained a side-line employment[44] of the NYAMAKALAU — who lived mainly from agriculture — for immediate needs or for exchange within the village; the NYAMAKALAU were drawn into the *économie de traite*, not through their crafts, but through their field production. Because of the generally low development of commodity-money relations on the flat land, the economic necessity for the existence of the crafts in their traditional form remained[45] and there was hardly any extension of the "market" for craft products within the village economy, so that only in exceptional cases was there any kind of transition to commodity production among the traditional crafts (near the cities)[46].

So seventy years of rule by monopoly trade capital created conditions in which the community economy, with its simple mechanism for reproduction of the means of subsistence was largely preserved.

Even if the commodity-money relations were able to penetrate very little, they began a process of gradual disintegration of the social relations, because "commerce ... has a more or less dissolving influence everywhere on the producing organisation which it finds at hand and whose different forms are mainly carried on with a view to use-value".[47]

However, there also existed two decisively inhibiting factors which countered these tendencies.

(1) The colonial nature of the development of commodity-money relations were not linked with an upsurge of the productive forces, because it was in the hands of foreign capital and sometimes local exploiters. While on the one hand they acquired the greater surplus labour of the community peasant (and at certain periods even some of the necessary labour) which arose through the commodity-money relations, on the other, they had no interest in developing the productive forces. This not only inhibited the unfolding of all economic and social processes, but also deformed and crippled them. The old production relations were undermined and eroded through the penetraiton of commodity-money relations and elements of new production relations arose. However, the stagnation of the productive forces caused by colonial exploitation meant that this process was extremely slow and in particular, there were lacking the economic prerequisites for a quick unfolding of the new productive and social relations corresponding to them. The decisive cause for the stagnation and deformation of economic and social processes under the conditions of colonial dependence and exploitation is thus, in the final analysis, not due to the fact that the unfolding of commodity-money relations were too slow, but that they were necessarily linked with colonial exploitation, in other words, with the stagnation of the productive forces.

(2) The disintegrating effect of trade was countered by the inner stability of the traditional community, because "... in how far it [trade – K. E.] causes dissolution of the old mode of production", wrote Marx, "depends on its stability and inner structure".[48] Marx points out that the Asian type of community showed particularly strong resistance to the disintegrating effect of trade.[49]

So while, during the colonial period, the system of economic and social relations within the community were shattered, tendencies of decay and elements of new relations appeared under the influence of the rising colonial agrarian market relations, as a whole there was no revolution in the mode of production, but instead the laws governing the processes of colonial exploitation and dependence stopped the unfolding of new production relations and largely determined the far-reaching persistence and increasingly crippled reproduction of traditional community relations.

Let us consider the extent of this persistence and its significance for non-capitalist agrarian transformation before we go into the details of the spontaneous disintegration of the traditional community relations.[50]

The low level of productivity and the small degree of production for exchange led to the economic basis for the traditional community and extended family relations being maintained in most Mali villages. The community and extended family remained necessary for the subsistence of all.[51] They continued as the basis for the social organisation of the Malinese village[52] up to the end of colonial rule. In 1960 some 70% to 75% of the village population still lived in economically functioning extended families which cultivated some 62% of the arable land.[53]

It persisted most strongly where the productive forces and commodity-money relations were least developed and the extended family was traditionally most stable. In the 1950s, this applied particularly to the areas of Senoufo[54] and Minianka[55] in south-east Mali, to the Malinké in the areas of Bakoy and Bafing[56] and to the Bambara of Kaarta[57]. And even where the disintegration was strongest — in the developed areas at the upper (Malinké)[58] and central (Bambara)[59] arms of the Niger River and along the Bamako to Kayes railway line[60] — the extended family still remained.[61]

The extended families had fifty and more members. E. Leynaud[62] gives the following results of a demographic inquiry among the families[63] living along the upper arm of the Niger River, according to size and persons:

Distribution of families along the upper arm of the Niger according to persons per family (1959)[64]

Persons per family	0—5	6—10	11—15	16—20	21—30	31 and more
percent of families	22.3	30.5	18.9	14.5	7.1	6.7

The medium extended family was made up of approximately 15–20 persons. Malgras gives the following typical case for the Minianka area.[65]

Demographic structure of a medium-size Minianka extended family (end of the fifties)

Family members	Adults male	female	children	total
Family head (FH) and his wife	1	1		2
1st son of FH, his two wives and their children	1	2	3	6
2nd son of FH, his wife and their children	1	1	2	4
Other children of FH	1		1	2
Relatives			1	1
	4	4	7	15

Sometimes, the extended family also included the brother (or brothers) of the FAKOROBA and his (their) children and grandchildren.[66] The FAKOROBA was always the oldest man of the oldest generation. Thus, on the upper arm of the Niger, some 85% of the FAKOROBA-families with over twenty persons (extended families) were older than fifty.

Distribution of family heads on the upper arm of the Niger according to the size of family (1959, in percent)[67]

Family size	Family heads' age				
	up to 40	40—50	50—60	60—70	70 and over
0—10	33	27	23	11	6
10—20	4	26	39	18	13
20—50	4	13	40	36	7
50—100	0	4	32	48	16
more than 100	0	10	0	40	50
more than 200	3	11	35	39	12

At the end of the 1950s the extended family remained, not only as a family relationship, but also as an economic unit, whose traditional system of production and distribution continued to function. Basically, the FOROBA mechanism was still completely intact.

Most of the immediate means of subsistence continued to be collectively produced on the Foroba (extended family field) on 4–6 days a week.[68] In 1960 altogether 67.6% of the cultivated areas were still Foroba, on which

62.5% of the millet was produced. In the natural form, this was most of the FOROBA administered by the FAKOROBA[69] and served the family subsistence.

Distribution of cultivated areas according to Foroba and DIONFORO
(1960, in percent)[70]

Crop	Foroba	DIONFORO	not defined[71]
Millet	73.8	19.1	6.1
Rice	57.6	14.7	21.7
other food crops	60.1	9.3	30.6
Cotton	51.3	22.5	24.2
Peanuts	59.7	27.4	12.9
Miscellaneous	60.7	17.2	20.1
Total	67.6	18.0	14.4

Not only did the system of production and distribution characteristic for the subsistence economy continue to function within the extended family but this system also absorbed the new beginnings of commodity-money relations. This is shown in the new aspects for composition and use of the FOROBA. Part of the Foroba was reserved for production of export crops (9,8%). This became part of the FOROBA, and no longer mainly in form of kind, but as money.

Distribution of crops on the Foroba (1960, in percent)[72]

Millet	Rice	Miscellaneous Food Crops	Cotton	Peanuts	Others
62,5	5,8	13,5	2,4	7,4	7,4

The FOROBA's financial income also resulted from marketing traditional (in their natural form) FOROBA products (hunted animals, fish, handicrafts, etc.)[73]. Apart from money gained through products from the DIONFORO, "all the money earned had to be passed over to the family head"[74], at least on principle. This applied above all to the money earned by migratory workers who come from areas with small cash crops and small market relations and went for a time to work in more developed agricultural areas and to the cities.[75]

The FOROBA's money served, above all, to pay taxes, contributions to the indigenous provident societes (S. I. P.)[76] and, perhaps to pay a money rent (apart from the rent paid in the form of products and labour) to the colonial *Chefferie*. Basic goods such as cloth, soap, household products, sugar, etc. and even means of production (plough, draught-cattle) were bought with FOROBA money. At least to the same degree, products were also exchanged to acquire other goods produced outside of the Lu (extended family) and made up its external economic relations.[77]

Thus, the extended family was maintained as a social system up to the end of colonial rule but without having to basically modify the traditional system of production and distribution for two reasons:
(1) economic necessity, and (2) its inner structural stability absorbed the economic changes.

Right up to the 1960s, the strong solidarity between the village members was maintained because of the necessity for collective forms of gaining subsistence, even if tendencies for a change in function and disintegration of the extended family – as we will show later [78] – became very noticeable.

This is evidence of the persistence of a traditional sense of responsibility within the village community up to the most recent past, particularly in the two main forms: the institution of mutual aid (LAMA) and the youth organisation (TON).

A survey taken by I. N. S. E. E. (Institut National de la Statistique et des Etudes Economiques) in 1960 showed that in each season, every family, or any other production unit, placed a worker at another's disposal for 55 working days, and a worker from another family worked for them on 75 days[79]. About half of this exchange of labour took place gratis, mainly on the basis of traditional LAMA relations.

Labour exchange for a farm in working days [80]

	Received	Given
Gratis	37.5	55
Paid	37.5	20
Total	75	55

A case study that I carried out in Nianzana[81] showed that of altogether 58 family production units, 11 (19%) ploughed the fields of other units on 140 days. Three of these units did the work gratis for 20 days (14.3%) within the LAMA framework. Thus, the mutual aid between the families within the community in the developed areas had decreased or had taken on a different social content, but still continued to exist and function.

Also the TON, which played a decisive role for aid on a village level in precolonial society, still existed in most of the Malinese villages at the end of colonial rule: some 75% of the villages had one or more TON[82]. Their inner structure[83] and membership was by no means different from the pre-colonial TON. It was a secular youth organisation with an average of 35 unmarried members[84] and an average age of 20 to 25[85], which represented 11% of the total population or 18% of the village population of working age.

All of the village I investigated[86] in 1967 had a TON. Here the average age was thirty which means that, as a whole, all the village youth belonged to it.

The basic features of the caste system were also maintained through the subsistence economy. N'Diayé writes: "... one must note that this influence [of the castes K. E.] has remained in the countryside. It is doubtless not as strong as previously, but it still penetrates the whole of social life ..."[87]

So the traditional community with its main social relations continued to function right up to the end of colonial rule. Although the forced integration of the community into the colonial market system introduced a process which began the disintegration of community relations, this process could not take its natural course because of the colonial conditions of reproduction in Mali up to the end of the 1950s. On the contrary, the community relations continued to be the main feature of socio-economic relations in most Malinese villages, even though in an increasingly undermined and crippled form.

3.2. Traditional structures — an obstacle for economic and social progress

The persistence of the traditional village community was of great importance for the Sudanese Union's attempts to carry out their conception for agrarian development. Their main orientation was to develop the material and human productive forces and create co-operatives on the basis of traditional community relations.[88]

The Malinese state allotted considerable sums for this task: From 1 July 1961 to 30 June 1966 (the period of the development plan) a total of 5.45 billion Franc Malien (FM) were spent on developing traditional agriculture.[89] Although this sum was only 55% of that originally intended for investment[90] — due to the growing financial difficulties[91] — it was very much more than any investments made during a comparable period before 1960.[92]

Modernising traditional agriculture meant — according to the development conception and the current economic and natural conditions — equipping the peasants with ploughs, ox-carts, harrows, simple sowing and spraying instruments, selected seed and fertiliser plus construction of irrigation and drainage systems in the rice-growing areas. During the course of the five-year plan much was achieved in this field, compared to the so-called modernisation measures during the colonial period. From 1960 to 1964/5 a total of 18,830 metres of canals, dams and dykes were built throughout the territory of Mali (outside of the Office du Niger) to irrigate 45,698 hectares of agricultural land.[93] During the same period, 29,556 ploughs[94], 1,082 ox-carts, 1,704 harrows, 5,877 spraying and 1,192 sowing instruments and several thousand tons of artificial fertiliser and insecticides were placed at the peasants' disposal through the S. M. D. R. and the G. R. P. S. M.[95] In addition, over 100 tons of selected peanut and rice seed plus 50 tons of cotton seed were distributed in the same way.[96] In general, however, it was not possible to equip traditional agriculture with modern means of production – in particular to modernise labour apart from ploughing – to the extent laid down in the plan.[97]

A further important measure was to set up a state development service. During the first phase it concentrated on creating the Zone d'Expansion Rurale (Z. E. R.) and building and equipping the seasonal schools, so that at the end of this period, 54 Z. E. R. had been founded, four seasonal schools (*Ecoles saisonnières*) equipped and another 50 were being built.[98]

From 1962 to 1964, the construction and equipment of the latter was generally complete.[99] From 1963 to 1966 the network of Z. E. R. was extended and the basic sectors were being founded, so by the end of 1965, the planned framework had been institutionally erected: At this time there existed six *Directions Régionales du Développement Rural*, 25 *Secteurs de Développement*, 150 Z. E. R., 400 basic sectors and 60 seasonal schools.[100] However, they were not all in operation. Above all, the basic sectors and the Z. E. R. needed cadres.[101] The seasonal schools took up their activities as late as 1964/5, and in 1965 began to train the first 1,000 "*animateurs*".[102] During the same period, measures were taken to improve training of agricultural cadres. At the same time as the rest of the school system, the Collège Technique Agricole de Katibougou was reformed, the Centre d'Apprentissage de M'Pesoba was extended and a second was founded in Samanko. However, the number of agricultural cadres trained did not correspond to the needs.

The *Service Civique* was built very quickly.[103] The first camps were set up in 1961 and by 1965 there existed some 40 to 50 camps training 40 youths each.[104] However, the number of 4,000 youth who were to have passed through the camps by the end of the plan, was not achived.[105]

The co-operative system was set up parallel to the system of development bodies during the first half of the 1960s.[106] By the end of the five-year plan, both had been basically established. It was during this period, that considerable investments were made for development of agriculture, even though less than intended. However, the economic results in no way justified the amounts spent and the effort put in.

A glance at the following tables makes this clear. It shows that increase (9–10%) in agricultural production for the most important agrarian products was far less than the plan intended. Particularly noticeable and relevant to our subject[107] is the fact that production of the most important food cultures – millet and rice – practically stagnated or decreased.

Production increase of important agrarian products 1959—65 compared to the plan (in 100 tons or billion FM) [108]

	1959 [109]		1964/65 [109]		Plan [110]		
Crop	Quantity	Value	Quantity	Value	Quantity	Value	Plan fulfilled (in percent)
Millet	800	8.80	678.0	7.46	1080	11.90	62.7
Rice	124	1.55	130.0	1.63	236	2.95	55.3
Maize	100	1.30	111.0	1.44	110	1.43	100.8
Peanuts	123	1.59	148.0	1.93	200	2.60	74.2
Cotton	5.4	0.18	32.5	1.10	25	0.84	130.9
Total	—	13.42	—	13.56	—	19.22	70.5

Development of agrarian production in Mali 1958/59—1967/68 [111]
(in 1,000 tons)

	58/59	59/60	60/61	61/62	62/63	63/64	64/65	65/66	66/67	67/68
Millet	800	765	800	850	940	750	678	734	825	557
Rice	124	188	170	185	190	165	130	91	99	134
Peanuts	123	125	110	110	120	130	148	157	117	96
Maize	100	55	65	65	72	70	111	76	66	66
Cotton	5	9	15	18	20	31	33	24	38	50

These economic results, despite the comprehensive investments and measures show that it is impossible to change traditional agriculture through material support, training and education alone, without changing socio-economic relations and taking into account a number of secondary factors which we will speak of later. They underline the interrelationship between development of the productive forces and the character of the production relations. The socio-economic relations of the traditional community — based on the undeveloped productive forces — became an obstacle for the advance of the productive forces.

A Soviet team of authors wrote: "The situation is that several features of the traditional land ownership are at present coming into contradiction more and more with the aim of social, economic and political developments of the independent African states and are a serious barrier to their efforts for the planned construction of a national economy." [112] Sobolev, Bénot, Arnauld and other Marxist writers draw similar conclusions about the inhibiting character of traditional community structures.[113]

The socio-economic relations which inhibit social progress and preserve the traditional community make themselves felt in various ways.

They become most obvious — particulary in economically undeveloped areas — in the passive resistance of the community peasants toward any economic innovations. On this basis, bourgeois writers try to limit the factors in the traditional community inhibiting progress to psychological aspects.[114] However, the fact is that the African peasant is by nature just as little opposed to progress as any other producer in any other society. On the contrary, unfolding of the productive forces and economic progress are objectively in his interest because it is the necessary prerequisite for overcoming a system of production relations which places very narrow limits on his possibilities for satisfying his material and mental needs. His subjectively passive attitude to and often even rejection of economic innovations, etc. does not come out of his human essence, but out of that system of production relations under which he reproduces his labour power. What appears to be a psychologically determined "typically African" mentality, proves, on closer examination, to be socially conditioned attitudes which, in fact, contradict the objective interests of the producer. Because for a system-conforming peasant, every extension of production is useless. The social system which ensures his survival lacks all inner driving force to develop the productive forces, it functions on the basis of a lack of ambition, unchanged reproduction, etc. The peasants' consciousness is adapted to this. Therefore, changes in production and his life in general must be strange and *appear* absurd to him.

The community system of production and distribution offers neither the economic necessity nor the stimulation to produce more, to develop the productive forces. As soon as he has made his contribution to the functioning of the system of collective subsistence, he is able to live. He has no incentive to produce more because the surplus productautomatically goes to the community. Because of the lack of a market the community does not use this product, but adds it to its treasures. In other words, the community system lacks all incentive for developing the productive forces.[115]

Thus the economic and social system of the community causes a lack of initiative and passivity which becomes a decisive obstacle for development of production and the productive forces. The producer who is fully integrated into the extended family has no subjective interest in extended production, in the use of sophisticated productive instruments, in applying modern methods of production. As Seydou Badian put very fittingly, he is happy "with the balance of poverty between man and nature".[116]

And then there is another aspect which western sociologists like to overlook: the colonial experience. During the colonial period, the peasants experienced that all "modernisation" led to increased exploitation.[117] R. Dumont[118] says quite correctly, that colonialism resulted in a fatalism towards technical innovations among the African peasants in general.[119]

Therefore, the efforts to set up a development service and other central organs, no matter how well organised, met with passive resistance from peasants living in still functioning extended families and community structures.

The "elders", the representatives of the traditional community are the least accessible for such innovations. For them, resistance to the new techniques and methods is not just a question of clinging to tradition. For them, the innovations are factors which disturb a whole system, in fact, may even destroy it; that system, which, up to now, had alone been able to guarantee the subsistence of the community of which they are a representative and for which they feel responsible. For this reason, the "elders" show strong enmity to the development service and its institutions. Their resistance is the personified expression of traditional production relations hindering the development of the productive forces.[120]

However, the obstacles growing out of the traditional system of social relations are not limited to the lack of initiative by its producers, to his contentment with the "balance of poverty", to the passive refusal of the producers to follow the efforts of the development service and other institutions to introduce new elements into agricultural production. Even any seed of modernisation which develops in the village itself or is brought in through outside factors is nipped in the bud by the traditional structures, i. e. they inhibit that process whereby the peasant producer becomes conscious of his objective interests and acts accordingly. Such seeds develop under many types of influences. The spread of commodity-money relations, contact with the city, the influence of the radio and press cause new types of needs to arise among the peasants – particularly among youth – and can lead to new attitudes towards increased production and developed productive forces.

Apart from these spontaneous and largely coincidental factors, such establishments as the development service and above all the *Service Civique* and the seasonal schools were intended to link up systematically with the objective interests of the peasant producers and awaken in them the subjective desire to modernise production, their way of life, etc. In these establishments they were trained to produce more and better with simple means.

Several *Service Civique* camps that we visited showed that under the consciously created changes in economic and social conditions, it is definitely possible to change the attitude of the young producers to economic and social progress and introduce them to more effective modern production. This is also shown by the yields per hectare of several well-functioning *Service Civique* camps.[121]

Comparison of hectare yields in *Service Civique* camps with average 1968/9 hectare yields (in kg per hectare) [122]

	Millet	Rice	Peanuts	Cotton
all Mali	582	660	775	564
Service Civique camps in:				
Dioila	1504	—	1470	505
Didiéni	1670	—	1700	—
Peguena	690	—	1100	2005
Dioro	585	1520	910	—
Sanando	1418	—	770	1965
Konodimini	1620	1000	1540	2131
Diankabou	—	1880	—	3240

Equipped with his new knowledge, agricultural means of production [123] and generally [124] the best of intentions, the young man returns to his village after one or two years of training. On arrival he becomes fully integrated into the traditional structure. The seed that has been planted with so much effort is buried under the weight of traditional society. The time needed to choke the awakened initiative differs according to area and level of development.

In areas with strong traditional structures and undeveloped economic conditions [125], the young "innovator" is faced with the determined resistance of the FAKOROBA. His two oxen become part of the FOROBA (as treasure), the plough remains unused – or is sold – and the young man himself becomes integrated into the traditional rhythms of work and life in the community.

It is impossible for him to carry out his intentions outside of the extended family, against the will of the FAKOROBA, because he would never receive the agreement of the "elders". However, this approval is the prerequisite for production, because without it he would never have access to the most important means of production: the land. He is then faced with two alternatives: either he gives his intentions up and allows himself to become fully integrated into the traditional way of life and subordinates himself to the FAKOROBA's authority, or he leaves the extended family and the village to live in the city.[126] In both cases, no progress is achieved for agriculture.

In the pre-colonial period the position of the FAKOROBA was justified, because he organised – as incarnation of the community whose subsistence he alone appeared to ensure – the whole economic and social life of the extended family and controlled its system of production and distribution. Due to the low level of the productive forces, this was the only form of social organisation possible. However, under the new conditions, this mechanism and its leadership inhibited the initiative of the dynamic, progressive youth. In the more developed areas, the traditional structures can take other inhibiting forms. It can happen that the FAKOROBA shows an open mind to the introduction of modern methods of production. They have seen that such methods can increase the extended family's surplus production. And, at least at the beginning, the fact that they can sell this surplus product on the market for their own personal gain is by no means the decisive factor.[127] More important for them is the possibility of enlarging the family reserve – the FOROBA – and the growing prestige of the family within the village community.

However, even if the FAKOROBA agrees to the introduction of new tools and methods or, in the extreme case, even encourages them, nothing changes from a socio-economic viewpoint for the producer within the extended family. Although he now works with a plough and with different methods, the conditions of production and distribution remain unchanged. His surplus product goes to the FOROBA; he has no economic incentive to do more work; thus, his initiative slowly but surely ebbs.

As the modern tools and the surplus products automatically become the possession of the FOROBA, this "modernisation" leads to a temporary[128] stabilisation of the traditional structure and also to even greater contradictions between the traditional conditions of production and the development of the productive forces.

The more the traditional system of production and distribution loses its economic basis – in developed areas – the greater is the contradiction with the development of the productive forces.

The more the traditional structure is undermined through the spread of commodity-money relations, the more it warps the characteristic subordination of the individual into a type of collective parasitism which finds its extreme form in the city. Here, the sense of responsibility that each has for the subsistence of the whole community (FOROBA system), leads to twenty, thirty and even up to one hundred persons – depending on the concrete circumstances[129] – living off the income of one person; not because they cannot find work[130], but because that individual's income is more or less sufficient to keep the others.[131] A very revealing article in *'Essor* describes the problem:

"Everyone knows that we have individuals (in large numbers) – be they relatives or not – who do nothing, and do not want to do anything. They lie in wait day after day, and if they see someone who has come from abroad or who owns something, then they hurry to him and suck him dry; and if their victim dares to show resistance, he becomes the black sheep of the family, a disgrace to his race, etc. He is reminded of the traditions inherited from our forefathers, whereby in Africa, one man works for a thousand mouths. Of course, one has a duty to one's mother and father. One should fulfill this as far as possible. However, we consider such duties of great hindrance where it concerns a brother who is incapable of giving meaning to his life, where it concerns people who attach themselves to another through some kind of social ties. This phenomenon can only be called parasitism."[132]

Jean Suret-Canale draws similar conclusions for Guinea and writes: "The familiar parasitism is a plague to the badly paid and honest functionaries who see innumerable idle relatives streaming into their houses."[133]

It is obvious that under the pressure of this parasitism, all interest in raising one's own labour productivity, interest in work as such, must dwindle both – in the example of the cities – for the earner as well as for the "parasites".[134]

Even if not in such an extreme form, because the contradiction between the traditional structure and undeveloped commodity-money relations is not so strong, this collective parasitism also acts as an obstacle to development of the productive forces in the countryside: the values created by the individual during migrant work outside of the community, or through a similar source of income, are taken over by the FOROBA, regardless of their size. Even that, which the individual creates through personal initiative and knowledge over and above his usual contribution to collective subsistence belongs to the community, each of its members has a direct claim to it.

A special variation of this parasitism is the acquisition by the family head of the surplus product of the extented family members or of the above-average income of an individual who uses more progressive methods of production.[135] Here, the parasitism of the community appears only in its personification. The head of the family personally acquires surplus product due to him as the embodiment of the community, raises himself above the community and turns the original collective parasitism into exploitation by the representative of the community.

This shows that a "psychological revolution" – demanded *inter alia* by S. Badian, obviously under the influence of western development strategists[136] – to educate the peasants to a different attitude both to work and to changing the methods and means of production must fail so long as it is conceived in the framework of traditional conditions. Education for new types of behaviour are only practical and effective in the spirit of Marx' third Feuerbach thesis[137], if it is carried out as part of necessary socio-economic changes, if it is combined with changes in material conditions which are the objective basis for inactivity.

The traditional structures prove to be an obstacle for socio-economic progress. Contrary to the assumption of the Malinese agrarian conception[138], they do not encourage the development of modern co-operative relations, but hinder them.

Although there are superficial similarities in the form of collective production and distribution between the primitive community and modern co-operatives, there exist fundamental qualitative differences which Marx pointed to when he wrote: "This primitive type of co-operative or collective production resulted, of course, from the weakness of the isolated individual and not from socialisation of the means of production."[139] Both forms of social relations, although apparently similar, are based on two historically completely different levels of development of the productive forces, they serve a completely different economic purpose and contain fundamentally different social relations.

Thus the establishment of co-operatives in traditional agriculture will not lead to a qualitative change in the social relations of the village, so long as the traditional community continues to function. The co-operative relations are modern, but only on the surface; their content remains traditional. They function not as modern but as traditional co-operative relations and therefore prevent the development of genuine socio-economic innovations.

In Mali, this became clear in the political leaders' conception of the collective field. The aim of the collective field, its technical and organisational essence lay on a completely different level to the traditional system of collective work within the framework of the extended family, in which there existed neither the necessity of the economic aims of the former (raising production, creating accumulation fund, etc.) nor the desire for them. Thus, the work on the collective field of the co-operative – in complete contrast to the aim of the development conception – became for the peasant a tribute to the state and appeared to him as a higher form of the community or a strange power standing over the community. The peasants identified the collective field with the chief's or king's field of the pre-colonial era. Each extended family placed one or two labourers – after the work on the FOROBA had been done – at the disposal of the co-operative and felt it was paying its traditional "tribute".[140] The extended families had no objection to doing this as long as it did not become too much, but this work in no way modified the traditional system, on the contrary, it fitted into it completely and was therefore without any effect for socio-economic progress. However, when the collective fields were to be enlarged, the extended families went over to passive resistance and the economic results were correspondingly low.

(1) The collective field remained very small. At first it was to be 0.1 hectare per family and to be extended to one hectare by the end of the five-year plan. Despite the greatest of efforts, the collective field reached an average size of 0.05 hectare per family by 1968.[141] When the collective fields were dissolved after the November 1968 *coup d'état*, the peasants agreed to this.

(2) The yields per hectare on the collective field remained well below that of the already low yields in the traditional sector.

Yields per hectare (in kg) in Mali 1967/68 [142]

	Millet	Rice	Peanuts	Cotton
Collective field	288	161	196	224
Traditional sector	780	727	885	584

The same tendency applies to other co-operative elements, even if not so obviously. Where the traditional system of production and distribution functions, there is no need for a co-operative accumulation fund. If it was created formally, it became part of the unproductive village or extended family treasure and the development officials complain that some "co-operatives" have huge sums in this "fund", but do not use it in any way.[143]

The traditional structures not only prevent the development of genuinely modern co-operative elements, but the founding of co-operatives in the traditional milieu objectively contributes — particularly when conceived as a revival of traditional community relations — to temporarily stabilising its inherently backward factors.

Even if the principle of reviving the traditional community through co-operatives was not everywhere and always applied[144], it was reflected in a whole number of basic measures and regulations. One of these was to give the village council the functions of the G. R. P. S. M. administration council and make the head of the village the latter's president. This meant that the traditional political structure of the village, which was already in contradiction with the socio-economic structure in the developed areas[145], became the basis for distributing the responsibilities in the co-operatives and consolidated the position of the representative of the traditional structure (the FAKOROBA in general and the traditionally most important extended families in particular) into the system of socio-economic relations, or even-re-established them to some extent in those areas where they were already largely undermined.

On the extended family level, the traditional structure was also basically accepted even when it was already disintegrated in its essential relations (as an economic unit).[146] The whole administrative, economic, political and development work was done on its foundations[147] so that it and not the effective economic unit was the officially accepted and registered organ in all decisive questions: payment of taxes, registering the cultivated land and number of animals, commercialisation, supplying industrial consumer goods, size of the G. R. P. S. M. co-operative field, payment of dues (to G. R. P. S. M., S. U.), etc. In the more backward areas where disintegration of the extended families has hardly begun, this practice can be interpreted as acceptance of existing conditions, but it was also practised in those areas where the nuclear family had already developed into the largest economic unit. In the latter cases, often the joint entry into the family book (*carnet de famille*) was the last link – sanctioned by the state administration – of each nuclear to the former extended family. This principle definitely strengthened the position of the FAKOROBA, because only he was officially recognised,[148] and it did not take into account the degree of disintegration that had already taken place.

In those areas which already had a relatively strong aristocratic element, the temporary consolidation of the traditional structure led to even greater exploitation of the community peasants. It took the form of the FAKOROBA or DUGUTIGI acquiring part of the surplus product through rent, mixed with developing forms of capitalist exploitation.[149]

Thus, the development conception contributed to temporarily consolidating traditional social relations in certain areas. In others, it was not able to stop the disintegration of traditional structures because here – through the relatively strong development of commodity-money relations – the spontaneous effect of objective economic laws was stronger, but it definitely had an inhibiting effect.

The measures stabilising the traditional structure also contributed to strengthening – or at least did nothing to overcome – those factors which were an obstacle to the economic aims of Malinese development policy.

This shows very clearly the anachronism of the attempts to re-establish the basic features of the traditional community.

So, the Malinese experiences as a whole teach us:
(1) The productive forces in the traditional sector of agriculture cannot be developed through an "education of the peasant for a will to progress" without overcoming the traditional socio-economic relations.
(2) The establishment of co-operatives on the basis of existing or revived traditional community relations must – so long as these continue to function – remain formal organisations and cannot bring about genuine social progress.

The experiences completely confirm what Engels said as early as 1894: "... It is a historical impossibility for a society at a lower stage of economic development to have to resolve the tasks and conflicts which have arisen, and could only have arisen, in a society at a much higher stage of development. All the tribal community forms arising before the emergence of commodity production and private exchange have only this in common with the future socialist society, that certain things, the means of production, are held as communal property and are in common use by certain groups. But this common feature alone does not yet enable the lower social form to grow into a future socialist society, that final product of capitalist society which it itself begets."[150]

This impossibility of economic and social progress on the basis of traditional community relations – as the Malinese experiences have shown – does not mean, however, that in areas with particularly strong traditional structures, certain elements and institutions of traditional relations cannot be used for non-capitalist development. They can and must be used as an instrument – no doubt temporarily and in a limited way – to solve concrete economic problems because there is no incentive for progress in these areas and the development policy cannot be carried out in a vacuum, but must be based on existing, concrete social conditions. However, such measures must not be an end in themselves and contain illusions about the traditional community, but must be an integral part of a conception to overcome traditional relations. The beginnings described here were not embedded into a more far-reaching conception and thus led up a blind alley. They could function, if combined with certain traditional forms of simple co-operation.[151] Even the collective village field could temporarily serve such a purpose, despite all questionability depicted on previous pages. Although the work on the collective field by no means destroys the traditional technical and social framework and its economic results are necessarily small, the use values or exchange values created over and above the normal extended family and village products could be used by the development service to develop the village economically. This applies even more to the conscious use of traditional forms of simple co-operation outside of agricultural-production, i. e. outside of the season when the peasant has traditionally nothing or little to do.[152] This means using such traditional institutions as the Ton, or the collective work of the whole village for infra-structural projects such as building and repairing irrigation systems, roads, schools, camps and offices (for the G. R. P. S. M.), medical and veterinary centres, etc.

The same can be said of the socio-economic character of this work as was said for the collective field, but despite the low productivity[153] the quantitative economic effect is bigger and this has a direct or indirect influence on raising agrarian production. The economic progress (or the raised educational level – to be dealt with later) directly accelerates the disintegration of traditional social relatious which means that as a whole the effect is progressive.

Such and other measures are possible and necessary, but they must not – and this cannot be stressed enough – be part of Narodnik utopian illusions for maintaining and reviving the traditional community, but must be seen as possible and necessary instruments for solving concrete problems and as part of a larger development policy for a fundamental revolution in the village. Then, and only then, can certain variants of traditional co-operation play a definite role even in a relatively developed phase of non-capitalist change, but only with a growing change in the social content, in other words: traditional only in form.

3.3. The traditional community and the political foundations for non-capitalist development

A basic prerequisite for success on the non-capitalist road is the firm alliance between the revolutionary democratic (and in future proletarian) leadership and the peasants, plus democratic transformation of political conditions in the village.

The peasants have played an outstanding role in the history of the national liberation struggle. They were the first to rise up against colonial exploitation and oppression (particularly against increased taxes, forced labour and conscription during the First World War): in 1908—10 the Dogon[154], in 1915 the Bambara of Bélédougou[155] and in 1915—16 the Bobo[156]. These uprisings showed the heroism and resistance of the peasants in these areas. They helped to shatter colonial rule and became one of the basic causes for the crisis of the colonial system that came later. However, these movements were spontaneous; socially they were still steeped in traditional structures and had no objective historical chance for success.

Only as a result of the Socialist October Revolution and under the influence of the general crisis of imperialism could new forms of anti-colonial struggle develop in the colony on the basis of socio-economic changes.[157] Under the leadership of the teachers Mamadou Konaté and Mamby Sidibé, organisations arose in the 1930s in Bamako which were the forerunners of the modern national liberation movement, although they were largely separated from the peasant masses and existed only in the cities.[158] New elements also arose in the peasant movement led by Sheikh Hamallah[159] from Nioro after the First World War[160], even though in a largely religious form through a radically democratic interpretation of Islam[161].

After the Second World War, the international and national conditions became ripe, during the second stage of the general crisis of imperialism, for the cohesion of all anti-colonial forces in a broad national liberation movement. The peasants formed the mass basis for the alliance, which was led by determined anti-colonial forces in the city. To the same extent as these leaders allied themselves with the peasantry, the peasants became the driving force of the struggle for national independence.

The process of mobilizing and integrating the peasants into the anti-colonial movement was long and complicated. It took the whole period from 1945 to 1958.[162]

The struggle to win the peasants for the national liberation movement was at the same time a struggle against the Progressive Party (Parti Soudanais Progressiste – P. S. P.)[163] and several administrative dwarf parties[164] in the country-side. These political organisations were an expression of the colonial system's adaptation to the changed conditions after the Second World War. The peasants had to be stopped from joining the developing anti-colonial movement by creation of pseudo-democratic organisations, as the system of colonial administrative *Chefferie*[165] in the old form no longer sufficed to oppress them.

The Sudanese Union had stronger influence among the peasants in the relatively developed areas along the main traffic routes (railway line Kayes-Koulikoro, Niger) because there the most favourable socio-economic prerequisites existed for their influence, and also in such areas where a militant Islam was deeply rooted from pre-colonial times with its strong anti-colonialist traditions (Malinké area, Timbuctoo-Songhai and the area of Sikasso with the pre-colonial Dioula-Kong dynasty).

The P. S. P. was able to maintain its influence longest in such areas which were either cutoff from economic development and hardly touched by changes in social structures or in which there was a general enmity to the militant Islamic rulers in the nineteenth century (Samory and Omar Tall) as the latter traditions were largely identified with the Sudanese Union, i. e. above all by the Bambara of Ségou and Bougouni and the Fulbe of Macina.

The gradual establishment of the alliance with the peasantry was most clearly manifested in the election results[166]: while in 1946 the S.U. won in only three districts (Kita, San, Sikasso), their influence increased by 1952 to five, then by 1956 to ten and by 1957 to 13 of the 15 districts.

The progress made by the revolutionary democratic forces in the country-side in the 1950s was considerably influenced by the trade unions extending their activities to the peasants after 1951. In that year a congress was held in Bamako of all trade unions affiliated to the C. G. T. with the support of the World Federation of Trade Unions, which decided to found peasant trade unions.[167]

Shortly after that, a Peasants' Trade Union was founded in Mali which existed up to 1962.[168] In January 1955 it organised the first West African peasants' congress where demands were made to decrease poll taxes, to improve conditions for credits and for receiving agricultural tools, to improve the social infra-structure and agricultural training in the countryside and to recognise trade union rights and democratic freedoms for the peasants.[169] After the congress, branches of the Peasants' Union were organised in all areas and regional meetings were held, such as that in Barouéli (April 1955).[170]

The successful struggle for an alliance with the peasants from 1945 to 1958, decisively contributed to the change in favour of the Sudanese Union on a national scale, so that after the March 1957 elections, it had the absolute majority in the Territorial Assembly and formed the *Loi-Cadre* government. In 1959 it was able to oust the P. S. P. from parliament altogether.

Election Results from 1946 to 1959 [171]

Year	Type of Election	Votes (S. U.)	Seats	Votes (P. S. P.)	Seats
Nov. 1946	Fr. Nat. Assembly	27,653	1	60,759	2
June 1951	Fr. Nat. Assembly	115,490	1	201,866	3
March 1952	Terr. Assembly	101,902	13	122,957	27
Jan. 1956	Fr. Nat. Assembly	215,419	2	161,911	2
March 1957	Terr. Assembly	472,208	57	218,668	6
March 1959	Legisl. Assembly	534,946	80	170,428	—

On the basis of its new political strength, the Sudanese Union used the concessions [172] forced out of the colonial rulers in 1959 and took measures to change the political structure and strengthen its own position in the countryside. While these measures were unable to shatter the rule of French monopoly capital [173] in any way at the time, because of the mechanism built up for domination within the *Communauté*, they had a far-reaching effect for political independence gained soon afterwards.

One of these measures was the destruction of the local colonial administration. It was begun by a decree of 10 April 1958 [174] on the basis of a Territorial Assembly decision of 12 February 1958 [175] which annulled the governor's order on the *Chefferie* system of 30 March 1935 [176]. This decree was first carried out in the districts of Ségou and Macina [177], but had not yet been extended to most of the districts by mid-1958. [178] Only after the "République Soudanaise" had been proclaimed (28 November 1958) was it possible to depose the *Chefferie* system and democratise the local organs throughout the country. The 16 districts and subdistricts of the colonial administration were eliminated. They were substituted by 21 *Circonscriptions* which were divided into *Poste administratif* and the *Poste village*. [179] A democratically elected council (*Conseil*) was set up in each *Circonscription*, to which the *Chef de Circonscription* (a Malinese) was responsible. [180] Electable councils were also set up in the villages and they had the power to propose a village head. The latter was appointed by the *Chef de Circonscription*. [181] The colonial *Chefferie* disappeared as an administrative institution.

The political organisations of the *Chefferie* were also eliminated in 1959: the P. S. P. dissolved itself after the big defeat of March 1959 and the administrative dwarf parties were banned. [182]

At the same time as the *Chefferie* and its political organisations were liquidated, the Sudanese Union set up its own country-wide organisational network. The third S. U. conference (September 1959) set the *Sous-Sections* (then district organisations) the task of forming S. U. committees in every village within two months. [183] The party leadership increased its efforts to organise the village youth by founding the national youth organisation (Jeunesse de l'Union Soudanaise).

These measures had great significance for the further development of the national revolution:

(1) When the *Chefferie* was overthrown and the P. S. P. dissolved or banned, the most important social and political pillars of colonial power in the village were liquidated.
(2) The reform of the administrative organs and the extension of the Sudanese Union's organisational system strengthened the political position of the revolutionary movement in the countryside.
(3) These political changes in the countryside were an essential prerequisite for gaining and safeguarding political independence immediately after 1960.
(4) The broad anti-colonial alliance of the working city people with the peasants, under leadership of the revolutionary democratic intelligentsia, were the pre-conditions for establishing a national-democratic state in Mali after political independence was achieved. The non-capitalist road which was begun in Mali after independence demanded continuation and deepening of the alliance between the revolutionary-democratic leadership and the peasants. It made greater demands on this alliance. Up to political independence, the common interest to eliminate colonial rule had formed the basis for a common platform; now it was necessary to jointly solve far-reaching social and economic, political and cultural tasks. The peasants had to be won for non-capitalist changes, for consolidation of national-democratic power.

In accordance with the objective necessity to consolidate this alliance, the revolutionary-democratic leadership perfected the system of political organisation in the village during the first years after independence, e. g. extension of the S. U.'s organisational network. By 1962 a committee had been formed in practically every village.[184] Further, the administration reform was continued in the course of which the system of party organs between the national leadership and the village was extended in accordance with the model set up at the 6th Party Congress [185] held at Bamako from 10 to 13 September 1962. Already in 1960/1, so-called parallel organisations – youth and women's organisations and "Vigilance Brigades", a para-military security organisation of the S. U. – were organised down to the villages.[186]

In 1960 the organs of state power were reformed on all levels.[187] The 21 *Circonscriptons* were re-organised into 42 districts and joined into six regions. The *Arrondissement* level was created between district and village (226 *Arrondissements*).[188] On each level there existed a governor (region), a commandant (district) and a chief (*Arrondissement*). All were representatives of the state and the latter was responsible for a number of local organs. At the same time, the institutions were established with whose help the leading role of the S. U. toward the administration organs was to be ensured.[189]

With these measures, the revolutionary-democratic leadership created important instruments for consolidating the alliance with the peasantry, to mobilise them for non-capitalist changes. In the meantime, the experiences of 1960 to 1968 show that effective political integration of the peasant masses is exceedingly complicated and is strongly inhibited by the persistence of traditional social structures.

Although elimination of the colonial administration in the countryside removed the social and political obstacle for further development, it also led to legalisation and sometimes a renaissance of political influence by the traditional leadership. Thanks to their position in the traditional system of social relations, the prestige they enjoyed, their religious influence and their family connections, it became possible for these forces to largely control the village organs (village head, village council) despite, or probably because of, the formal, absolutely democratic character of the local village elections. Even if the S. U. succeeded in replacing a village chief who had openly collaborated with the colonialists by a progressive man in the 1959/60 elections, it was quite possible that at the next opportunity (at the 1964/5 local elections) the former again became village head [190] because he came from a traditional DUGUTIGI family.

Thus in the 1960s, the absolute majority of the village heads were traditional DUGUTIGI[191] whose extended families were often still the most stable in their village. One example is D. S., head of the Niola village basic sector Soliko, Z. E. R., Barouéli), Ségou region. He was the FAKOROBA of the largest of the altogether 13 families in the village. Altogether it had 38 persons (12 persons was the average membership of an extended family in the village), six nuclear families (average was 2.39 families), 10 labourers (average 3.69). His extended family also had a fully functioning FOROBA mechanism. He cultivated 12.5 hectares (average 4.93) of which 24% (25.1% was the village average) was used for export crops. He owned 210 mango trees (out of 395[192]), five oxen (of 11), 12 cows (of 21), one horse (of three), two ploughs (of eight), one cart (of three), one scuffler (of two) and the three spraying instruments existing in the village. Of altogether 30 TON days, he claimed six for himself.

The traditional leadership generally also ruled in the village councils, even if the influence of economic and political developments could also be felt there. Characteristic of less developed areas, perhaps even for most of the areas, was the composition of the Niamana[193] village council:[194]

Name	Age	Social Position [196]	Member since:
(1) B. K.	65	F	end of war
(2) N. K.	55	F	end of war
(3) G. T.	70	F	end of war
(4) N. K.	40	K (i)	1960
(5) O. S.	65	F	end of war
(6) D. K.[195]	85	F	end of war

This council is almost completely composed of the FAKOROBA from the traditional extended families. They have been council members for at least 20 years. The only exception is N. K. (No. 4 in above table) who served in the colonial army in the 1950s and is therefore the only one in the village able to speak a little French. However, he is fully integrated into his extended family. The council in such relatively developed villages as Nianzana and Kintan-B. is already somewhat different:

Nianzana Village Council [197]

Name	Age	Social Position	Member since:
(1) F. K.	32	K (s)	before 1965 [198]
(2) S. K.	36	K (s)	before 1965
(3) S. K.	70	F	before 1965
(4) D. K.	60	K (s)	before 1965 [198]
(5) M. K.	40	K	1965
(6) N. K.	80	F	1967 [199]

Kintan-Bamana Village Council [200]

Name	Age	Social Position	Member since:
(1) A. D.	70	F	before 1960
(2) B. D.	42	F	before 1960
(3) Z. D.	30	K (i)	1960
(4) N. D.	41	K (i)	1960 [201]
(5) S. D.	41	K (s)	1960
(6) K. D.	60	F	1960 [202]

In these councils, the FAKOROBA are by no means in the absolute majority. Two of the Kintan council members elected in 1960 — Nos. 3 and 4 — are economically fully integrated into the extended family, and the third (number 5) is the son of the village head. On the other hand, in Nianzana, already three members are heads of nuclear families who have emancipated themselves economically within the extended family. One member (number 5), first elected in 1965, is head of an economically independent nuclear family. His family consists of three persons, he cultivates three hectares (on one he grows export crops), owns a plough and two oxen. It is significant that three of the seven members who are not FAKOROBA graduated from the agricultural school in Barouéli.

It is typical for the strongly conservative character of the village, that even in these two developed villages, the council members – without exception all male – originate only from the traditionally ruling clan of the Konaté or Diarra, although the Konaté in Nianzana make up only 31% of the families and 32% of the inhabitants, and the Diarra in Kintan-B. only 62% of the families and 73% of the inhabilitants.

So, in the 1960s the representatives of the traditional socio-economic structures exercised the greatest influence in decisive local political institutions such as the positions of village head and in the village council, even in those areas where the disintegration of traditional conditions was already far advanced.

The traditional village leadership had not proved an obstacle in the struggle for national independence.[203] On the contrary, they headed the first anti-colonial movements. They were actively integrated into the modern national liberation movement with all those classes and strata who did not collaborate with colonialism on the basis of an anti-colonial platform. They were able to use their influential position in the village to mobilize the whole population for struggle against colonial rule[204].

After political independence had been achieved and it became necessary to introduce social and economic changes, the traditional leaders inevitably became an obstacle in mobilising the peasants for the non-capitalist road. As representatives and the embodiment of the old system they were necessarily conservative in their attitudes to social and economic changes and had neither an objective nor a subjective interest in such changes. The traditional political leaders became a barrier between the peasant masses and the revolutionary-democratic leadership.

The traditional structures had a similarly inhibiting effect on the work of the local organisations of the national-democratic mass party. They were also permeated by traditional social structures, even if not so strongly as the communal organs.

An investigation held by the Malinese sociologist, Jango Cissé is very revealing in this respect.[205] Through the example of the Kita area, he shows that the party branches were built up on the basis of the traditional clans.[206] "Here we can see an over-laying, a real overlapping of traditional and modern structures."[207]

This often led to difficulties in carrying out progressive political measures:

"... the existence of certain conservative aspects which one did not want to acknowledge was the cause of often strong reactions which made it necessary to send representatives of the National Political Bureau to Kita."[208]

An *L'Essor* editorial of 25 March 1968 shows up some of the difficulties: "... one should seek the cause of these difficulties [in making the S. U.'s agrarian conception reality – K.E.] in the almost systematic attempts to keep the peasant youth away from responsible positions. In our villages, only the elders are elected to such posts, or to be more exact, appointed, and this, not because of any capabilities, but simply through their age. The elders ignore the role played by youth for progress in all societies of the world, and jealously guard the rights they enjoy out of such subjective reasons as certain traditions and customs ... It is important to allow the village youth more active and more effective participation in managing the economy and in taking over adequate, responsible functions in the villages, the mass organisations, the party organisations and the village councils."

On the basis of traditional social institutions, the inner relations in the committees were determined by the traditions to the same extent as these continued to function. In the traditional community, the individual never took up direct contact to the superior institution, but only through the FAKO-ROBA so that the committees were also run on this basically gerontocratic principle, i. e. the "elders" automatically became the leaders of the village party committees. This structure paralysed the village party group as an instrument of non-capitalist transformation in two respects. Firstly, the representatives of the traditional structure in the committees did not pass on the impulses given from the central leadership, so that the latter was unable to effectively mobilise the peasant masses. Secondly, the "rule of the elders" choked any initiative shown by the "younger", i. e. the mass of the producers. Direct and effective relations could not be built up between the leadership in the city and the peasant ally, who was the ordinary producer, although he had an objective interest in non-capitalist change, in contrast to the traditional leaders.

So, one must agree with Bénot when he writes about the Sudanese Union and similar parties: "... they could not become the instrument for economic development and social change, because they are permeated by the existing social structures from the bottom to the top with a power that has been so far invincible."[209]

Even if it was most obvious there, the inhibiting effect on the mobilisation of the peasant masses by the traditional structures expressed itself not only through traditional "elders" ruling the modern political organisations and institutions on a local level. Consolidation of the alliance between the revolutionary leadership in the city and the peasantry was inhibited by the colonial backwardness of village conditions as a whole. The low level of the productive forces, the isolation of the natural economy, integration into the rigid social structures of the community and the extended family, religious superstition, ignorance and illiteracy hindered the peasant producer from unfolding his potential as ally to the revolutionary-democratic forces, even where it had been possible to largely remove the traditional leadership from the village organs.

In the same way, the traditional structures necessarily hindered the spread of a revolutionary ideology. The peasants' consciousness, stamped by the traditional community and its ideological structures, necessarily resisted any revolutionary ideology, as, in line with its function within the extended family and the community, it was directed at reproduction of that which existed and not at change, because "... for the forefathers, any advance meant a return to the origins; man and society progressed only to the extent that they reproduced the old models. This mentality continues to exist in traditional Africa. That is why old people are treated with such respect: they are a living witness of the models of the past. However, in the modern sense of the word, this is the opposite to progress."[210]

Therefore, it is taking a formal approach and strategically wrong to try to identify the traditional collectivism of the extended family with socialist ideology or to presume that the existence of the former can accelerate the permeation of socialist ideology. On the contrary, as long as the extended family and the traditional community function as a socio-economic system, they continually reproduce traditionalist ideological elements in the whole movement, i. e. they will always nourish those illusory conceptions of the allegedly socialist character of traditional relations and are an objective hindrance to the ideological process of cognition that is necessary for working class ideology to be able to penetrate the whole movement.

Thus, the persistency of traditional structures in Mali is a decisive objective cause for the revolutionary-democratic leadership — despite great efforts — failing to consolidate the alliance with the peasant masses in such a way that it could become a pillar of political stability.[211]

The leadership of the Sudanese Union recognised fairly quickly that the strong influence of the traditional leaders in the political institutions were an obstacle to non-capitalist transformation but not in its full connotations. For example, in the commentary to a law from 1961/2 it is stated: "... in practise it is sometimes difficult for the young people and women to put their opinions against those of the elders ..."[212]

However, ensnared as they were in their Narodnik-like illusions, the revolutionary-democratic leadership was unable at that time to see the whole problem or draw the necessary conclusions.

Only after a longer period of experience on the non-capitalist road, were Mali's leaders able to see some of the basic factors. At a co-operative seminar in 1968, they acknowledged patriarchal gerontocracy as a "retrograde force" which they had underestimated up to then. In comparison, the youth, the women and the poor peasantry were classified as a revolutionary potential which had not yet been sufficiently mobilised for democratic changes in the village.[213]

Political conclusions were drawn from this reassessment to strengthen party positions against the "retrograde forces".[214] In particular, the committee and the village council — both were largely ruled by the traditional leaders — were to be eliminated as institutions and replaced by a *Comité Révolutionnaire de Base* (C. R. B.). The C. R. B. was to become an effective party instrument for mobilizing the masses and had the task of managing economic questions of the co-operative through its secretary.[215]

Although the three months from summer to November 1968 were too short for these measures to prove themselves in practise, the principle of basing oneself on those groups in the village whose interests contradict those of the traditional forces (and capitalist elements) seems to be the way for non-capitalist changes. However, due to left-wing sectarianism, these groups were taken too narrowly in Mali in 1968 so that important allies were antagonised.

Thus the Malinese experience showed that the social relations of the traditional community are a serious obstacle to economic, social, political and ideological progress towards non-capitalist development. The Malinese experience not only reduces to absurdity the illusion that the village community makes the march to socialism easier, but it again confirms the words of Lenin, still fully valid for all developing countries, that "capitalism can be 'prevented' in China and that a 'social revolution' there will be made easier by the country's backwardness, . . . is altogether reactionary".[216]

REFERENCES

1 In the 1890s the people and states in Mali were systematically militarily oppressed by France. The military campaigns of the 1870s and 1880s (particularly the thrust from Senegal to the Niger River near Bamako in 1883) served as its preparation. For details of the conquest and a Marxist assessment, see J. Suret-Canale, *Schwarzafrika*, loc. cit., pp. 240—52 and 256—77. The Mali Federation was given political independence on 20. 6. 1960. After the Federation disintegrated, the Republic of Mali was proclaimed on 22 September 1960.

2 For details of colonialism as an integral part of imperialism, see particularly, V. I. Lenin, *Imperialism, the Highest Stage of Capitalism. A Popular Outline*,

in: *Collected Works*, vol. 22, Moscow 1964, pp. 185–304 and S. Tyulpanov, *Das Kolonialsystem des Imperialismus und sein Zerfall*, Berlin 1959.
3. Afrique Occidentale Française (A. O. F.) – founded in 1895 and constituted in 1904 – included the French colonies in West Africa up to 1958. They were: Mauretania, Senegal, Sudan, Upper Volta, Guinea, Niger, the Ivory Coast (for details see J. Suret-Canale, *French Colonialism in Tropical Africa, 1900–1945* [translated from the French by T. Gottheiner], London 1971, pp. 86–90).
4. According to an investigation by S. H. Frankel (*Capital Investment in Africa, its course and effects*, London 1938) French capital export to Africa before the Second World War was 2.1 per inhabitant. In contrast, the other imperialist "Mother countries" invested £ 3.9 in the densely populated Nigeria, £ 9.8 in the Portuguese colonies, £ 13 in Belgian-Congo and £ 38.4 in Rhodesia (see *Le travail en Afrique Noire*, Paris 1952, p. 219).
5. See V. I. Lenin, *Imperialism, the Highest Stage of Capitalism*, in: *Collected Works*, vol. 22, Moscow 1964, p. 243.
6. A study made in 1943 by the Colonial Ministry on French capital export to the French colonies in West and Central Africa and to Togo and the Cameroons (1910–40) is very revealing. It states that 39% of capital exported was invested in trade, and only 9.6% into industry, 7.5% into mining, 3.6% into transport, 18% into plantations, 12.5% into forestry, and here, one must remember that plantations, mining and forestry developed mainly in Central Africa (see J. Dresch, "Les Investissements en Afrique Noire", in: *Le travail en Afrique Noire*, Paris 1952, pp. 234–5).
7. The most important were S. C. O. A., the C. F. A. O., branches of the Unilever trust and such Bordelais firms as Peyrissac, Maurel et Prom, Vézia. As I can describe only the most important and most general characteristics of the economic exploitation in the French West African colonies here, I would point to the excellent depiction in "Physiognomy of the Financial Oligarchy" in Suret-Canale's book *French Colonialism in Tropical Africa* (loc. cit.) particularly on pages 167–83. The bourgeois economist, M. Capet, gives a good survey on the structure and activities of the trade monopolies in *Traité d'économie tropicale. Les économies d'A. O. F.*, Paris 1958, pp. 121–134. A highly apologetic description is given in: Jean and René Charbonneau, *Marchés et marchands d'Afrique Noir*, Paris 1961.
8. See J. Woddis, *Africa: The Roots of Revolt*, London 1960, pp. 1–108.
9. J. Dresch, "Les trusts en Afrique noire", in: *Servir la France*, 1946, p. 30. J. Suret-Canale gives the most comprehensive and thorough Marxist analysis so far of the essence of the *économie de traite*. (*French Colonialism in Tropical Africa*, loc. cit., pp. 4–58 and 159–306).
10. J. Suret-Canale gives a very fitting background to the economic causes of the anti-slave attitudes of high finance when he writes: "In brief, for important businessmen who were opposed to slavery it was not a question of abolishing it to ease the fate of the slave, but rather of making them do more work 'under the stimulus of self-interest', which, in fact, was confused with necessity – to the advantage of the colonisers. As for the former slave masters,

they were to be turned away from the 'easy and lazy life', in other words put to work under the same terms as their former slaves, and for the profits of the same colonisers." (*French Colonialism in Tropical Africa*, loc. cit., p. 61). However, as a whole the colonial "slave liberation" policy was very contradictory, because it lay in their interests to maintain traditional, social antagonisms (see J. Suret-Canale, *French Colonialism in Tropical Africa* loc. cit., pp. 60—7).

11 The fact that the traditional community gradually disintegrated through the penetration of commodity-money relations together with the *économie de traite*, is quite a different question.

12 K. Marx, *Capital*, vol. 3, Foreign Languages Publishing House, Moscow 1962, p. 232.

13 République du Mali, *Comptes économiques de la République du Mali 1959*, Clichy 1962, p. 159.

14 The colonial Office du Niger was founded in 1932 and in 1959 controlled an artificially irrigated area of 47,000 hectares in the so-called dead Delta of the Niger which was cultivated by African settlers. Its purpose was to make France independent of English cotton imports and supply the A. O. F. with rice.

15 See J. Suret-Canale, *French Colonialism in Tropical Africa*, loc. cit., pp. 228—35.

16 K. Marx, *Capital*, vol. 3, loc. cit. pp. 325 ff.

17 One canton usually consists of 10—20 villages.

18 They were to guard "public order" in the villages and cantons and immediately report to the district commandants "all actions and propaganda aimed at disturbing public order". They also had the task to divide up the "collective duties" (taxes, forced labour, recruitment, forced cultivation and delivery, S. I. P. contributions) among the various villages and families and ensure they are carried out. See "Arreté du Lieutenant-Gouverneur p. i. portant réorganisation de l'Administration indigène dans la Colonie du Soudan Français", in: *Journal Officiel du Soudan Français*, 693/1935, p. 232. For further details see ibid. pp. 233—4. See also the detailed description in J. Suret-Canale, *French Colonialism in Tropical Africa*, loc. cit., pp. 71—92 and R. Cornevin, "L'évolution des chefferies dans l'Afrique noire, d'expression Française", in: *Recueil Penant*, 686/1961, pp. 235—50; 687/61, pp. 379—388; 688/61, pp. 539—56). Special literature on the *Chefferie* in Mali is the work by G. S. Kondratyev, "Ob institute kantonalnych i derevenskich voždej v Respublike Mali", in: *Narody Asii i Afriki*, 4/1965, pp. 36—40 and the apologetic article by the former colonial administration officer, F. Fournier ("Aspects politiques du problème des chefferies au Soudan présahélien", in: *Revue juridique et politique de l'Union Française*, 1/1955, pp. 147—82). A. B. Letnev (*Derevnja zapadnogo Mali*, Moscow 1964) also deals with some socio-economic aspects of the colonial *Chefferie* on pages 62—81.

19 Although some of the *Chefferie* (particularly the village heads) were recruited from among the traditional leadership, in their essence they were fundamen-

tally different from them. The leadership which either stood at the head of community as its embodiment and raised itself above it as the ruling aristocracy, was replaced by an arbitrary instrument of the colonial administration which oppressed and exploited the community and its members in the interests and for the benefit of the foreign monopolies.

20 See Letnev, *Derevnja zapadnogo Mali*, loc. cit., pp. 73—81; Fournier, *Aspects politiques*, op. cit., p. 175.
21 The trade monopolies guarded their monopoly position with economic and administrative means (refusal of licences, prosecution of unlicensed buying of export crops) (see A. B. Letnev, *Social'naja differencija v Mali*, loc. cit., p. 77).
22 This was, above all, traditional trade with dry fish, live animals, some food crops, etc. (see mainly J. Tricart, "Les échanges entre la zone forestière de la Côte d'Ivoire et les savannes soudaniennes", in: *Les Cahiers d'Outre-Mer*, Bordeaux, 35/1956, pp. 209—38).
23 The *économie de traite* system is often compared with a pyramid with the trade monopolies as importers and exporters at the top. Below them are the French and Lebanese wholesalers and retailers; dependent on them were the small African merchants (see J. and R. Charbonneau, op. cit., pp. 58—61).
24 As the banks did not give credits to the peasants, they had to turn to the merchants and were forced to pay very high interest rates (30—50%). (See H. Capet, op. cit., pp. 173—178)
25 R. Barbé describes this process as neo-colonialism of the largest trade monopolies, because it was their reaction to the approaching independence (see R. Barbé, *Les classes sociales en Afrique Noire*, Paris 1964, pp. 100—2.).
26 The first — and up to the end of the Second World War decisive — task of the colonial administration in exploiting the producers organised in the traditional community for the trade monopolies was the use of non-economic force. In addition, and often linked with the first, it also had the task to "modernise" traditional agriculture in such a way that it was able to satisfy the needs of the *"métropole"* for agricultural raw material in the required assortment, quality and quantity; and to see to it that the economic conditions for acquisition of the peasants' surplus labour by the monopolies were maintained and if possible, extended. The essence of this "modernisation policy" was that a small part of the surplus product which was pressed out of the producer (in the form of taxes and other tributes) was then channelled through the colonial administration into the traditional agriculture in order to enable the amount of surplus products to grow for the monopolies. The results were very poor because, also in this field, the colonial administration concentrated only on creating the necessary prerequisites to enable the *économie de traite* to function. Up to 1946, the colonial administration made absolutely no productive investments into traditional agriculture (See S. Amin, *Trois expériences africaines de développement: le Mali, la Guinée et le Ghana*, Paris 1965, p. 38). From 1947—59, they invested four billion Fr.-CFA, i. e. a yearly average of 310 million, (ibid., p. 39) which was only a fraction of the profits made by the

trade monopolies and was generally paid out of the colonial budget, with only a very small part financed from state-monopoly means (FIDES, FERDES). (See "La République du Mali", in: *La Documentation Française. Notes et Etudes Documentaires*, 2 739/13/1/1961, pp. 46—52).

27 République Du Mali, *Enquête agricole au Mali 1960*, Paris 1964, p. 37. Distribution of the ox-drawn ploughs differed greatly in the various regions. It was highest in Ségou (22.1% of all farms), followed by Mopti (15%), Sikasso (9.3%), Bamako (9%) and Kayes (6.7%).

28 See République Soudanaise, *Le Problème de la fumure au Soudan*, Bamako 1958 (photostat). The peasants were too poor to buy artificial fertiliser, and the traditional separation between agriculture and animal breeding prevented use of natural fertiliser. Apart from that, the necessary means of transport did not exist. So the use of natural fertiliser was limited only to small areas (gardens) near the village, as in precolonial times.

29 *Enquête agricole 1960*, op. cit., p. 59. One must take into account that agriculture, above all rice, was grown on fixed fields (69% of all rice fields were continually cultivated) because it was dependent on an irrigation system. Outside of these irrigation systems, 80—90% of the area was cultivated on continually shifting the fields.

30 *Enquête agricole 1960*, op. cit., p. 55.

31 *Comptes économiques 1959*, op. cit., pp. 32—37.

32 *Enquête agricole 1960*, op. cit., p. 61. The 80.2% were composed of 58% millet, 6.9% rice, 15.3% other foods.

33 Ibid.

34 For millet, the marketing was 7.5% and for rice 8% of the production (see *Comptes économiques 1959*, op. cit., p. 32 and 34).

35 With marketing quotas of 71% (cotton) and 74% (peanuts). See ibid., p. 36.

36 The S. E. R. E. S. A. study (*Etude sur l'économie agricole du Soudan*, loc. cit., p. 30) gives a figure of 80% for self-supply in the traditional sector. S. Amin (*Comptes économiques*, op. cit., 1959, p. 12) assesses that 62% of agriculture is run as natural economy, but includes the Office du Niger into his calculations. Both studies also include into their calculations the animal and fish production, where commercialisation grew enormously in the 1950s.

37 République du Mali, Mission socio-économique. *Enquête budgétaire dans le Delta Central Nigérien*, Paris 1961, p. 20 (photostat). Budget studies are also contained in the papers by Malgrad (ibid., pp. 295—6), Cl. Grandet ("La vie rurale dans le cercle de Goundam", in: *Les Cahiers d'Outre-Mer*, 41/1958, pp. 41—43), G. Dupeyron ("Bintagoundou village du Faguibine; budgets et niveau de vie", in: *Les Cahiers d'Outre-Mer*, 45/1959, pp. 26—55) and H. Labouret (*Les paysans d'Afrique Noire*, loc. cit., pp. 211—16). However, because this is only a case study, it is not as convincing as the representative survey by the M. I. S. E. S. However, I mention them because in part they are more concrete.

38 See *Enquête budgétaire*, op. cit., pp. 68—70.

39 See ibid., p. 47.

40 Here it is mainly rice (47.1%) which plays a similar role for this area (because of the natural conditions) as an export crop, as cotton and peanuts do in the dry areas.
41 The relatively high amount of fish (14.8%) is also geographically determined.
42 See *Enquête budgétaire*, op. cit., p. 52.
43 See S. E. R. E. S. A. *Etude sur l'économie agricole du Soudan*, loc. cit., p. 32.
44 See R. Barbé, op. cit., pp. 18—19; *Enquête agricole 1960*, op. cit., pp. 17—18 and République du Mali, Mission socioéconomique 1956—58. *Enquête démographique dans le Delta Central Nigérien. 2e Fascicule. Résultats détaillés*, pp. 49—57.
45 Therefore, traditional handicrafts were not largely ruined, as was the case with strongly developed commodity-money relations (Senegal, Ivory Coast). (See J. Suret-Canale, *French Colonialism in Tropical Africa*, loc. cit., p. 294).
46 Here, it is simply that traditional goods (*dabas*, mats, etc.) were produced with traditional methods, but more and more for sale in the cities and thus became commodities. However, there was almost no (not even personal) continuity from traditional to modern handicrafts (in the cities). The tailors, mechanics, builders, bakers, butchers, etc. were not recruited from among those people who had traditionally done similar work (see M. Capet, op. cit., p. 171).
47 K. Marx, *Capital*, vol. 3, loc. cit., p. 326.
48 Ibid., p. 328.
49 Ibid., p. 328.
50 See chapters 4 and 5 of this book.
51 J. Suret-Canale writes quite correctly: "So long as the traditional self-sufficient economy dominates (which is expressed in the main role played by food crops), the patriarchal community, even if shaky, continues to remain an economic reality." (J. Suret-Canale, "Les fondéments sociaux de la vie politique africaine contemporaine", in: *Recherches Internationales*, 22/1961, p. 23).
52 Traditional structures were also maintained and reproduced in the cities, although of course, to a lesser degree. (See I. Diallo, "Economie urbaine et formes de participation traditionelles", in: *Etudes Maliennes*, 1/1970, pp. 21—28).
53 See *Enquête agricole 1960*, op. cit., p. 54.
54 See B. Holas, *Les Senoufo (y compris les Minianka)*, Paris 1957, pp. 105—7.
55 See R. P. D. Malgras, op. cit., p. 279—80.
56 See S. E. R. E. S. A. *Etude sur l'économie agricole du Soudan*, loc. cit.
57 See ibid.
58 See E. Leynaud, *Les cadres sociaux*, op. cit., pp. 156—63.
59 See V. Paques, op. cit., p. 78.
60 See S. E. R. E. S. A. *Etude sur l'économie agricole du Soudan*, loc. cit.
61 For the situation in the developed areas, see pages 177 ff.
62 E. Leynaud, *Les cadres sociaux*, op. cit., p. 158.
63 Here the term "family" is used because in the group "0—5" and also partly "6—10" the extended family is not meant.
64 The M. I. S. E. S. survey deviates sometimes considerably from these values in the Mopti and Macina districts.

Persons per family	0–5	5–9	10–14	20 and over
Percentage of families	46.8	36.5	16	2.0

However, this is less an expression of stronger disintegration of the extended family in this area than the high percentage of ethnic groups (Fulbe − 22%, Rimaibê − 25.4%) who traditionally have an undeveloped extended family structure (see République du Mali. Mission socio-économique 1956–58. *Enquête démographique dans le Delta Central Nigerien. Résultats détaillés*, Paris, n. d., p. 24).

65 R. P. D. Malgras, op. cit., p. 281.
66 See V. Paques, op. cit. p. 52–3.
67 E. Leynaud, Les cadres sociaux, op. cit., p. 162.
68 See S. E. R. E. S. A. *Etude sur l'économie agricole du Soudan*, loc. cit. p. 37–8.
69 "The family head decides on how the harvest from the collective field is to be used (often he alone has the key to the food store), but must ensure the family subsistence . . ." (République Soudanaise. Ministère de l'Agriculture et des Eaux et Forets. Direction de L'Agriculture. "Programme de Développement Rural de la Haute-Vallée du Niger", Bamako 1958, p. 11 [photostat]).
70 *Enquête agricole 1960*, op. cit., p. 58.
71 These are the fields of the nuclear families which had separated from the extended families. For details, see further on.
72 *Enquête agricole 1960*, op. cit., p. 58.
73 See E. Leynaud, *Les cadres sociaux*, op. cit., pp. 222–5.
74 *Programme de Développement Rural*, op. cit., p. 11.
75 The income which was actually placed at the disposal of the extended family differed in different areas and was largely determined by the degree of disintegration in the traditional structure. In the area of Kita, the returning migrant workers, for example, had to give at least three-quarters of the money they had earned to the FAKOROBA. (Information S. K., May 1965). On questions of the socio-economic status of the migrants, see further on.
76 The S. I. P. (Sociétés Indigènes de Prévoyance) were forced co-operatives during the colonial period, which embraced the population of a whole district. Their contributions were collected together with the taxes and were an additional source of income for the colonial administration. For details on the structure and how the S. I. P. functioned − although from an apologetic viewpoint, see M. Boyer, *Les Sociétés Indigènes de Prévoyance, de Secours et de Prêts Mutuels Agricoles en Afrique Occidentale Francaise*, Paris 1935. For a Marxist assessment of the S. I. P., see J. Suret-Canale, *French Colonialism in Tropical Africa*, loc. cit., pp. 235–44.
77 See the family budget analysis above and M. Capet, op. cit., pp. 48–50.
78 See pp. 117 and 172 ff.
79 See *Enquête agricole* 1960, op. cit., p. 23. The difference of 20 days resulted from the TON activities which are contained in the labour power used.
80 Ibid.

The traditional community today 107

81 Nianzana is a large, relatively developed village with differentiations within it in the Barouéli *Arrondissement*, Ségou district.
82 See *Enquête agricole 1960*, op. cit., p. 29. The study by the S. E. R. E. S. A. (*Etude sur l'économie agricole du Soudan*, loc. cit., p. 49) also points out that in almost all villages a Ton existed. The same conclusions were reached in the regional studies of S. de Genay (op. cit., p. 425) for the area of the Bambara in Ségou, E. Leynaud ("Fraternités d'âge et société de culture dans la Haute-Vallée du Niger", in: *Cahiers d'Etudes Africaines*, 21/1966, p. 51) for the Malinké area on the Upper Arm of the Niger, R. P. D. Malgras (op. cit., pp. 276–98) and J. Gallais (*La signification du village*, loc. cit., p. 145) for the Minianka in the Koutiala-Kimperana area. R. Dumont (*Afrique Noire. Développement Agricole. Réconversion de l'économie agricole: Guinée, Côte d'Ivoire, Mali.* Paris 1961, p. 166) also points to the widespread existence of the Ton.
83 As I cannot go into the inner structure of the Ton in this book, see E. Leynaud, *Fraternités d'âges*, op. cit., pp. 43–57.
84 Of these, 73% were male (see *Enquête agricole 1960*, op. cit., p. 30). Leynaud, who made a thorough examination of the Ton in the Haute-Vallée, states that the average size of the Ton in this area is 45 persons (*Fraternités d'âges* op. cit., p. 52).
85 E. Leynaud, *Fraternités d'âges*, op. cit., p. 52. According to the *Enquête agricole* (p. 31), the various age groups were distributed as follows:

Age group	Percent of Ton members
less than 30	71
30–49	25
50 and over	4

86 This investigation was made in nine villages of the Barouéli *Arrondissement*, Ségou district.
87 B. N'D iayé, op. cit., p. 118.
88 See pp. 33 ff.
89 See *Annuaire statistique 1966*, op. cit., pp. 162–3. This sum corresponds to about 11.2% of the total investments in the plan.
90 Originally, 9.958 billion FM were to be allotted. (See *Eléments du Bilan économique 1963*, loc. cit., pp. 7–13). Only 55% of the 5 year investment plan for the traditional sector of agriculture was fulfilled. The general plan for investments was fulfilled by some 72.5% – of the 67.438 billion FM intended (see ibid., p. 13), altogether 48.85 billion FM were actually invested (see *Annuaire statistique* 1966, loc. cit., p. 163).
91 Mali's growing financial difficulties arise mainly from the colonial backwardness of the Malinese economy and the increasing exploitation of Mali – and other developing countries – in the framework of the capitalist world market mechanism. Mali had huge losses through the steady decrease in the price of raw material and the increase for industrial products on the world market. (For details, see *L'Essor*, 19. 6. 1967). Other causes were, the stagnation of agrarian production, the enormous development of the black market and

smuggling, wrong investments and errors made in organising the economy (see also L. Nègre, "La Dévaluation du Franc Malien", in: *L'Essor*, 9. 5. 1967).

92 It lies far above the total sum for investments into the traditional sector of agriculture made during the whole post-war period up to and including 1959.

93 See "Le Développement de notre Monde rural", in: *Le Mali*, 3. 9. 1965, pp. 14—15. All the projects are described there in detail. The five-year plan laid down that altogether 70,000 hectares were to be irrigated (see République du Mali. *Où en est le Plan Quinquennal. Première Campagne 1961—1962. Résultats*, Bamako 1962, p. 6.)

94 The five-year plan intended to equip one third to one half of all farms with an ox-drawn plough by 1964/65. This would have meant some 15—20,000 ploughing units annually.

95 See *Le Développement*, op. cit., p. 14.

96 See ibid.

97 See République du Mali. Ministère d'Etat chargé du plan et de la Coordination des Affaires Economiques et Financières. "Rapport définitif de l'Enquête agricole 1964—65", Bamako n. d., p. 11. (photostat) and M. Keita in: *L'Essor*, 3. 1. 1966.

98 See Secrétariat d'Etat à l'Agriculture et aux Eaux et Forêts. "Réalisation ... depuis le Congrès Extraordinaire du 22 Septembre 1960", Bamako 1962, pp. 5—7 (photostat). On the development stage of the Z. E. R. see Chambre de Commerce, d'Agriculture et d'Industrie de Bamako. *Circulaire Mensuelle d'Information*, January 1963.

99 See Ministère du Développement. "Rapport sur l'exécution par le Ministère du Développement de la Deuxième Tranche 62—63 du Plan Quinquennal", Bamako 1963, pp. 3—5 and (Service de Développement) "Rapport d'Activités 1963—64", Bamako 1964, pp. 18ff. (photostat). This also contains a list of seasonal schools.

100 See "Le Développement de notre monde rural", in: *Le Mali*, 3/1965, p. 15. Unfortunately, I have no information on whether the plan to found 150 C. C. E. M. A. was realised. According to information from the S. D. R. Ségou, this aim was only partly achieved.

101 See (Ministère du Développement). "Programm Mil", Bamako 1965, p. 54 (photostat).

102 See Séminaire du Développement. Résolution générale, in: Chambre de Commerce, d'Agriculture et d'Industrie de Bamako. *Circulaire Mensuelle*, April 1964, p. 2 and *L'Essor*, 14. 6. 1965. Altogether 7,000 were planned.

103 The great interest of the Malinese government in the development of the *Service Civique* (S. C.) is seen from the fact that instead of the originally intended allottment of 48 million FM, the S. C. received 220 million FM during the course of the development plan (see *Eléments du Bilan économique 1963*, op. cit., p. 7 and *Annuaire statistique 1966*, op. cit., p. 163).

104 According to information from the national leadership of the *Service Civique*.

105 In 1963 the first one thousand youth were released from the *Service Civique* and in 1966 the second one thousand (see *L'Essor*, 11. 2. 1963 and 4. 4. 1966).

106 For details see pages 141ff.
107 For in the areas with very strong traditional structures, almost solely these crops were cultivated.
108 The calculation of the value of production was made on the basis of official buying prices for agrarian products in 1964/5 (see *Annuaire Statistique 1966*, op. cit., p. 143 and Comptes économiques 1965/6, op. cit., p. 9: millet: 11, rice: 12,5, maize: 13, peanuts: 13, cotton: 34 − first quality − FM per kg).
109 See *Comptes économiques 1959*, op. cit., pp. 32−7 and *Comptes économiques 1964/65*, op. cit., pp. 7−24. The *Comptes économiques 1958* were set up for the *calendar* year of 1959, while the Comptes économiques 1964−5 were set up for the *financial* year (from 1 July 1964 to 30 June 1965). So the production figures for 1959 correspond to the 1958/9 season.
110 See *Plan Quinquennal*, op. cit., pp. 15−16.
111 See *Annuaire statistique 1961*; *1962*; *1963*; *1964*; *1965*; *1966*; *Comptes économiques*, op. cit., pp. 32−7; *Principaux résultats de l'enquête agricole*, of 1967 and 1968, Bamako 1969, p. 15; *Rapport de l'enquête agricole 1968−1969*, Bamako 1970, p. 37.
112 *Klassen und Klassenkampf in den Entwicklungsländern. Probleme der ökonomischen Unabhängigkeit*, vol. 2, Berlin 1970, p. 170.
113 "In the form in which it exists, the community", writes Sobolev, "cannot be the source of socialism. Strictly speaking, it does not ease the forward march to socialism, as many believe, but puts on brakes" (A. Sobolev, "Einige Probleme des sozialen Fortschritts in Afrika", in: G. Liebig, *Nationale und soziale Revolution in Afrika*, Berlin 1967, p. 90. See Y. Bénot, *Idéologies des indépendances africaines*, Paris 1969, p. 280 and J. Arnauld, *Du colonialisme au socialisme*, Paris 1966, p. 270−1).
114 See P. Viguier, *L'Afrique de l'Ouest vue par un agriculteur*, Paris 1968 and M. Petit-Pont, *Structures traditionelles et développement*, Paris 1968.
115 Sobolev writes: "The clan and tribal community lack dynamics − because it is undeveloped, conservative in the organization of production and long out-dated in the system of distribution − so it has no effective reasons and serious inner sources for development of the productive forces, for extended reproduction" (A. Sobolev, op. cit., p. 90).
116 "Here one produces only for immediate use. A type of balance has developed between man and nature, but a balance of poverty. The individual and the collective are free of all ambition, prosperity is unknown, the issue here is sheer existence" (Badian uses a play on words in this passage. In French *"bien-être"* means prosperity and existence, while only *"être"* means being − K. E.). (S. Badian, op. cit., p. 86).
117 See pages 84ff.
118 See R. Dumont, *Développement agricole africain*, Paris 1965, p. 83.
119 I. e. also in those areas in which the inhibiting factors arising out of the traditional system slowly lose their effect through the disintegration of traditional relations.

120 We will not deal here with the aspect, linked to this, that in reality, under certain conditions, the "elders" oppose change because it destroys the basis for their personal enrichment.

121 The average results of the *Service Civique* camps (plus state farms) show, however, that it was not possible to achieve higher production in all camps: millet 570 kg, peanuts 705 kg, cotton 780 kg. This has reasons like a lack of cadres, bad organization, material difficulties, etc. which do not directly affect our subject (see *Rapport de l'enquête agricole 1968–69*, Bamako 1970, Tableau 37).

122 Compiled from: *Rapport de l'enquête agricole 1968/69*, op. cit., p. 37 and Service d l'Agriculture. *Rapport Annuel 1968–69*, pp. 130–56.

123 After his training in the *Service Civique* is finished, every youth receives an ox-drawn plough and a pair of oxen.

124 Some 10% of the *Service Civique* members do not return to their village after training.

125 The following remarks are based particularly on experiences in the south east of Mali.

126 This affects the whole question of flight from the countryside and migrant labour. See further on.

127 This aspect plays a role in a more developed phase to which I return on pages 172ff.

128 In the long run it does lead to the traditional structures being destroyed. See following chapter.

129 That is, dependent on the size of income, size of family, their geographical distribution and economic situation.

130 Of course this also plays a role. But the mere fact that there is always someone in the city who is traditionally obliged to provide food and lodging makes the city so attractive and so much easier to take this step into what would otherwise present a very uncertain future. And this obligation to assist applies not only to the members of the extended family in the narrower sense. It includes the whole clan and even territorial bonds. E. g. former members of the same youth organisation, those of the same age from a village (i. e. those who were circumcised in the same year) have greater obligations to each other than to real brothers or sisters who are not of the same age (see E. Leynaud, *Fraternités d'âge*, op. cit., p. 46–51).

131 The Malinese sociologist I. Diallo points out in a very interesting study that of the adult population in Bamako almost 50% (some 40,000 out of 90,000) exist without a regular income (see I. Diallo, *Economie Urbaine*, op. cit., pp. 21–8).

132 *L'Essor*, 7. 1. 1971, p. 4.

133 J. Suret-Canale, *Die Tradition in den westafrikanischen Gesellschaftsordnungen*, loc. cit., p. 132. However, at the same time he points out that the out-dated structures can just as well become the starting point for bourgeois developments. We will come back to this.

134 In his book, already quoted, Arnauld repeated a very typical discussion

held with the director of a state Malinese firm. He writes: "In the traditional society, M. T. adds, every individual places his labour power at the disposal of the community and has his needs satisfied. Individual property was unknown. Equally, there was no idleness, except the cripples for whom there was great solidarity. Everyone gave in accordance with his abilities and received in accordance with his needs. Then wage labour was introduced, i. e. individualisation of work. But the communal way of life remained. With my wages, I support some 20 of my relatives who come to me, stay several days and then return to the village. What is mine is also theirs. Under such conditions it is very difficult for a young wage-labourer to save. He would have to neglect his obligations. Thus those who receive wages and salaries cannot lay the basis for a savings account which would help development. This is tremendous waste" (J. Arnauld, *Du colonialisme au socialisme*, Paris 1966, p. 270).

135 On these phenomena in the disintegration of traditional relations, see further on.
136 See *Colloque sur les politiques de développement*, loc. cit., p. 172.
137 K. Marx, *Theses on Feuerbach*, in: K. Marx/F. Engels, *Selected Works*, vol. 1, Progress Publishers, Moscow 1973, p. 13.
138 See pages 33 ff.
139 K. Marx, *First Draft of the Reply to V. I. Zasulich's Letter*, in: K. Marx/F. Engels, *Selected Works*, vol. 3, Moscow 1973, p. 155.
140 Similar phenomena could be observed in Guinea (see J. Suret-Canale, *Die Tradition in den westafrikanischen Gesellschaftsordnungen*, loc. cit., p. 134.
141 See *Enquête agricole 1967—68*, op. cit., pp. 5f.
142 Ibid., table 45 and 47.
143 See speech by M. Keita at the 5th economic conference in Bamako, in: *L'Essor*, 25. 1. 1965, p. 7.
144 As already mentioned on pages 33 ff., at the beginning of the sixties there were elements in the conception of the co-operative which contradicted the „Remise à pied" principle of the traditional community (e. g. giving an „animateur" control of administrative affairs, etc.). However, these were caused more by administrative organisational necessity, rather than a fundamental doubt about the possibility of „socialist" re-establishment of the traditional community. The officials in the development service neglected this principle far more, because their main aim was to see to it that certain economic and technical innovations were used.
145 For details see following chapter.
146 Here is expressed a basic conception contained in the „transformation socialiste" — never formulated but always implied — that the extended family should be retained as the social and economic basis for the future „socialist" village community. This conception was confirmed to me at least as his personal view in a long talk I had with A. D., head of the Cooperation Division in the Development Ministry on questions of co-operative development. He was of the opinion that the extended family was *the* African form of social organisation

and its disintegration was a bad thing. However, this view is by no means shared by all members of the development service. In a talk I had with M. L. F., leading member of the S. M. D. R. in Sikasso, he expressed the view in May 1965 that as a social system, the extended family is outdated, inhibits economic development and, therefore, must give way.

147 The fundamental administrative document for this is the family book (*carnet de famille*), in which were entered all members of a family in the traditional sense who lived in a village. It is the basis for organization of the village population for every purpose (administration, party, co-operative, development service).

148 A very clear example is what I was told in 1967 in Ségou as being quite usual: in order to control the migrants, it was decided that those who want to leave the village must present the family book to the district or *Arrondissement* administration for registration. However, the family book is kept by the family head who, of course, will not pass it over if he does not agree that the family member emigrates.

149 See pages 183 ff.

150 F. Engels, *On Social Relations in Russia* (Afterword), in: K. Marx/F. Engels, *Selected Works*, vol. 2, Progress Publishers, Moscow 1973, p. 403.

151 See J. Suret-Canale, *Die Tradition in den westafrikanischen Gesellschaftsordnungen*, loc. cit., p. 136.

152 Basically, it is a question of overcoming the underemployment in agriculture (spread over the whole year) caused by traditional organisation (see R. Dumont, *Développement agricole africain*, op. cit., pp. 36—9).

153 Generally, little exact material exists on the productivity of such work. In the Z. E. R. Barouéli and other areas I found many good results from this orientation, but had neither the time nor opportunity to make productivity calculations, although the following figures about the Joliba village are revealing: here four groups of 60 men made bricks out of clay mixed with 30% cement for housebuilding. Three times a week, the whole village participated in the work. It consisted of 813 men, 415 women, 245 children and 40 elders (the last two groups probably gave more moral than actual support). At first 250 bricks were produced daily. With the help of a competition this was increased to 3,400. Leaving aside the help given by the whole village, this meant 14 clay bricks per labourer or two to three per working hour. If one adds the help by the whole village three times a week, then the result is just five bricks per labourer, per day. This is definitely a representative case because Joliba was a model village with the best prerequisites (see *L'Essor*, 14. 6. 1965).

154 See "La pacification du pays Habé", in: *L'Afrique française. Renseignements coloniaux*, 3/1911.

155 See Issa Baba Traoré, *Un héros: Koumi-Diossé*, Bamako 1962, pp. 44—56.

156 See *Révolte dans le cercle de San* (1916), Archives of Koulouba.

157 As a result of the penetration of commodity-money relations into agriculture, the traditional structures gradually disintegrated and new social forces

came into being. For details, see pp. 117 ff. Particularly in the cities, the new social forces (teachers, subaltern employees, merchants, etc.) took up new forms of anti-colonial struggle. For questions of urbanisation, see J. Dresch, "Villes d'Afrique occidentale", in: *Les Cahiers d'Outre-Mer*, 11/1950, pp. 200—30.

158 This is the Association des Anciens Elèves de Terrason (1931), the Syndicat des Instituteurs and the Association des Lettres du Soudan (later Foyer du Soudan), founded in 1937. However, these organisations contained only a few members (above all teachers, subaltern officials and employees in the trade societies). Every political activity was denied them by the colonial administration (see Th. Hodgkin/R. Schachter-Morgenthau, *Mali*, loc. cit., pp. 229—230).

159 See J. Suret-Canale, *French Colonialism in Tropical Africa*, loc. cit., pp. 435—6.

160 Although the Hamallah movement never had a political program nor did it wage a political struggle against the colonial power, it was bitterly persecuted by the colonial administration because it robbed the traditional marabouts of whom the majority supported the colonial-administrative *Chefferie* of huge numbers of its members. Hamallah himself was deported in 1930 and died in 1943 of a "heart attack". In August 1940, his supporters were massacred. The most prominent representative of Hamallism supported the R. D. A. after the Second World War, in the period of harshest oppression by the colonial administration (1946—51).

161 "Hamallism set men free — whether within groups created by colonialism or in tribes; whether in huts or under tents; or — in the very heart of the family — women and adolescents. "(A. Gouilly, *L' Islam dans l' Afrique occidentale française*, Paris 1952 [quoted by J. Suret-Canale, *French Colonialism in Tropical Africa*, loc. cit., p. 436]).

162 See Circulaire No. 11, op. cit., pp. 2—4.

163 The leadership of the P. S. P. was mainly recruited from the *Chefferie*: F. D. Sisoko was chief of the Bafoulabé canton, his right-hand man, H. Dicko, son of a Fulbe chief in the Douentza canton. The absolute majority of the village and canton chiefs supported the P. S. P. and used their administrative functions (one was to organise the elections) to ensure that the P. S. P. candidates were elected (see Th. Hodgkin/R. Schachter-Morgenthau, *Mali*, loc. cit., p. 234—235).

164 The parties, led by the administrative *Chefferie* along ethnic lines, were inspired by the colonial administration in order to control the local representative bodies. Their activities remained very limited; they had neither a statute nor a program and functioned only during election campaigns. They were above all the „Union Dogon" in the Bandiagara district, the "Union Démocratique Ségovienne" and the "Union Démocratique de Kayes". (see G. S. Kondratyev, op. cit., p. 37—38 and Th. Hodgkin, *African Political Parties*, London 1961, p. 4).

165 For details on the colonial administrative *Chefferie* see p. 71.

166 J. Delval, "Le R. D. A. au Soudan Français", in: *L'Afrique et l'Asie*, 16/1951, pp. 56—8.
167 See G. N. Skorov, *Francuzskij imperializm v Zapadnoj Afriki*, Moscow 1956, p. 206.
168 See W. Wilke, "Die Entstehung und der Kampf der Gewerkschaften in den französischen Kolonien Westafrikas gegen den Kolonialismus (1945—1957)", in: *Arbeiterklasse, Gewerkschaften und nationale Befreiungsbewegung*. (Hochschule der Deutschen Gewerkschaften "Fritz Heckert". Fakultät für Ausländerstudium, Bernau 1964, p. 62. This work (pp. 54—85) gives a good survey of the development of the trade union movement in West Africa during that period.
169 See Congrès des paysans du Soudan, Bamako 23—24 January, 1955. Textes adoptés, pp. 4—5. Altogether 59 delegates and observers took part from the whole of Mali.
170 See Barakela, 4—10 April 1955, p. 3. 342 delegates from 67 villages around Barouéli (Ségou district) took part in this regional meeting.
171 Compiled from Th. Hodgkin/R. Schachter-Morgenthau, *Mali*, loc. cit., p. 232—3.
172 In 1956/7 the so-called *Loi-cadre* was introduced, the competency of the territorial assemblies was extended to limited legislative rights in the budget — and other local questions, and territorial governments were created which were responsible to the French governor (and not to the territorial assembly). However, all decisive fields remained the responsiblity of the governor as a "*Service d'Etat*". In 1958, the French constitution of the Fifth Republic changed the Union Française, which had grown out of the Empire Française in 1946, into the Communauté Franco-Africaine. The individual colonial territories as "republics" received their own government and were given an "inner autonomy". For details see N. I. Gavrilov, *Zapadnaja Afrika pod gnetom francii (1945—1959)*, Moscow 1961.
173 See Gavrilov, op. cit.
174 See Arreté Territorial, 191 D. 1—3/10—4/1958; *Journal Officiel du Soudan Français*, 1379/1958, pp. 405—6.
175 See ibid., p. 405.
176 See footnote 18, page 102.
177 See *Afrique Nouvelle*, Dakar, 546/1958.
178 See G. S. Kontratyev, op. cit., pp. 38—9.
179 See *La République du Mali*, op. cit., pp. 13—15.
180 See ibid.
181 By the Ordonnance No. 43 portant organisation des villages au Soudan et créant des Conseils de village du 28 mars 1959, in: *Journal Officiel de la République Soudanaise*, Numéro spécial, 1er avril 1959, pp. XXXV—XXXVIII.
182 See Décret portant dissolution de l'association dénommé "Union Démocratique Ségovienne" du 5 février 1959, in: *Journal Officiel de la République Soudanaise*, 15/1959, p. 240 and Décret portant dissolution de l'association

dénommé "Union Dogon" à Bandiagara du 15 Mai 1959, in: *Journal Officiel de la République Soudanaise*, 23/1959, p. 456.
183 See Parti de la Fédération Africaine. *L'Union Soudanaise – R. D. A. à la veille de l'Indépendence. Résolution sur l'organisation.*
184 In 1962 there were altogether 9,758 comités de villages, de fractions et de quartier (see VIe Congrès, loc. cit., p. 146).
185 See page 37f.
186 See VIe Congrès, loc. cit., p. 146 and 2e Séminaire, loc. cit., pp. 32–3.
187 See VIe Congrès, loc. cit., pp. 65–7.
188 See Chambre de Commerce d'Agriculture et d'Industrie de Bamako. *Annuaire Administratif de la République du Mali*, Bamako 1964, pp. 25–30.
189 See for further details 2e Séminaire, loc. cit., pp. 30–43 and S. M. Sy, *Recherches sur l'exercise du pouvoir politique en Afrique Noire (Côte d'Ivoire, Guinée, Mali)*, Paris 1965, pp. 186–202.
190 A very characteristic case occurred at the turn of the year 1964/5, in Somo. In the course of a "democratic" election, M. T. was able to take over the village chieftanship from B. K. who had had this function since 1960. M. T. came of a traditional DUGUTIGI family in Somo and was then still keeper of the village fetish. His then deceased father, village chief up to 1960, had founded the P. S. P. in Somo and had been replaced by B. K., founder and leader of the S. U. in Somo, in 1960 because of his close collaboration with the colonial power.
191 Even in the most developed villages I visited, the village chief came from the traditional DUGUTIGI family and had become chief in the traditional way, i. e. at an advanced age, see the following surveys on the councils in Niamana and Kintan-B. R. Dumont (*Afrique Noire est mal partie*, Paris 1961, p. 119) points out that the village chiefs in Mali come almost exclusively from the traditional *Chefferie* and were generally around 70.
192 The figures in brackets refer to the total number in the whole village.
193 Niamana is a relatively small village (150 inhabitants) in the basic sector N'Djeni in the Barouéli *Arrondissement*. As it is somewhat isolated, it has been little affected by economic developments.
194 Elected on 16. 12. 1965.
195 Village chief since end of the war.
196 F – FAKOROBA, K – head of an economically independent nuclear family, K(s) – head of a nuclear family which is independent within the extended family, K(i) – head of a nuclear family which is fully integrated into the extended family.
197 Elected on 24. 12. 1965.
198 Graduates of the Ecole rurale Barouéli.
199 In 1967 N. K. (sixth in the example) replaced his father, who had died in that year.
200 Elected on 19. 12. 1965.
201 Graduates of the Ecole rurale Barouéli (1938–43).

202 K. D. (sixth in the example) replaced his brother, who had been village chief up to then in 1960, but had to give this position up for health reasons.
203 Exceptions are, of course, the traditional leaders who supported the colonial-administrative *Chefferie* and became a pillar of colonial power.
204 See M. Bourjol, "Essai sur les transformations et l'évolution dialectique de la famille africaine de la 'gens' au 'ménage'", in: *Revue juridique et politique de l'Union Française*, 1/1957, pp. 92—93.
205 *Structures des Malinké de Kita*, Bamako 1970. Dr. Dj. Cissé is at present Director of the Ecole Normale Supérieure, the most important college in Mali.
206 In Kita there are three clan groups: 1. the Camara and Tounkara, 2. the Keita, 3. the Cissé, Diallo and Sow. They make up the suburbs Same-Dugu, Makandiabougou, Moribougou and Segoubougou with corresponding suburban committees (see ibid , p. 280).
207 Ibid.
208 Ibid, p. 272.
209 Y. Bénot, "Développement accéléré et révolution sociale en Afrique Occidentale", in: *La Pensée*, 126/1966, p. 36.
210 Amadou Seydou, Director of the UNESCO Cultural Department in an interview with the Paris O. R. T. F. (see *L'Essor*, 30. 1. 1970, p. 2).
211 Other factors must be added, like the development of bureaucratic-bourgeois tendencies in the party and state apparatus, or in the developed areas, the contradictory attitudes of the peasant producers which accompany the spread of small commodity production. We will return to this later.
212 "*Encadrement rural en République du Mali*", *Action rurale*. Edition spéciale, p. 7.
213 See *Rapport de Synthèse*, op. cit., p. 13.
214 See ibid., p. 15.
215 See ibid., p. 17.
216 V. I. Lenin, *Democracy and Narodizm in China*, in: *Collected Works*, vol. 18, Moscow 1963, pp. 166ff.

4. Spontaneous decay of traditional structures and the problems of non-capitalist transformation

The objective social processes show that the preservation of traditional, allegedly socialist conditions is not only a strategic error, but that, in the long run, it makes non-capitalist development impossible. The economic development destroys these traditional social conditions, independent of the subjective will expressed in any development conceptions. As Marx declared in a similar context, this dissolution is historical progress, because it corresponds to the "... development of the forces of production which is only limited, and indeed limited in principle. The development of the forces of production dissolves these forms, and their dissolution is itself a development of the human productive forces".[1]

4.1. Foundations, phenomena and causes of decay in traditional structures

The basic cause of the gradual decay of traditional social conditions is the penetration of commodity-money relations into the village community.

This process began during the colonial period. It was the necessary outcome of the forced integration of traditional peasant producers into the colonial market economy and its intensity and extent was determined by colonial profit interests.[2]

The commodity-money relations developed above all in those areas where the best natural and infra-structural conditions for exploitation existed. In colonial Mali, this applied mainly to the territory along the Kayes-Bamako railway line and the navigable part of the Niger River from Koulikoro to Ségou. It was here that the first cash crops were planted[3] and here that 75–80% of the peanut production was grown in the mid-fifties.[4]

During the course of time, the points of concentration within this zone changed. While up to the Second World War cash crops were concentrated on the area between Kayes and Bamako, after 1945 they were moved more and more into the Bamako-Ségou area with some in Mopti and Koutiala because of soil exhaustion. Increase in rice production outside of the Office du Niger (at the upper arm and in the Niger delta)[5] and cotton production[6] (above all in the Koutiala-Kimparana area) during the 1950s contributed to this.

After political independence, basically new conditions arose for the unfolding of the productive forces and thus for the economic driving power within the social processes. They were no longer determined solely by the profit interests of monopoly capital, but were growingly influenced by the non-capitalist development policy of the national democratic state.[7] Thus after 1960 there was a speedier growth of the productive forces and strong commodity-money relations in the countryside, despite the inhibiting effects of the traditional community.[8]

The development of the agricultural productive forces after independence can be seen by the number of ploughs used:[9]

1960	1964/65	1967/68
44,720	71,900	90,300

According to Samir Amin, in Mali in the 1960s the progress made in spreading the ox-drawn plough was "probably the greatest in all West Africa".[10] Considerable successes were achieved in equipping the peasants with other means of production and transport, such as harrows, spraying instruments and ox-carts.[11]

Apart from this, the extension and intensification of the development service[12] was an essential aspect for the development of the productive forces, as was also the further construction of the infrastructure of the country. The same applies to the economic[13] as well as the social infrastructure.[14]

Interwoven with the development of the productive forces were also the commodity-money relations. The share of export crops compared to general agrarian products almost doubled from 1959 to 1969.

Export crops compared to agrarian products (percent of the value)[15]

1959	1964/65	1968/69
14.5	22.3	26.6

Commodity production rose (in comparison to general production) from 15.7% (1959) to 19.2% (1964—5) and reached some 25% in 1968.[16] Although the Malinese state tried to bring about a proportional development in agriculture, the productive forces and commodity-money relations grew unevenly in the various territories.

In areas where commodity-market relations had been only superficial during the colonial period, the economic processes stagnated temporarily after independence when the colonial administration stopped forcing the inhabitants to produce for a market. This resulted in market relations receding and greater natural economic self-isolation of the traditional community for a time.[17] Here the resistance of the traditional structure was stronger than the efforts of the development service.

In areas where commodity-money relations had already become an integral part of the economic relations and had partly superseded the subsistence economy, the productive forces developed quickly and market relations spread. It was from here that the commodity-money relations – together with the factors named above – penetrated into the less developed areas.

The difference in the level of the productive forces can be seen when comparing the number of ploughs per 1,000 agriculturally active inhabitants in the five southern regions in which very similar natural conditions exist for its use (1968/69:[18]

Mali	Kayes	Sikasso	Bamako	Ségou	Mopti
18.4	4.3	16.4	24.2	44.3	12.2

Within each region, the figures differ considerably above and below these averages.

Very characteristic for the relatively developed areas is the Z. E. R. Barouéli in which the ox-plough (52 per 1000 inhabitants in 1966/67) found general use. On the basis of relatively developed productive forces [19], the development of commodity-money relations and of commodity production reached a much higher level than the average of the other areas of Mali. The amount of commodity production compared to the agrarian product in the Z. E. R. Barouéli is around 35–40%. This is an expression of a higher share of export crops compared to the crops planted and a higher degree of commercialisation of each of the crops.

Percentage of export crops and commodity production
in the Z. E. R. Barouéli (1966/67) compared to Mali 1964/65 [20]

	Share of the cultivated ground		Commodity production compared to gross product	
	Barouéli	Mali	Barouéli	Mali
Millet	68.6	66.5	15.0	8.5
Cotton	10.8	6.6	70.0	70.0
Peanuts	15.6	10.4	60.0	50.6
other crops	5.0	16.5 [21]	5.0	5.0
Total	100.0	100.0	37.0	19.0

Apart from the economic, other factors – administrative, political and ideological – also influence changes in the traditional social structures.

Such factors appeared already during the colonial period: measures for so-called slave liberation [22] or to liquidate the traditional aristocracy [23] and larger movements of the population – particularly against conscription to the colonial army [24] – and against the spread of bourgeois ideology and way of life [25]. These measures and processes had the spontaneous effect of shattering and undermining the traditional system of material relations and ideas. Their object was to ensure the functioning of the colonial system of oppression and exploitation and their objective phenomena, and had nothing to do with any alleged acculturation.[26]

The Hamallah movement and the early forms of the national liberation movement in the 1930s – although territorially limited – had a considerable political and ideological influence on the decaying process of the traditional structures.[27]

After the Second World War, the gradual integration of the peasantry into the anti-colonial struggle made clear that the national liberation movement stimulated the decay of the traditional structures. New ideas and values came to the village through the Sudanese Union which no longer corresponded to the organisational structures and forms of thinking in traditional society. The peasants were torn out of village isolation and their political and ideological narrowness, to be integrated into a movement with a national and democratic character.[28] This necessarily undermined the traditional structures, even if the Sudanese Union based its village branches on the existing structural elements for a very long time.[29]

After the Second World War, the Sudanese Union played the role of a political force which, for the first time, actively worked for slave liberation [30] and for liquidation of the colonial *Chefferie* which they eliminated by the end of the fifties.[31]

After independence, this process continued apace. The extension of the system of political organisations (particularly of youth and women) and the intensification of ideological work continually brought new impulses which contributed to the increased decay of the traditional structures through the faster development of the human and material productive forces and a greater spread of commodity-money relations which, in turn, led to new social relations arising.

As a result of the spread of commodity-money relations and further development of the agricultural productive forces after political independence, plus the influence of non-economic factors, spontaneous social processes took place in Malinese agriculture which *generally* tended in the direction of decay in traditional and formation of new social relations. However, these processes – taking place under conditions of colonial and not yet overcome neo-colonial dependence and exploitation – were very slow and contradictory. The new social relations were impeded spontaneously, carriered the sign of colonial and neo-colonial deformation of social evolution and in multifarious ways were over-lapped by traditional relations. At the same time, the traditional relations were preserved and reproduced, but gradually changed their social content. Characteristic of this process of decay was the gradual loosening of the family ties and final dissolution of the extended family as a social and economic entity. It is the direct result of the penetration of commodity-money relations in the community which awakens in the producer the desire to sell his surplus product on the market. This desire must place him in contradiction to the production and distribution system of the extended family – with its FOROBA mechanism – and must end in opposition to the extended family and its foundations.

In the economically more developed areas, in which this process is fastest and most intense, the significance of the individual field (DIONFORO) grows because the producer can use its products at will, without coming into direct conflict with the norms of the extended family.[32] The producer takes more time and care for its cultivation while his interest in the Foroba dwindles. V. Paques wrote down some interesting relevant observations: "The family field, today less cared for than in the past, loses its significance in favour of the individual field. Before, the family field was at the end of a path lined with small, individual fields. Thus, before or after collective work on the family field, every peasant could reach his individual field quickly and cultivate it. Today we can observe that the individual fields are laid down in the bush, far from the path to the family field. This clearly shows the desire of the individual to detach himself from the extended family, to evade control by the head of the family and acquire individual gain over which the family has no control."[33]

To a growing extent, cash crops (including rice) are being planted on the DIONFORO because they are sold on the market most easily for the highest profit.[34] That is why a far larger amount of cash crops is grown on the DIONFORO than on the Foroba.[35] In 1960, an average of 23.3% of the DIONFORO were used for cash crops, while only 15.6% of the Foroba were planted with cotton (2.4%), peanuts (7.4%) and rice (5.8%).[36]

Most important crops grown on the DIONFORO (1960 in percent)[37]

Millet	Rice	other food crops	Cotton	Peanuts	Miscellaneous
61.3	6.4	7.6	4.1	12.8	7.8

So at first, the extended family producer continues to remain fully integrated in the natural economy mechanism of the extended family. He still works for the FOROBA and receives his main means of subsistence from the extended family. But at the same time he begins to appear on the growing market with his part of the DIONFORO product. These new relations become the decisive stimulus for the producers' striving to have a steadily growing part of his product at his own disposal. He extends cultivation of his own DIONFORO which grows in size and economic importance. The production of his DIONFORO gradually becomes the basis for his existence so that his nuclear family becomes a separate entity within the extended family, but is now economically independent of the FAKOROBA and the primary community.[38]

As the economic importance of the DIONFORO can only grow at the cost of the Foroba, i. e. of the traditional system of production and distribution, this leads to a conflict sooner or later between the producer and the extended family – usually represented by the FAKOROBA. Basically, it is the social expression of the contradiction between the necessity of the productive forces to develop and the historically out-dated character of existing production relations.

The conflict between the producer and the head of the extended family is generally sharpened by the fact that under the new economic conditions the latter develops a greater interest in maintaining the Foroba and even extending it, because the sale of the extended family's surplus product on the market leads to greater prosperity for the FAKOROBA himself.[39]

The contradiction between the interests of the extended family's member and of the extended family or its head also penetrates into the field of so-called secondary activities. Often the conflict will start in these fields because the secondary activities such as hunting, fishing or handicrafts do not contribute to the immediate subsistence of the family as do the agricultural products, so that secondary production takes on a commodity character much more quickly. One can observe a general tendency whereby the members of the extended family show a growing resistance to passing over their income from these secondary activities to the FOROBA.[40]

Migratory work plays a special role in the process of forming independent economic units within the extended family, leading to conflicts with the traditional structures. In Africa it is a widespread phenomena in the disintegration of traditional modes of production and establishment of new social relations.[41] The main reason for migratory work in West Africa is not separation of the producer from the means of production,[42] but the system of colonial exploitation and the changes it caused in the economic and social conditions of the village. Backwardness, poverty, exploitation, gerontocratic tutelage and illusions drive youth into the cities or to more developed areas.[43]

Unfortunately, there are no exact figures available on the amount of migrant labour compared to the total agriculturally active population in Mali. However, if one accepts those ascertained by the *Enquête démographique du Delta Central Nigerien* of 12.2%[44] as general, then the number who leave their village each year to seek more work elsewhere for a shorter or longer period would be around 180,000[45]. The vast majority of these migrants are young men[46] aged up to 40.

Migrants according to age groups (in percent)[47]

15—19	20—24	25—29	30—39	40—49	50 and over
19.9	20.3	15.7	23.5	11.2	9.4

The majority of the young men leave the village for only a short time to work in neighbouring villages or nearby towns and cities.

Migrants grouped according to length of absence (in percent)[48]

up to 1 month	1—5 months	6—11 months	1 year and over	not declared
(1)	(2)	(3)	(4)	(5)
42.2	33.3	5.8	18.5	0.2

Those who leave the village for a longer period either go to Senegal[49] and the Ivory Coast, into the Malinese cities (above all Bamako)[50] or to the more developed agricultural areas of Mali[51]. This migratory labour considerably helps to destroy the traditional structures[52], and the contact to the towns not only awakens and nourishes[53] a desire among the young Lu members for personal ownership of their surplus product: the money they earn[54] make economic emancipation (at first within the extended family) possible. Firstly, the migrant worker is able to set up his own nuclear family[55] and secondly, he has the means necessary to acquire his own tools. Thus, he refuses more and more to hand over his savings to the Foroba.[56]

So the economic and non-economic factors undermine the social system of the extended family and finally destroy it via the intermediate stage of the economic emancipation of the nuclear family within the Lu. This development began in the 1920s and 1930s[57] and became widespread after the Second World War. A global impression of how much the extended family had fallen into decay by the end of the 1950s, is given by the following figures: in 1960 the average family (in the countryside) contained 11.8 persons and 2.3 nuclear families[58] and the medium farm[59] was run only by 1.7 nuclear families and 10.3 persons.[60]

The picture presented by social reality, however, was not that of an extended family farm on the one hand and a nuclear family farm on the other. There existed all possible stages in between from completely independent nuclear families and their total social and economic integration into the patriarchal extended family.[61]

The decay of the extended family can be expressed only inexactly in figures. According to the *Enquête agricole*, which investigated 280,260 farms in 1960, there existed the following number of nuclear families per farm:

Distribution of farms according to the number of nuclear families per farm [62]

	0 [63]	1	2—3	4—5	6—10	more than 10	not defined
absolute	12,790	142,090	71,600	22,060	12,060	6,720	12,940
percent	4.6	50.6	25.6	7.9	4.3	2.4	4.6

These figures are only an inexact reflection of the decaying process because they are based on the definition by the National Statistical Institute (Institut Nationale de la Statistique et des Etudes Economiques – I. N. S. E. E.)[64] of the farm and do not take into account that in many cases, the nuclear families which produce their main means of subsistence on the individual field (DIONFORO) – in fact, as an independent economic unit – are still grouped into the extended family under the authority of the FAKOROBA[65]. However, the figures do make clear that by the end of the colonial period, large-scale economic emancipation of the nuclear family (inside or outside the extended family) had begun. And one must not forget that the percentages given in the second column of the above table (50.6%) by no means corresponded to the same percentage of the population on each farm. Unfortunately, in 1960 the *Enquête agricole* offers no relevant information. If one assumes that the medium-size nuclear family is 5.2 persons[66] and lives basically independently, whether grouped into the extended family or not[67], then the number of persons subsisting from farms run by economically independent nuclear families, either inside or outside of the extended family would amount to approximately 740,000 or 25.6% of the total population living in the traditional sector of agriculture.[68] Since 1960 the process of decay in the traditional structures has continued.

Although the sources available about the whole process are still very limited and the time too short to make comparisons, the existing data shows that the tendency of the traditional social structure to decay is stronger and the more determining factor, than their temporary consolidation in certain areas. E. g., a comparison of data from 1960 and 1964/5 given by the *Enquête agricole* shows a general reduction from 10.3 persons[69] to 10.0 persons[70] in the number of people working on the average farm and a general growth in the number of farms with one to five persons from 29.6%[71] to 33%[72]. From these figures one can conclude the growing disintegration of the extended

Persons per farm in the five southern regions of Mali[75] from 1960 to 1964/65

Persons per farm	Kayes 1960	Kayes 1964/65	Sikasso 1960	Sikasso 1964/65	Bamako 1960	Bamako 1964/65	Ségou 1960	Ségou 1964/65	Mopti 1960	Mopti 1964/65
1— 5	23.3	34	29.4	23	28.2	32	31.3	33	44.1	39
6—10	35.9	38	33.9	28	32.1	31	40.7	36	33.7	34
11—15	17.5	14	17.4	19	18.9	17	14.2	17	12.5	17
16—20	9.1	6	7.4	12	10.2	5	5.8	6	4.8	5
21—25	5.0	3	4.1	7	4.4	3	2.5	6	1.9	3
26 and over	9.2	5	7.2	11	6.2	12	5.5	2	3.0	2

family and a growing number in the nuclear families. The *Enquête agricole* ascertained 9.83 persons[73] per farm in 1967/8 and draws the same conclusions in a report: "The outcome of three surveys for the whole country shows a very small but steady reduction of the persons per farm. This can be explained by the tendency for the extended family to dissolve into nuclear families."[74]

The distribution of farms in accordance with the number of persons working there and with the various regions shows that for some areas, there is a growth in the number of farms with only a few persons, whereas the opposite is the case in other areas. This signifies an uneven and even contradictory course of the social processes. On the one hand we are faced with an accelerated decay of traditional structures and on the other with their temporary consolidation. Unfortunaltey, it is exceedingly difficult to express the actual processes going on in statistics. The territorial units are so large and so heterogenous in their inner development that contradictory tendencies within one region are usually compensated for when shown in figures.

As the existing material allows only very inexact conclusions on the concrete forms and phenomena of the decaying process taking place in the traditional structures at the present time, I tried to take this aspect into special consideration during my surveys in 1967.

Even if these investigations were necessarily limited to a very small section of Malinese reality (the Z.E.R. Barouéli) and are concretely valid only for this, the results can be presumed to be characteristic in so far as the area examined is economically one of the most developed in the country so that the decaying process has reached a relatively advanced stage. Under these conditions the decaying process of traditional

Changes in the number of persons on a farm in the five southern regions
of Mali from 1960 to 1964/65 [76]

Persons per farm	Kayes	Sikasso	Bamako	Ségou	Mopti
1— 5	+10.7	—6.4	+3.8	+1.7	—4.1
6—10	+ 2.1	—5.9	—1.1	—4.7	+0.3
11—15	— 3.5	+1.6	—1.9	+2.8	+4.5
16—20	— 3.1	+4.6	—5.2	+0.2	+0.2
21—25	— 2.0	+2.9	—1.4	+3.5	+1.1
26 and over	— 4.2	+3.8	+5.8	—3.5	—1.0

structures is altogether more advanced in the Z. E. R. Barouéli than in Mali as a whole. The share of nuclear families which have become independent economic units inside and outside the extended family has grown to 61.4% of the farms and 35.3% of the population.[77] The medium-size farm comprises here only 8.1 persons and 1.8 nuclear families; and one family has an average of 2.7 nuclear families.

In the decaying process, the following noteworthy aspects can be seen in the Z. E. R. Barouéli. Investigations in seven villages showed[78] that in the relationship extended family – nuclear family – economic unit (farm)[79], four different types, stages or variants have developed:

(1) (Variant I) An extended family, consisting of several nuclear families make up an economic unit (farm). This variant which basically[80] represents the traditional extended family farm composes 36.9% of the families, 25.2% of the farms and 46.1% of the inhabitants in the villages examined. The typical (or medium-size) family in this variant has 14.9 persons, 3.2 nuclear families and 4.2 persons of working age. It cultivates 7.7 hectares, of these 2.0 hectares are used for industrial crops. It has 0.88 ploughs, 1.95 draught oxen, 0.34 carts, 5.91 cows and 0.49 horses. The extremes in the number of persons are 51 and five, and in the number of nuclear families eleven and two. Most of the families (73.2%) – 54% of the total inhabitants – consist of only two or three nuclear families.

Distribution of families in variant I in accordance
with the number of nuclear families per family

	Number of nuclear Families			
	2	3	4	5 and over
Percentage of families	48.8	24.4	14.6	12.2
Percentage of population	31.6	22.4	20.1	25.9

Division of the extended family farms in accordance with the number of nuclear families shows that the first two sub-divisions which consist of two or three nuclear families each with 9.5 and 13.7 persons, are preponderant over the last two sub-divisions of four or five nuclear families with 20.05 and 31.6 persons. This points to the fact that a considerable number of the extended family farms are no longer extended families of the "classic" type (in size and inner structure), but are already the product of a process of disintegration, even if the basic features still remain. A clear stage or product of this process is already the second variation.

(2) (Variant II) Several economic units exist within an extended family. However, they are smaller in number than the nuclear families. This means on the one hand that while the process of inner decay of the extended family has already begun in the economic field which caused the development of several economic units within the extended family, it has not yet led to the economic independence of every nuclear family (an average of two nuclear families – 1.9 to be exact – form an economic unit). On the other hand, the extended family continues to exist as a social entity, the economic units remain integrated within it. This integration applies above all to non-economic fields, but also has its economic aspects. The extended family remains the bond and – represented by the FAKOROBA – continues to carry out its customs and traditions, in particular, regulation of marriages (including payment of bride-price, the FURU-NA-FOLO), representation of the family within the village community, payment of taxes – which are shared by all the separate economic units, care of any collectively owned means of production (plough, cart, etc.), and mutual support in the field of production. The economic power of the FAKOROBA (e. g. through his personal ownership of modern means of production), combined with his traditional prestige, may form the basis of the ties between each element of the extended family. However, these ties are then based on the greater or lesser economic dependence of these elements on the FAKOROBA.

In the surveyed village, the second variant makes up 11.7% of the families, 25.8% of the farms and 27.7% of the inhabitants. The typical family in this group comprises of 25.4 persons, 6.2 nuclear families, 3.2 economic units and 6.8 persons of working age. It cultivates 11.9 hectares, of this 3.2 hectares with industrial crops and has 1.5 ploughs, 4.2 draught oxen, 0.5 carts, 14.5 cows and 0.5 horses. The extremes in the family size according to inhabitants, nuclear families and farms range from 42 and seven members, 13 and three, and five and two.

Characteristic for the inner structure of this group is the large number of families with more than four nuclear families on the one hand and with few nuclear families per economic unit on the other.

Distribution of families in variant II according to the number
of nuclear families per family

	\multicolumn{4}{c}{Number of nuclear families}
	3	4	5	6 and over
Percentage of families	15.4	7.7	23.1	53.8
Percentage of population	9.5	8.2	19.5	62.8

Distribution of families in variant II according to the number
of nuclear families per farm

	\multicolumn{4}{c}{Number of nuclear families}
	1.1—1.5	1.6—2.0	2.1—2.5	2.6—3.0
Percentage of families	30.8	38.4	15.4	15.4
Percentage of population	27.5	32.9	14.9	24.7

(3) (Variant III) Here, all the nuclear families within the extended family have become economically independent, but because of the same factors as apply to variant II, are still part of the extended family and exist as a social unit. However, in this group, mutual aid on an equal basis within the extended family plays a far larger role than in group II, because (still within the extended family) the social prerequisites for it exist here – full emancipation of all nuclear families within the extended family – and because the relatively large number of people to be supported from land with few modern means of production makes this economically necessary.

The third variation in the villages examined, make up 14.5% of the families, 23.8% of the farms, 13.5% of the nuclear families and 13.1% of the inhabitants. This makes it the smallest group of families. The typical family in this group comprises of 10.8 persons, 2.4 nuclear families, the same number of economic units and 3.3 persons of working age. It cultivates 7.04 hectares, of this 1.7 hectares is used for export crops. It has 0.5 ploughs, 0.9 oxen, 0.13 carts, 0.25 cows, 0.13 horses. Characteristic of the inner structure of this group is the absolute majority of families with two nuclear families.

Distribution of families in variant III according
to the number of nuclear families per family

	Number of nuclear families		
	2	3	more than 3
Percentage of families	75	18.75	6.25
Percentage of population	54.1	22.1	23.8

(4) In variant IV, the nuclear family has completely separated from the extended family and becomes an independent unit in itself. It is now registered by the administration as a "family" in the same way as the extended families of variant I to III.

This group makes up 36.9% of all families, 25.2% of all farms and 14.2% of all nuclear families and 16% of the inhabitants in the villages investigated. Thus it is the second smallest group of families.

The medium family here comprises of 5.1 persons and 1.7 persons of working age, who cultivate 3.5 hectares, of this 0.9 hectares with industrial crops. They own 0.37 ploughs and 0.95 draught oxen, 0.1 carts, 0.93 cows and 0.15 horses. The size of the family (according to persons and those of working age ranges from one to 18 and one to five, respectively. The following table gives a comparison of the four variants according to their most important features:

Features	Variants			
	I	II	III	IV
Percentage of families	36.9	11.7	14.5	36.9
Percentage of farms	25.2	25.8	23.8	25.2
Percentage of population	44.6	27.7	13.5	14.2
Persons per family	14.9	25.4	10.8	5.1
Persons per farm	14.9	7.8	4.4	5.1
Nuclear families per family	3.2	6.2	2.4	1.0
Nuclear family per farm	3.2	1.9	1.0	1.0
Farm per family	1.0	3.2	2.4	1.0
Persons of working age per family	4.2	6.8	3.3	1.7
Person of working age per farm	4.2	2.1	1.3	1.7
Area per family	7.7	11.9	7.04	3.5
Draught oxen per family	1.95	4.2	0.9	0.95
Ploughs per family	0.88	1.5	0.5	0.37

With the disintegration of the extended family as a social and economic unit and structural element of the village community, the basic relations within the community are modified, without at first destroying them completely or even questioning the existence of the village community. The fundamental relationship between the community and the individual producer to the most important conditions of production (land) are maintained. As small commodity producer he does not take up a free relationship to them, nor does he become subordinate to them (slave or serf), nor is he separated from them (wage labourer). The pre-conditions for use of the land, which remains the inalienable possession of the community[81], continues to be membership of the community. The permanent right to use the land or to own considerable parts of it is passed on to the nuclear family and the individual producers as the extended family disintegrates. Even though individualisation of land ownership is a step towards private property[82] and leads directly through spontaneous "normal" development to division of community land into privately owned units[83], one must not confuse the one with the other if one is not to draw false conclusions regarding non-capitalist development.[84] In contrast to the pre-colonial communities, the relationship of the producer who has freed himself from the extended family to the land is no longer mediated twice – through membership of the clan, lineage or extended family, and of the territorially organised community in which the members of the various kinship groups live together – but directly through his membership of the community. In other words, the territorial and neighbourly relations within the community are finally freed from the ties of blood relationship[85] because a producer arises who replaces the extended family sub-system and takes up a direct relationship to it as a structural element of the community.[86]

It is necessary to underline that the producers now liberating themselves are not – not yet – small commodity producers or petty-bourgeois peasants, as we know them in Europe.[87] Not only do the fundamental conditions of ownership make this impossible, but the colonial and neo-colonial conditions of reproduction also do not allow a "normal" development of these individual small producers into independent small commodity producers. They not only determine the far-reaching persistence and reproduction of basic community relations, but also condemn the individual small producers to extremely backward conditions of production and economic weakness, which do not allow them to extend their production and produce commodities to any significant extent. In fact, in order to ensure subsistence, the small producers are usually forced to ask the community and family relations for help and thus make themselves dependent on the rising village upper strata. In return they have occasionally to sell their labour power or put themselves at the mercy of trade and usury capital.[88]

The disintegration of the traditional structures is a multifarious and complicated process. It affects not only the extended families of the free community members (HORON)[89] and their relations inside the community, but it also applies to the members of castes (NYAMAKALAU) and the slaves (DYON).

Bokar N'Diayé clearly shows in his paper[90] how castes disappear in the city milieu.[91] Even if he ascertains for the village that „... the peasant still does not dare to oppose these institutions openly ..."[92], he finally comes to the conclusion that "it is obvious that under the influence of the new ideas and technical progress the castes generally continue to lose ground"[93].

The disintegrating process is much more noticeable among the DYON than among the NYAMAKALAU.[94] The general tendency of the DYON who are not integrated into the extended family is that they have freed themselves from dependence on their former masters and come nearer to the HORON in their socio-economic position.

This begins with the emancipation of the DYON in regard to the most important means of production, the land. They are no longer exploited by the HORON.[95] The former DYON now cultivates the land under the same conditions as the HORON. The DYONS' relationship to the community means that he is allowed to use the land. This process is, in fact, a socio-economic levelling out within the village community, it is a process of liberation from forms of pre-capitalist exploitation which is actually foreign to the constitution of the community. The concrete form this takes is that the former DYON cultivates either the same land or another piece granted him by the community, under the same socio-economic conditions as the HORON, i. e. without having to pay tributes or do compulsory labour for others.[96] In Nianzana[97] this situation[98] takes on the following concrete form: Six of the total of 42 families are of such former DYON. They are 19.5% of the population in the village[99] and cultivate 67 hectares or 25.1% of the cultivated area in Nianzana under the same conditions as the rest of the village inhabitants. This is clearly expressed in their share of the land, compared with the medium-size farms of the village.

Former DYON families in Nianzana[100]

	Families	Farms	Population	Persons of Working Age	Cultivated Area	Ploughs	Oxen
Absolute	6	15	77	27	67	4	8
% of whole village	14.3	26.8	19.5	26.0	25.1	18.2	16.4
per farm	0.40	—	5.14	1.80	4.47	0.27	0.53
per average farm in the village	0.75	—	7.06	1.86	4.79	0.39	0.91

The changes in social relations both within the extended family and between the community members are very little different for the socio-economically emancipated Dyon than for the Horon. From the investigations in Nianzana one can see the same tendencies for disintegration of the extended family as an economic and social entity for the former Dyon as for the extended families of the Horon.

	6 former Dyon families	Nianzana average	Average in investigated area	Mali average [101] (1960)
Nuclear families per farm	1.2	1.47	1.8	1.7
Persons per farm	5.14	7.06	8.1	10.3

However, one must take into consideration that the former Dyon are drawn into this process under relatively less favourable conditions than the Horon, above all because of their slave position in the precolonial society and the brutal exploitation they suffered at the hands of the colonial administration in the *"villages de liberté"*[102]. On the other hand, for various reasons the Dyon was often the first social group to come in touch with commodity production and a modern education[103], so that, as a whole, the concrete socio-economic position of the former Dyon or his descendants in the present-day village is determined by many often contradictory factors, without, however, disturbing the general tendency. In contrast to the basic economic emancipation of the former Dyon, it can be noted that in the non-economic field, the process of social emancipation took much longer. The Dyon continued to have less social prestige than the Horon because the traditional norms and social values continued for a long time.[104]

Apart from the general change in the social position of the Dyon, another tendency must be mentioned which was most widespread in the early colonial period and in those areas which were especially backward economically or had a strong aristocratic element which found formal continuation in the colonial *Chefferie*. These conditions were to be found mainly in the areas on the periphery of the Sahel.[105] Here the disintegration of slavery took place at a slower rate. In the relationship between the Dyon and the *Chefferie* (apart from the relationship between *Chefferie* and community) slavery took on new forms.[106] After independence, the old slave relations were often taken as the starting point in these areas to build up elements of capitalist exploitation on the basis of traditional structures.[107]

The slave who lived within a free extended family (Woloso) was generally drawn into the social changes within it. Here too, gradual emancipation of the producers from the extended family takes place. It should be noted that the material prerequisites for the WOLOSO to separate from the extended family are generally less favourable than those aplying to free extended family members. Therefore, the tendencies for change in inter-family relations are different for the WOLOSO. They will be dealt with later.

In general, one may say that the DYON (in both pre-colonial variants) is in the process of disappearing, at least from a socio-economic viewpoint, as a special social stratum within the village community by merging into other social groups. As Bokar N'Diayé summed it up, "be it as it may, the least that one can say is that the old social structures are in the process of decay in all fields." [108]

4.2. New conditions for economic and social progress

The decay of the traditional structures, particularly of the extended family as a system of social and economic relations, is of fundamental importance in economic, social and political development. Through this, there mature new spontaneous social conditions for economic development and for consolidating the alliance of the revolutionary-democratic (and in future proletarian) leadership with the peasants.

The disintegration of the traditional system of production and distribution and the development of an individual producer create the new objective prerequisites and a driving force for development of the productive forces and of production. Liberated from the burden of his FOROBA duties, the producer has a new relationship to his work and his product. He can now sell his surplus product on the market and is interested in increasing it. The direct contact to the market is for him a continual stimulus to produce more commodities and develop the productive forces. And away from the extended family and its collective subsistence, he is also economically forced to do this. As he can no longer depend on the reserves and support of the primary community,[109] he must reach a higher level of productivity in order to be insured against natural catastrophe, illness, etc. Further, the character of his farm now forces him into increased commodity production, because it is impossible for his family alone to produce their needs as the extended family can, and they become dependent on exchange. This becomes very clear when comparing the farms of type I to IV in the Z. E. R. Barouéli. Despite greater accumulation and investment difficulties [110], the farms of the nuclear families on an average use more ploughs and draught oxen and in particular, have a larger cultivated area per head of the population.[111]

Ploughs, draught oxen and cultivated area per 100 inhabitants
and ten persons of working age in variants I—IV

	I	II	III	IV	I—IV
Ploughs					
per 100 inhabitants	5.9	6.0	4.7	7.1	5.9
per 10 persons of working age	2.1	2.1	1.5	2.1	2.0
Draught Oxen					
per 100 inhabitants	13.2	17.3	8.2	18.5	14.3
per 10 persons of working age	4.7	6.2	2.7	5.5	4.9
Area					
per 100 inhabitants	52	47	63	69	55
per 10 persons of working age	18	17	22	20	19

The structure in the agrarian product per capita in the *Arrondissement* Barouéli shows very clearly the new economic interest of the producers in commodity production.

Agrarian production per capita in Mali and the Z. E. R. Barouéli
(1966/67) according to food and industrial crops (in FM) [112]

	Mali	*Barouéli*
Food crops	2,929	4,110
Industrial crops	782	2,912

The new economic interests can also become the basis for a development service or other state organs to modernise agriculture. Freed from the burden of traditional structures and with an economic interest in extending his production, the producer has a completely different relationship to this institution and its aims. He no longer offers passive resistance to its efforts to introduce new production tools and methods, but is willing, on principle to modernise his production.[113]

The experience of the last ten years in Mali shows that the work of the development service has borne fruit above all in those areas where the process of decay in traditional structures was already fairly advanced.[114] This applies particularly to the Ségou area and radiated to Koutiala and Dioila. The use of the plough and fertiliser — to name only two modernising elements — has made significant progress there in the past ten years. The table on page 119 makes obvious that the increase in the use of the ox-plough is concentrated in this area. The same applies to the greater use of fertiliser.[115]

It became very clear in the modernisation of cotton production.[116] In

Spontaneous decay of traditional structures

1968/9 some two thirds of the cotton area were ploughed[117] in the area cultivated by the French cotton firm, C. F. D. T. (Compagnie Francaise pour le Développement des Fibres Textiles).[118]

In Ségou, the area of cotton ploughed was almost 90% and in Koutiala and Dioila some 70%. On the other hand, in the San sector where commodity-money relations had hardly affected the traditional structures right into the 1960s, the percentage was well below average.

Ploughed area for cotton planting in the various C. F. D. T. sectors (in percent) [119]

Sector	Ox-plough	*daba*
Bamako	37.6	62.4
Bougouni	41.2	58.8
Dioila	69.4	30.6
San	24.9	75.1
Ségou	85.4	14.6
Sikasso	52.9	37.1
Koutiala	72.7	27.3
All sectors	65.6	34.4

The progress made in the use of organic and mineral fertiliser — almost unknown up to the end of colonial rule[120] — is even more significant. From 1963/4 to 1968/9, the use of organic fertiliser for cotton planting more than doubled and that of mineral fertiliser increased by almost ten times.

Use of fertiliser for cotton planting [121] (in percent of the cultivated area)

	organic fertiliser	mineral fertiliser
1963/64	8.6	3.1
1968/69	21.2	30.6

Most mineral fertiliser was used in the Sikasso, Ségou and Koutiala sectors in 1968/9 with 35%, 35% and 32.5% of the cultivated areas respectively. The highest use rates of organic fertiliser were in the Bougouni (52%), Sikasso (49%) and Ségou (40%) sectors.[122]

In the more advanced areas, fertiliser was also used for other crops.[123] Organic fertiliser was used particularly for cultivating food crops. In the Ségou and Koutiala districts some 10% of the millet and 50% of the maize fields were organically fertilised in 1965/6.[124]

Closely linked to overcoming traditional methods of production is the transport problem. Fertiliser in particular can no longer be transported by the customary means [125]. So an essential element of agricultural modernisation is the introduction of means of transport adapted to the material and infrastructural conditions. Ox-carts have been found particularly useful in the last few years.[126]

In 1968/9, 16,758 such carts were counted in the whole of Mali.[127] This was 200% more than in 1960[128]. On an average, four such carts existed for 1,000 inhabitants.[129] Again, the Ségou area was most developed.

Carts per 1000 inhabitants according to districts 1968/9 [130]

Kayes	Bamako	Sikasso	Mopti	Ségou	Z. E. R. Barouéli (1966/7)
0.5	5.7	4.3	0.5	13.6	23

The transition to modernised agrarian production — which means the use of the ox-plough, organic fertiliser and ox-carts — in the developed areas shows that it has been possible here to achieve the first successes in overcoming the traditional separation of agriculture and animal husbandry along tribal lines. My own research in 1967 showed (see following table) that in the Konodimini-M'Gara area (Ségou district) traditional peasants such as the Bambara and Marka were beginning to own draught animals, whereas traditional cattle-breeders (the Fulbe) were beginning to plant food and use their animals productively. Even members of the Somono fishers, part whom have a caste status and who have a particularly strong sense of responsibility for traditional employment, have begun to do farming and look after draught animals in this area.

Distribution of agriculture and drought-cattle in selected villages of the Z. E. R. Central-Ségou 1966/7 [131]

Village	Ethnic group	Cultivated area (hectare) per inhabitant	Ploughs per 100 inhabit.	Draught oxen per 100 inh.
Konodimini	Bambara	0.7	8.6	20.3
Sidabougou-Wéré	Fulbe	0.4	5.4	9.9
Somonodougouni	Somono	0.7	11.3	25.1
Gouréli	Marka	0.3	4.3	16.7

The examples given prove that the decay of the traditional system of production and distribution opens up fundamentally new possibilities for the development of the productive forces, which in turn creates new opportunities for socio-economic progress, for forming co-operatives and for consolidating the alliance with the peasants.

As already emphasized, the small producers liberating themselves from the traditional system are generally not "normally" developed small producers. As a result of colonial exploitation and backwardness they possess very backward means of production and very small means of accumulation. Therefore, they can cultivate only small areas of poor quality soil, because the best land in the village usually belongs to the traditional economic units – the extended families. Generally, they have not the money to buy a plough, vehicles, draught animals or special agricultural tools. So one can say, that most of the producers who make themselves independent of the extended family have an objective interest in raising production and producing more commodities for exchange, but their economic weakness gives them only limited opportunities for doing so. The following list of prices illustrates this, particularly if one keeps in mind that in the second half of the 1960s, the average annual income of the Malinese country population was 2,000 to 2,500 FM.[132]

Prices for agricultural tools and vehicles in 1968/9 [133]

	FM
Plough	6,500
Harrow	21,000
Cart	22,500
Sprayer (for cotton)	14,000
Pair of oxen	30,000

The only way to solve this problem in the interests of the producers is the co-operative, is to jointly buy and use the necessary tools and transport. In other words, decay of the traditional socio-economic relations gives rise to the objective need for modern – although simple – forms of co-operative relations whose foundations and laws of development are fundamentally different to the traditional system. The driving power which develops through the disintegration of traditional structures can only be used to accelerate economic growth in agriculture via the co-operative.

However, the co-operative gains basic significance for yet another reason. To the same extent as the producers free themselves from the subsistence economy and go over to commodity production, they are gradually integrated into the growing local market. Under colonial conditions, this market is necessarily capitalist and dominated by monopoly trade capital.[134] The relations take on the form of a *Traite*-pyramid.[135]

Economically weak, separated from the traditional community and thus without its protection [136], the small producer is inevitably caught up in the wheels of the *économie de traite* and ground down by it. Thus the small producer has an objective interest in removing the domination of foreign trade monopolies and in curbing trade and usury capital on the local market, and replacing them by co-operatives which can buy and sell the products. In other words, this stratum has a direct economic interest in replacing existing capitalist relations on the agrarian market by non-capitalist – state and co-operative – relations. Thus, out of the decay of the traditional mode of production, there arise not only new possibilities and driving forces for economic progress, but these possibilities can be realised only via social progress, i. e. via the non-capitalist transformation of agrarian relations, because the social laws governing colonial and neo-colonial dependence and exploitation do not allow the "normal" changes in production relations or a speedy development of the productive forces.

This disintegration also creates new conditions for consolidating the alliance between the revolutionary leaders and the peasantry.

During the process of decay of traditional structures, new social forces namely, the small producers arise, and here there is a better prerequisite for such an alliance than with the traditional peasant because of the fundamentally new attitude of the former towards economic progress, and their links to the local market. These forces have an objective interest in the aims of the national-democratic revolution, both as individuals and as a social stratum. Their social interests are:

(1) a speedy development of material and human productive forces, a broad unfolding of commodity production and development of the local market;
(2) far-reaching social and economic changes such as overcoming the traditional system of production and distribution, removing the domination of foreign capital, curbing local trade and usury capital and the agrarian bourgeois elements, plus creation of non-capitalist transitional relations to develop the productive forces;
(3) far-reaching democratisation of political conditions and maximum stabilisation of the national-democratic state and its foundations as the main prerequisite for a quick non-capitalist development;
(4) far-reaching changes in ideas and cultural life.

The small producers become the main potential ally for the revolutionary-democratic forces in the countryside, insofar as they free themselves from traditional structures.[137]

When the subsistence economy and its methods of production and distribution decay, the foundations of the political role played by the traditional chiefs in the village is undermined, and so new conditions arise for increasing the influence of progressive forces in the political institutions of the village. This becomes clear through the composition of the party committee in Nianzana:

	Name		Age	Social Position	Comments
1. D. K.		General secretary	60	K (s)	Konaté
2. S. K. 1		Deputy gen. secretary	33	K (s)	"
3. S. K. 2		Treasurer	70	F	"
4. F. K.		Organisational secretary	32	K (s)	"
5. M. D.		Deputy treasurer	73	F	Fulbe
6. O. B.		Propaganda	54	F	"
7. Y. K.		"	69	F	Konaté
8. K. C.		Conflicts	54	F	Coulibaly
9. B. C.		"	50	K	"
10. B. O.		Youth	42	K	Quaré
11. M. D.		Women	45	K	Woloso

Here one sees several elements which are characteristic for the decline of the traditional chief's political influence in this leading organ of the Sudanese Union in the village. First, the large number of dynamic social forces, particularly heads of nuclear families, is conspicuous. Secondly, the party committee (as opposed to the Nianzana village council)[138] does not consist of only the traditional leading clan, the Konaté, but also contains two members of a non-leading clan which is also part of the Bambara ethnic group (the Coulibaly). In addition, and this is so particularly characteristic, the Fulbe (from another ethnic group) and a former Woloso are represented. This still appears impossible for the village council. Further, the large number of persons under sixty is also conspicuous.

So, as a whole, new and favourable objective conditions arise for development of the productive forces and production, for social and economic changes and for consolidating the alliance with the peasantry out of the disintegration of traditional structures. However, this does not mean that non-capitalist development comes automatically. The spontaneous social processes lead in quite a different direction.

Parallel with the growth of commodity production and agricultural commodity-money relations, capitalist relations also intensify. From national trade and usury capital there grows a social force which – apart from monopoly capital and its agents – consciously opposes any non-capitalist changes in agriculture, particularly on the agrarian market.

The development of commodity-money relations within the framework of a national market dominated by local and foreign private capital, inevitably has considerable repercussions for further social processes in the field of production. With the growth of agricultural commodity production there is a spontaneous increase in the number of producers who experience the transition from the traditional system of production and distribution, to become small commodity producers, without actually being able to develop into such under the given colonial and neo-colonial conditions of reproduction. Yet this tendency still breaks up the socio-economic basis of the community, the producer takes up free and direct relations to his means of production (the soil), even if the legal basis for private property is not laid down for a longer period by the continued existence of the norms attached to communal property. The way private property and – even if slow and deformed – small commodity production tend to develop are the reason for the penetration into the village of the attitudes of the petty-bourgeoisie, of whom Marx said ". . . contradiction is the basis of his existence"[139]. On the one hand, the co-operative road corresponds to the small producer's objective interests because the capitalist road would lead to his economic ruin, whereas on the other, as a small owner he spontaneously favours "free" market relations in the hope of selling his goods at higher prices. However, the small commodity producer is also nothing but the intermediary product of spontaneous social developments, because "small-cale production *engenders* capitalism and the bourgeoisie, continually, daily, hourly, spontaneously, and on a mass scale"[140].

The more capitalist market relations develop, stamped by colonial and neo-colonial dependence, the more strongly its inherent economic laws function. The tendency grows for pauperisation of the mass of small producers and for their increasing subordination directly or indirectly, to monopoly-capital, to local trade and usury capital, to bureaucratic capital and to the rising village bourgeoisie; and it is not possible, under the given conditions of colonial and neo-colonial dependence, for the productive forces and the production relations to become genuinely revolutionised in a capitalist way.

So according to the level of maturity which the social processes have reached[141], the non-capitalist transformation of relations in the agrarian market becomes a decisive link in the whole non-capitalist development of agriculture. Non-capitalist (i. e. state-co-operative) market relations make it possible to limit the effects of the social laws arising from colonial and neo-colonial dependence and exploitation, to create conditions favouring the development of the productive forces, and to contribute to consolidating the alliance between the revolutionary-democratic forces and the producer, newly freed from the traditional structures. There, relations are therefore the necessary prerequisite for those economic, social and political processes which take agriculture along the non-capitalist path.

4.3. *The struggle for non-capitalist agrarian market relations*

The conditions and requirements for economic progress, for socio-economic changes and for the alliance with the peasantry, which arise from the spontaneous decay of traditional systems of production and distribution, objectively [142] corresponded to a number of measures taken by the Malinese party and state leadership during the *"action rurale"* program. This applies — apart from the development of the productive forces, which has already been dealt with [143] — to the struggle for non-capitalist relations on the agrarian market. The first decisive measure in this direction was the gradual curbing and expulsion of foreign monopoly capital from the circulation sphere and creation of state import, export and wholesale companies.

This process was of fundamental importance for the success of non-capitalist development as a whole because of Mali's economic structure.[144] It is to be considered here mainly from the viewpoint of non-capitalist changes in agriculture. Two aspects are of special significance: the creation of the state trading organisation (S. O. M. I. E. X. and O. P. A. M.) and the granting of a special status for the mixed company C. F. D. T.

The Société Malienne d'Importation et d'Exportation (S. O. M. I. E. X.) was founded on 29 October 1960 during the process of implementing the decisions of the Extraordinary Congress of the Sudanese Union on 22 September 1960.[145] It had the task of "improving the sale of products of the Republic of Mali and supplying the state apparatus, state trade organisations and co-operative institutions with commodities under favourable conditions ..."[146] For this purpose it received the export monopoly for peanuts and an import monopoly for the most important requirements (sugar, flour, salt, cement, matches, cigarettes, oil, soap, etc.).[147]

Apart from this function, S. O. M. I. E. X. acted as wholesaler on the inland market for the retail and intermediate traders and — of particular interest — for the Société Mutuelle de Developpement Rurale (S. M. D. R.).[148] S. O. M. I. E. X. had the buying monopoly for peanuts [149] and supplied the S. M. D. R. with all imported products. In addition, S. O. M. I. E. X. acted as retailer.[150]

The Office des Produits Agricoles du Mali (O. P. A. M.) was founded on 13 March 1965 to replace [151] the Office des Céréales.[152] It was given the monopoly for commercialisation and for export and import of all agricultural products which were not traded by other state bodies.[153] On the home market, its partners were the S. M. D. R. and the co-operative bodies subordinated to it for buying, and the consumer co-operatives for selling products [154] which were dealt with by O. P. A. M. The position of French monopoly capital was clearly weakened in Mali when S. O. M. I. E. X. and O. P. A. M. were formed.[155]

The S. U. leadership thus considered S. O. M. I. E. X. "the decisive instrument for independence ... and of economic policy ..."[156]

In the sector of traditional agriculture these measures greatly limited the direct rule of monopoly capital in its traditional field – agriculture – although the exploitation of the country did not stop but was simply transferred to the level of foreign trade, which continued on a non-equivalent basis because the Republic of Mali remained within the capitalist world market and was thus subject to its laws[157]: Through the new state wholesale companies and their agrarian market monopoly a completely new quality of non-capitalist transition was created[158] – which gave the market relations a new non-capitalist character and was a potential instrument for changing socio-economic conditions – through market relations – in the sector of traditional agriculture. However, the character and function of state-controlled market relations are not automatically established by a judicial act, but are largely determined by the efficiency of state market institutions. The state market can be made ineffective by another – illegal – influential market (of private traders), or by inefficiency caused by inexperience, lack of cadres and material, or by the development of a bureaucratic bourgeoisie within the state distribution system – a definite possibility at the present stage of non-capitalist development. Both are genuine problems of non-capitalist transition to be dealt with further on.

Foreign monopoly capital continued to function in Malinese agriculture in the form of the French cotton company C. F. D. T. (Compagnie Française pour le Développement des Fibres Textiles).[159] The C. F. D. T. extended its activities to Mali in 1952/53, since when its role in the Malinese economy steadily grew with the growth of cotton production.[160] In February 1964, a convention was signed between the company and the Malinese government which regulated the work between them.[161]

According to this convention, valid for ten years, the C. F. D. T. received a monopoly for the development of cotton production, its commercialisation and ginning (removing cotton from its seeds) on the territory of the Mali Republic with the exception of those zones reserved for the Office du Niger. It had to pledge subordination of its own activities to the development plan.

In the field of cotton production, the C. F. D. T. was attached to certain Z. E. R.s where its cadres – or those placed at its disposal by the Development Ministry – were obliged to do development work in the same way as the state development service.[162] In these zones, the C. F. D. T. marketed the cotton at state prices[163] and did the ginning in its own machines.[164] Malinese industry had a prior claim on the ginned cotton; in case of export, the C. F. D. T. had to follow the regulations of the Malinese government. For the period of the convention, the C. F. D. T. was guaranteed free transfer of all its annual gross profits. After this period, the Malinese government was to take over all buildings and installations belonging to the C. F. D. T. witbout paying compensation: these have to be in a good condition. Finally, the C. F. D. T. pledged to train Malinese cadres for agriculture and operating the ginning machines.

This convention was, of course, a compromise with monopoly capital, which became necessary because of the difficult financial and cadre situation and the necessity for speedy development of cotton growing as a prerequisite for building up Mali's own textile industry and extending exports. It seemed a justified attempt to integrate the C. F. D. T. into the state development and marketing system and to subordinate its activities to that of the state, and from this viewpoint presented a transitional solution, in contrast to the unlimited parasitic rule of trade monopolies in the period before 1960. Another decisive problem for a state-controlled agrarian market was to curb national trade and usury capital and establish co-operative bodies for buying and selling agricultural products.

In the last few years before independence, private trade capital was given a large boost [165] by the neo-colonialism of the big trading companies, and after 1960 it hoped to take over their positions. However, the Sudanese Union's conception was gradually to eliminate all private trade from the agrarian market.[166] This was not immediately possible in the first years because no state buying organisation existed with a sufficiently widespread network for commercialisation, nor was the co-operative system strong enough to take over these tasks. So during the first phase after political independence, private traders were integrated into the marketing system and placed on the commission of the state buying societies [167] which were founded in 1959 in connection with the establishment of the Office des Céréales.[168] However, it was soon observed that the mass of the private traders did not keep the agreements to re-sell the commercialised agrarian products to the state buying organisation, but sold them on the black market or exported them illegally.[169] That is why the setting up of the agricultural co-operative system was accelerated at the beginning of the 1960s, after the foundation stone had been laid in 1959.[170] By 1962 some 3,000 G. R. P. S. M.s (Groupement Rural de Production et de Secours Mutuel) existed in Mali,[171] and in 1965 almost every village had a G. R. P. S. M. (official statistics stated that there were some 7,000).[172] The setting up of the G. R. A. (*Groupement Rural Associé*), begun in 1963, was also generally completed by 1965, when over 500 existed.[173] Then in 1965–7 F. P.s (*Fédérations Primaires*) were founded in most of the *Arrondissements*.[174] So when the period of the first development plan ended, the co-operative system was generally completed – although with delays.

By 1964/5 the private traders were completely excluded from commercial activity, and this was passed over to state and cooperative bodies only.[175] At about the same time (March 1965) a new trade decree was issued which laid down strict regulations for trading.[176]

The founding of agricultural co-operatives was a historic step for non-capitalist development. This system, which must not be confused with socialist co-operatives[177], has its own internal laws growing out of the function and structure which set free important driving powers for further unfolding non-capitalist economic, social and political changes:

(1) The co-operative organisation for marketing commodities and supplying the producers with tools, seed and consumer goods, the co-operative credit system plus the collective buying of larger machines and improvement of the local infrastructure give the optimum economic and social prerequisites for developing production and sets free important stimuli to develop the productive forces.

(2) The acceleration of the material and human productive forces and exchange relations possible within the co-operative inevitably contributes to a quicker decay of traditional relations which still exist. And for the revolutionary-democrats, the co-operatives are *the* instruments for speeding up this process through purposeful granting of credits, equipment with modern tools, seed, fertiliser, etc. Co-operative organisation of the agrarian market can control the spontaneous effects of the law of value and thus limit the social differentiation into classes. This possibility for speedier development of the productive forces and of the cultural, political, ideological level in the village can also lead to prerequisite being created for a higher level of co-operative relations.

(3) The integration of the producer who liberates himself from the traditional structures into non-capitalist co-operative relations creates completely new prerequisites for consolidating the alliance with the peasantry and thus also helps to stabilise national-democratic power. With the formation of non-capitalist co-operative relations, the economic foundations for the creation of a new political nucleus begins to develop which then becomes the main pillar of the revolutionary-democratic forces in the village.

However, the social reality of the Malinese village is that these co-operative relations could not be established immediately as a firm system. The degree of their development was determined by both subjective and objective factors. It depended, first, on the level of the productive forces and the stage of economic development throughout the country and in the various districts; secondly, it was determined by the speed of the spontaneous decay of the traditional socio-economic relations and social norms of behaviour, and the penetration of petty-bourgeois and embryonic capitalist socio-economic and ideological elements; and finally, it was largely determined by whether and to what extent the conceived model of co-operative relations corresponded to the objective conditions, and with what intensity and by what methods the model was implemented by the political leadership.

At the beginning, co-operative relations in the Malinese village were doubtless most highly developed in the field of exchange. The reason was that despite the big territorial and structural differences, the most mature development existed there. In addition, the aspect of marketing and supply within the whole co-operative conception corresponded most to the level of the village – despite conceptual defects to be dealt with later. So in the mid-1960s, the producer who had liberated himself from the traditional system of production and distribution, became integrated into the co-operative system of exchange to the extent that he no longer produced either subsistence products only and also no longer produced all the goods he needed for himself, and no longer received the latter through direct exchange within the traditional community. He sold his commodities via the G. R. P. S. M. at fixed prices and received from it, also at fixed prices, means of subsistence and production. This stimulated him to increase production and protected him from exploitation by private trade capital.

Beginnings of modern co-operative relations also resulted in some forms of accumulation. Even if fewer prerequisites existed for accumulation, the co-operative relations were particularly important in overcoming economic backwardness and developing the productive forces. A start was made by some co-operatives towards buying their own tools and transport and financing local infrastructural projects. For example, in the F. P. of M'Pésoba[178] the following projects were carried out (1964/5): The F. P. bought a lorry for marketing purposes, and to supply the G. R. P. S. M. with consumer goods, a millet mill was installed, the construction of a bakery and a dispensary was financed[179], and a mango grove with 6,000 young plants set up. Each G. R. A. was equipped with a cart and two draught oxen. There are similar examples from other areas.[180]

The co-operative relations in the sphere of production are a special problem. The S. U.'s conception of how to develop co-operative production relations via the collective field was in obvious contradiction to the existing conditions in the Malinese village. Even the developed areas[181] lacked the prerequisites for modern co-operative production in the 1960s. First, the level of the productive forces was much too low. On the DABA or ox-plough basis, which characterises the level of the productive forces, co-operative production was economically pointless and meant politically discrediting the co-operatives and, in the long run, socialism. Ideologically, too, the liberated producers were not prepared for co-operative production. They were still very close to the traditional system of production and distribution and so necessarily saw in the collective field a type of relapse into the Foroba era, particularly as its propagation was accompanied by the glorification of traditional forms of production. That is why they were so very reserved vis-à-vis the collective field.[182]

On the other hand, a form of co-operative production arose sporadically during the process of spontaneous social development after 1960 which, in my opinion, is of greatest significance for non-capitalist changes and can become a genuine first step towards a later socialist co-operative organisation of production in agriculture which corresponds to the objective and subjective conditions. It is a form of mutual assistance of the small producers in agricultural production on the basis of equality, independent of traditional ties and therefore free of the traditional forms of collective production which inhibit the development of the productive forces. This mutual aid in cultivation and harvesting makes possible the efficient use of such modern tools as the plough, sprayers, and so on.[183]

The S. U. conception was not expressly oriented towards such forms of collective production, so their development was left to chance. In the mid-1960s, despite the formal 100% existence of co-operatives, the process of building up effective, modern co-operative relations was only in its first stages. This was not only because there were objective limits to the creation of co-operative relations in certain economic fields, such as production, because all the village inhabitants were in the G. R. P. S. M. and consequently were closely linked with the traditional system[184]; but it also applies to those fields in which the development of modern co-operative relations was both possible and necessary, i. e. exchange and, to some extent, accumulation. So in 1964/5 — although legally the co-operatives had a marketing monopoly — co-operative sales amounted to only 11,7% of agrarian production and 62,5% of commodity production.[185] This corresponded to a value of only 400 FM per head of the rural population and 4,900 FM per farm.[186] In the developed area of Barouéli in 1966/7 [187] the co-operatively commercialised agrarian and commodity production was about 28% and 76%, and represented a value of 1,900 FM *per capita* and 15,500 per farm.[188] In buying consumer goods for the peasants, the co-operative market's share was much lower.[189]

The accumulated capital of the G. R. P. S. M. was still fairly low in 1965.[190] The 7,000 G. R. P. S. M. existing in that year had a total capital of 105 million FM,[191] i.e. about 15,000 FM per G.R.P.S.M. The averages in the various regions and districts differed considerably around the 15,000 FM mark.[192]

Survey of average capital per G. R. P. S. M. on 30 May 1965 according to regions and districts (in 1,000 FM)

Region	Kayes	Region	Bamako	Region	Ségou	Region	Sikasso
Kayes	43	Bamako	16	Ségou	17	Bougouni	3
Bafoulabé	18	Banamba	9	Macina	22	Kadiolo	25
Kita	17	Dioila	17	San	7	Kolondiéba	8
Kéniéba	9	Kangaba	72	Niono	11	Koutiala	20
Nioro	11	Kolokani	4	Tominian	5	Yorosso	19
Yélimané	9	Koulikoro	18			Sikasso	24
		Nara	13			Yanfolila	11
Region	22	Region	14	Region	12	Region	12

Thus, by the second half of the 1960s, the national democrats had not yet succeeded in using the potentials that grew out of disintegration for creating non-capitalist agrarian market relations, i. e. they could not integrate producers leaving the traditional system into co-operative relations.

This had various reasons. The main one was the resistance of the national trade and usury capitalists to the non-capitalist changes in agrarian market relations. In the class struggle that ensued, it had not been possible to break this resistance, because it had been under-rated owing to Narodnik-like illusions. From 1964, however, in all documents and statements of the S. U. leadership and the Malinese government on questions of marketing and, in particular, on supply difficulties, the attitude of the merchants was stated to be the main cause of these difficulties and was described as an "openly hostile attitude towards our socialist alternative"[193].

After the private merchants were excluded from marketing of agrarian products, partly at the beginning of the 1960s and completely from 1964, they organised a "parallel market" which effectively sabotaged "official commodity circulation". They paid 2—5 francs more than the state[194], exploited all the cooperatives and state market's difficulties and mistakes and used their greater experience and many connections with the agricultural market.[195]

The traders were most interested in those products which they had traditionally bought and sold, and in agriculture these were mainly millet, rice, maize and secondary food culture.[196] According to official figures, the amount of millet traded on the "parallel market" in 1964/5 was some 70% of the commodity production (40,000 of 57,200 tons) and of rice – outside of the Office du Niger – even over 85% (12,000 of 14,000 tons).[197] For all other food cultures (including maize) the amount traded on the official[198] market was inconsiderable.

Private trade capital made a profit of 466 million FM through marketing of food crops (except fruit, vegetables and rice[199]) on the "parallel market" in 1964/5.[200]

Private trade capital was less active in the marketing of export crops. This is shown by the absolute decline in official peanut marketing (despite a slight increase in gross production) and the general decline of officially marketed production compared to the gross production of peanuts and cotton.[201] The 1965/6 R. F. D. T. report states: "Marketing countinues actively on the local markets and causes many buying losses, particularly in the most recently pioneered zones and the Barouéli Z. E. R."[202] This tendency was probably stronger for peanuts, as the local market was more capable of absorbing peanuts and peanut products than cotton.[203] In my opinion, the quantities of peanuts and cotton traded on the "parallel market" in 1964/5 must have been about 30,000 tons (peanuts) and 1,000 to 2,000 tons (cotton), which corresponds to about 40% and 5%, respectively, of this production.

However, the private merchants were not only very active in marketing, but they also controlled what the peasants received in the way of industrial consumer goods. According to information from the Ségou-San area and general information, one can assume that in the mid-1960s at least 75–80% of the consumer goods bought by the peasants came to them from the "parallel market". A millet study set up in 1965 even assumes that in an average district, more than 50% of all economic operations (including, for example, payment of salaries in the administrative services) was carried out by private trade.[204] Thus the merchants were able to largely assert their positions on the agrarian market.

The private traders' struggle against the non-capitalist changes on the agrarian market was objectively aided by a number of conceptual and practical weaknesses in the S. U.'s and the Malinese government's agrarian policy – caused, in the final analysis, by the petty-bourgeois character of the whole movement.

Because of its illusions regarding the character of the traditional community[205] – resulting in an under-estimation of the objective social processes – the Malinese agrarian conception was too little differentiated in its whole tactical and strategic line; it therefore paid too little attention to the disintegration process that the traditional structures were undergoing and to winning the small producer for political, economic and social non-capitalist changes in the village. This was expressed in the first half of the 1960s not only in the already mentioned weaknesses of the political organisation in the village[206], but also in an underestimation of the importance of stimulating the small producing economic ally to become integrated into the co-operatives. This aspect becomes clear when one examines the buying prices for agrarian products.

Official buying prices for agrarian products 1958/9—1965/6 [207]
(in FM per kg)

	1958/9	1961/2	1962/3	1963/4	1964/5	1965/6
Millet	16	10	10	10	11	11
Rice	12,5	8	11	11,5	12,5	12,5
Peanuts	14,75	14	14	14	13	13
Cotton	34	34	34	34	34	34

On an average, they were lower than the 1958 level. For the three main crops and for millet the difference is very unfavourable, while during the period 1961—6, the prices for the most important consumer goods rose by 50%.[208] This meant that the producer had absolutely no interest in raising commodity production and selling the goods on the state co-operative market.[209] The sale of agrarian products to these bodies must have seemed to him pointless, since they supplied him with very few industrial goods. Only in the mid-1960s did this supply begin to function, especially for such products as cloth, soap, salt, cigarettes, etc. In the developed Ségou district only some one-third of the needs were satisfied in 1966/7, so that the peasant was forced to buy what he needed on the market which meant at high prices.[210] Under these conditions, a millet peasant received about 60 FM per working day if he marketed his goods as the law prescribed, and for this he was able to buy 100 grams of sugar or a packet of cigarettes.[211]

Likewise, important economic incentives in the field of accumulation, which would have consolidated the co-operative were ignored. Co-operative capital came mainly from two sources, both unsuitable for winning the producer over to the co-operative. One source was from annual dues which had severe material[212] and moral limits,[213] and the other was from the profits of the co-operative field. The co-operative was not allowed to keep any profit from its commercial activities for accumulation — especially that gained through buying agrarian products from the village member — although this is one of the advantages of co-operative market relations. Added to this were bureaucratic-bourgeois tendencies which also had a negative effect on the non-capitalist changes in agriculture. These tendencies were the signs of a general process of social differentiation which also included petty-bourgeois cadres and officials in the party and state apparatus. The U. N. T. M. general secretary sharply condemned this process: "It is no longer a people's revolution, but a revolution for intriguers, courtesans, opportunists, black-marketeers and smugglers who have succeeded in developing methods whereby to misuse the party for their personal advantage and to replace the party's political line through a system of monkey-business."[214]

The activities of the bureaucratic-bourgeois elements opposing non-capitalist development in agriculture took on two pricipal forms.[215] They misused their official position for personal enrichment in many ways such as embezzlement, smugling, nepotism, etc.; however, the dominant method in the mid-1960s was probably to use the industrial consumer goods intended for the village inhabitants and the marketed food crops for the needs of themselves and their friends and relatives, and in extreme cases for large-scale black-marketeering.[216]

On the first variation, the millet study comments laconically — but revealingly — when listing the reasons for supply difficulties for the peasants from the competent bodies that "most of the S. M. D. R. and S. O. M. I. E. X. goods remain in the towns where the officials are their main consumers. The peasant in the distant village cannot be at all certain ..."[217] In 1965/7 in the San this led to several hundred tons of millet being sold, but not one gram of it left San through the official channels.[218]

Just as the activities of such officials — their number is difficult to assess — damaged the non-capitalist changes in market relations and sometimes reduced them to a mockery, their attitudes towards the peasants considerably hindered non-capitalist development in agriculture at the basic — i. e. village — level. This relationship between the "administrators" and the "administered", often condemned by Modibo Keita as "political or administrative feudalism",[219] was specially marked in the attitudes of certain officials towards the uneducated peasant masses.[220] Often this administrative-authoritarian method was only the other side of the coin of their incompetence, inflexibility and self-enrichment. In practice this meant, for example, that party work was reduced to collecting the annual dues. It was organised as an administrative campaign with a tax-list, so that to the ordinary peasant it had to appear that the attempts from "above" to get him into the party were only an easy excuse for additional taxation.

In marketing too bureaucratic methods were well entrenched. The peasant did not know how much and how often he was to deliver millet, rice, etc. Several campaigns buying up these products were carried out, their intensity and number depending on the first and second campaigns and also partly on the distance of the village from the administrative and transport centres.[221] The peasants therefore gave as little as possible to the marketing groups right from the beginning.

The marketing often became a campaign which differed from confiscation only in that the peasant received money for his product, but because he could not buy cheap consumer goods for it, it was of no use to him. The millet study formulated the natural reactions of the peasant: "Why should the peasant deliver millet if he receives only money and no consumer goods? ...

Spontaneous decay of traditional structures 151

One demands of the peasant that he engage himself, but the officials cannot satisfy his needs."[222]
The direct outcome of the unsolved problems on the local market was a considerable decrease of official marketing of the three most important agrarian crops (millet, rice, peanuts).

Development of officially marketed production
1958/9—1965/6[223] (in 1,000 tons)

	1958/9	1961/2	1962/3	1963/4	1964/5	1965/6
Millet	60.0	20.9	27.1	16.3	17.3	25.9
Rice	14.0	0.4	4.8	3.9	2.0	1.4
Peanuts	86.0	66.4	70.7	75.2	44.1	27.2
Cotton	3.8	5.9	12.3	15.8	21.8	16.2

The decline in officially marketed production — because agriculture held such an important place in the Malinese economy — was largely responsible for the retrograde development of exports and therefore for the growing foreign trade deficit.

Development of foreign trade 1959—65[224]
(in mill. FM value 1964/5)

	1959	1964/5	Index
Import	13,322	18,748	141.7
Export	10,811	9,517	88.0
of these: agricultural products (including first processing)	10,811	9,343.1	86.5
of these: peanuts	2,060.0	1,984.0	96.5
cotton	260.0	1,284.5	492.0
rice and millet	981.0	249.6	39.3
cattle	2,990.0	3,120.0	104.5
goats-sheep	1,645.0	705.0	42.8
fish	1,500.0	1,500.0	100.0

In the above survey on exports of the most important agricultural products, one must remember that the export of 54,560 tons of peanuts worth 1,984 billion FM was an exception compared to the previous and following years and came about because a large part of the previous harvest (32,400 tons)[225] was still exported. The export figures from 1962 to 1966 shows that the peanut export was lower in the average years:

Peanut export 1962—6[226] (in 1,000 tons)

1962	1963	1964	1965	1966	Annual average 1962—1966
41.8	29.9	49.9	29.9	21.0	34.5

This average quantity corresponds to a value of 1.26 billion FM or 61.8% of the peanut export of 1959, so that for (respectively) peanuts, cotton, rice and millet, the actual figures are 3,101 million FM (1959) and 2,794.1 million FM (1964/5) (as against 3,518.1 million FM actual exports). In other words, for the four most important agrarian products there was a downward tendency (index 87.6) despite the increase in cotton exports; the insufficient development of official commodity production resulted, through the decline in exports and balance of trade, in a negative balance of payments, and was thus a decisive internal cause of the acute worsening of the financial situation in the mid-1960s.[227]

The decline in official marketing, particularly in food crops, also caused considerable difficulties — for the first time on a large scale in 1964/5[228] — in supplying the city population and those living in the Sahel zones. At this time, through the fast process of urbanisation,[229] the amount of millet needed rose far above the quantities supplied through controlled marketing.

Demand for millet and its provision through official marketing 1964—6 (in tons)[230]

	1964/5	1965/6
Demand	37,600	55,495
Marketed millet	17,250	25,900
Deficit	20,350	29,595

As this deficit in millet could not be compensated for by the similarly declining marketing of rice from the traditional sector, it had to be done by using precious hard currency to import millet and stopping the export of rice from the Office du Niger.[231] In addition, the shortage led to a huge rise in prices for millet and rice in the retail trade (outside the co-operatives, which had stable prices but insufficient goods):

Index of market prices for millet and rice in Bamako[232]

	1962	1963	1964	1965	1966
Millet	100	109.1	139.4	297.0	339.4
Rice	100	116.3	140.5	243.2	281.1

However, the difficulties in integrating the peasant producers not only had indirect and direct economic effects, but were also of considerable political significance. The far-reaching boycott of the state co-operative marketing bodies by a large number of peasants meant politically that an alliance with them was impossible. Apart from some agrarian-bourgeois elements[233] who entered into a more or less conscious alliance with the merchants against the non-capitalist road, the people concerned were those small producers who were gradually going over to commodity production after freeing themselves from the traditional structures, and were thus the main peasant ally for the revolutionary-democratic forces. This meant that from a political point of view, the unsolved problems of non-capitalist agrarian market relations were a great danger to the future of the national-democratic revolution. Further, the agricultural difficulties led to supply problems in the cities, which in turn undermined the alliance of revolutionary democrats with the city workers.

Due to growing complications in the economic situation and the sharpened class struggle[234], Mali's revolutionary leaders recognised the dangers of the current developments for agriculture in the mid-1960s and began to take measures which aimed to generally consolidate the alliance with the peasantry.

The Sudanese Union's first reaction to the great marketing and supply difficulties in 1964 was to intensify its ideological work among the peasants. For this purpose, 23 production zones were formed at the beginning of 1966 for which a member of the Political Bureau and a political commissar or regional governor were responsible.[235] Under their leadership, all cadres from the party and state apparatus were mobilised to convince the peasants that it is necessary to produce more and sell their products to the state co-operative marketing bodies. This campaign was continued in 1967 and took on a new urgency after the August events in 1967.[236]

In connection with measures against the bureaucratic bourgeoisie taken after 22 August, 1967 these elements in the state co-operative marketing bodies and the state apparatus above village level were sharply criticised and reprimanded, and some were dismissed.[237] At the same time, steps were taken to strengthen the role of the young dynamic forces in the political and administrative life of the village.[238] A second group of measures aimed at using economic incentives for formation of the co-operatives.

From 1966 to 1968 the buying prices for agrarian products (particularly food crops) were gradually increased.

Development of buying prices for agrarian products
1965–1967/8 (FM/kg)[239]

	Millet	Rice	Cotton	Peanuts
1965/6	11	12.5	34	13
1966/7	15	16	34	16
1967/8	16	18	40	24

At the same time, greater efforts were made to supply the peasants with consumer goods by the G. R. P. S. M.,[240] and the steps were taken to allow the co-operatives to participate in the profits from the sale of their products.[241]

A third group of measures were to intensify and differentiate the development work. The peasants were equipped with more modern tools[242], special development schemes were worked out for the main crops,[243] and a literacy campaign was carried out together with the UNESCO in the Ségou region[244]. All these measures corresponded to the tasks necessary for the non-capitalist changes in traditional agriculture, particularly for winning over the small producers for the co-operative. They were the practical expression of the realisation that the Narodnik-like glorification of the traditional community was unrealistic; it was the beginning of a scientific approach to questions of non-capitalist development. In agriculture the measures led to several positive results. Progress was made in the marketing of agrarian products, especially millet.

Official marketing 1964/5—1967/8 (in 1,000 tons)[245]

	1964/5	1965/6	1966/7	1967/8
Millet	17,3	25,9	56,6	60,3
Rice	2,0	1,4	7,0	5,8
Peanuts	44,1	27,2	40,2	31,3
Cotton	21,8	16,2	21,7	29,9

This meant the stabilisation of the G. R. P. S. M., which was expressed also in the growth of co-operative accumulation.

G. R. P. S. M. development in the Bamako region 1963/4—1966/7[246]

	1963/4	1964/5	1965/6	1966/7
Number of G. R. P. S. M.	217	974	1,225	1,512
Accumulated total sum (mill. FM)	1,7	13,0	20,0	28,7
Accumulated sum per G. R. P. S. M. (thous. FM)	7,9	13,6	16,3	19,0

As a whole, these measures were able to strengthen the political and ideological influence of the revolutionary democrats in the villages.

However, within the short space of 2—3 years (for some questions even less) the many problems involved in non-capitalist transitional relations, particularly the burning issue of firmly integrating the producer who had freed himself from the traditional structures into a co-operative, could not be permanently solved. The positive results amounted to only the first steps in the solution of these problems.

The positive aspects of the new orientation were impaired by a number of ultra-left tendencies accompanying it. These were that the transition to co-operative production was placed on the agenda at a time when non-capitalist development demanded that the freed peasant be integrated into the state co-operative marketing system and the necessity existed to win him over to the non-capitalist path in order to create the material, social and ideological prerequisites for the higher form of co-operative production. Instead, the task was set to gradually eliminate the individual fields, and to extend the collective fields and make them the kernel of large-scale co-operative production.[247] As a result, no material support was given to individual producers, but only to co-operative farms.[248]

This policy antagonised just those social forces which had the greatest objective interest in a non-capitalist path and should have become the main peasant ally of the revolutionary democrats. Thus, all existing possibilities of taking first steps for non-capitalist transformation of agriculture were made more difficult and, in the long run, it became *the* obstacle that closed the road to co-operative production altogether.

REFERENCES

1 K. Marx, *Foundations of the Critique of Political Economy*, loc. cit., p. 496.
2 For details see pages 53 ff.
3 Until just before the First World War, the monopolies were most interested in the natural rubber which they demanded in 1896 from the inhabitants (sometimes in the form of tax in kind). By 1907 it reached 720 tons, but decreased from 1910 onwards due to the crisis in natural rubber, and was replaced by peanuts, particularly after the Kayes-Bamako (1904) railway line was finished. Only small before the First World War (1907 : 400 tons), peanut production grew rapidly between the two wars (1928 : 35,000 tons, 1939 :105,000 tons) and after a sharp decrease during the Second World War gradually reached the 1939 level (see J. Suret-Canale, *French Colonialism in Tropical Africa*, loc. cit., pp. 42—5; Governement Général de l'Afrique Occidentale Française. *Colonie du Haut-Sénégal et Niger*, op. cit., p. 47 and p. 51 and S. Amin, op. cit., p. 24).
4 In 1956, the districts of Kayes, Kita, Bamako and Ségou had 77.47% of the peanut production (see République Soudanaise, Ministère de l'Agriculture et des Eaux Forêts. Direction de l'Agriculture. "Arachide", Bamako 1958, p. 2 − photostat).
5 Up to the Second World War, the food deficit existing in Senegal since the 1930s (through the larger peanut production) was balanced out by import-

ing rice from Indo-China. Cut off from East Asia during the Second World War, French imperialism finally lost its colonies there altogether after 1945. This is why at this time, the production and marketing of food crops (above all rice and millet) was of great significance for French imperialism.

6 The production of cotton (outside of the Office du Niger) rose from 220 tons in 1952/3 to 3,825 tons in 1958/9 (see Chambre de Commerce d'Agriculture et d'Industrie de Bamako, *Elements du bilan économique 1964*, Bamako 1965, p. 113).
7 See pages 29 ff.
8 See pages 79 ff.
9 See *Enquête agricole 1960*, op. cit., p. 57;
Enquête agricole 1964/65, op. cit., p. 18 and
Enquête agricole 1967/68, op. cit., p. 8. The number of ploughs rose per 100 farms from 15 (1960) to 23 (1967/8).
10 S. Amin, op. cit., p. 225.
11 For details see pages 79 f.
12 See ibid.
13 From 1960 to 1970 1,225 km of road were asphalted (see *L'Informateur*, 9/10/1970, p. 17).
14 In the field of health, the following developments took place in the countryside:

	1958	1967
District hospitals	17	44
Medical centres	137	293
Social centres	0	57

(See *Le Guide du Mali*, Bamako n. d., p. 48).
There was a particularly steep rise in the number of primary schools in the countryside:

	1959/60	1969/70
Primary schools	425	807
Primary school teachers	1,408	6,405
Primary school-children	48,594	218,194

(See Annuaire statistique 1966, op. cit., p. 45 and L'informateur, op. cit., p. 14).
15 Here, the issue is the share of cotton and peanuts in the whole agrarian product (millet, rice, maize, peanuts, cotton). The basis for calculation were the 1964/5 prices (see *Comptes économiques*, op. cit., pp. 32—7. *Annuaire statistique 1966*, pp. 57—64 and 142, and *Enquête agricole 1968/69*, op. cit., p. 37).
16 For 1959 see *Comptes économiques 1959*, op. cit., pp. 32—7 and for 1964/5 du *Comptes économiques 1964/65*, op. cit., pp. 7—24. The 1967/8 figure is only an

estimation because no information exists which is anywhere near exact. The officially marketed production, which was generally 4 to 5% below the total commodity production, was 20%. (See *Rapport définitif de l'Enquête agricole 1967/68*, op. cit., p. 79). The 1964/5 buying prices were the basis for calculation.
17 In this connection, Julis says that "... the village community withdraws into a type of collective individualism" (C. Julis, op. cit., p. 12).
18 According to the *Enquête agricole 1968/69*, op. cit., table 90.
19 For further details, see annex.
20 The figures for the Z. E. R. Barouéli were calculated with values given by the Z. E. R. heads; the values for Mali are based on the 1964/5 *Enquête agricole*.
21 Of this, rice, which is not planted in Barouéli, with 9.1%.
22 See page 70 and the literature listed in footnote 10 on pages 101 f. In my doctor's thesis on pp. 99—102, I described the causes for and character of this elimination of slavery.
23 The traditional aristocracy was liquidated as an institution, and some even physically, during the course of or shortly after colonial conquest, and replaced by the colonial-administrative *Chefferie*.
24 Mali was "favoured" for recruitment. Revealing are the figures published about the recruits gained in 1959 in the various ex—A. O. F. countries:

Mali	30,202	Ivory Coast	9,883
Upper Volta	17,492	Dahomey	5,987
Senegal	15,498	Niger	2,677
Guinea	13,443	Mauretania	1,215

(See "Chroniques de la Communauté". *La Documentation française*, 3/1960, p. 11).
25 In the thirties, the broad propagation of bourgeois ideology and way of life began through film, radio and the beginnings of a school system, and this increased after the Second World War.
26 The theory of acculturation which is currently widespread in the bourgeois sociology of developing countries, tries to interpret the changes in the social relations of these countries or the former colonies as a "process of imitation and adoption of originally foreign cultural elements into their own culture", as a "meeting between various and different types of cultures ... whereby the more developed (and therefore more active) system opens its influence to the less developed (and therefore, first of all passive and weaker) system and begins to penetrate and change it" in order to veil over the imperialist character of colonial rule. (R. F. Behrendt, op. cit., p. 116—17).
27 See page 91.
28 See pages 91 ff.
29 So, in the final analysis, the preserving aspects of the traditional structures were eliminated and the elements which stimulated disintegration proved stronger.
30 J. Gaillais also reached the following conclusion: "The theoretical elimination of slavery by the French administration only became fully effective when a

democratic political life developed: i. e. some ten years ago." (J. Gallais, *La signification du village*, op. cit., p. 149). H. Gerbeau reaches the same conclusion. (H. Gerbeau, *La Region de l'Issa-Ber*, op. cit., p. 116).

31 See pages 93 to 94.
32 See page 55.
33 V. Paques, op. cit., p. 78.
34 Taking into account the average yields per hectare, the buying prices in 1964/5 after deducting the seasonal expenses for seed, irrigation and insecticides (not taken into account here are the long-term expenses for ploughs, spraying instruments etc.), marketing the product of one hectare brings the peasants the following income:

| millet | 8,200 FM | rice | 12,500 FM |
| peanuts | 12,000 FM | cotton | 17,000 FM |

35 Compare the table on p. 77 for the most important crops on the Foroba.
36 This is a very significant development, because at the beginnings, the export crops — as forced crops — were mainly planted on the Foroba.
37 *Enquête agricole*, op. cit., p. 58.
38 See E. Leynaud, *Les cadres sociaux*, op. cit., p. 161.
39 See pages 172 ff.
40 See *Programme de Développement Rural*, op. cit., p. 11.
41 See further down for details of production relations among migrant workers.
42 It was different in East Africa where masses of peasants were purposely expropriated to become a labour reservoir for the European farmers and the extractive industry. (See J. Woddis, *Africa — The Roots of Revolt*, loc. cit., pp. 90ff. and V. V. Krylow, op. cit., pp. 9–11).
43 See R. Barbé, *Les classes sociales en Afrique Noire*, Paris 1964, pp. 61–4. In many cases — particularly in the economically backward areas — the migrant's income was the only larger source of money income and therefore vital for the existence of the extended family. Young family members were thus sent by the FAKOROBA into the more developed areas or the cities in order to earn money for the extended family.
44 *Enquête démographique dans le Delta Central Nigerien. Résultats Détaillés*, Paris n. d., p. 119. Here and in the following, I speak only of persons from the agricultural sector who have left their villages, but still belong to them and generally return. However, all other economic sectors are not taken into account, because the large number of fishers and cattlebreeders who normally leave their villages for a certain time would give a wrong picture for our purposes.
45 With a total of 1,484,000 labourers (see *Enquête agricole 1960*, op. cit., p. 6).
46 Only 1.2% of the migrants were women (see *Enquête démographique*, op. cit., p. 119).
47 Ibid.
48 Ibid., p. 122.
49 According to the statistics, some 15,000 seasonal workers went to Senegal

from the most important areas of West Mali as *navétanes* in the last forty years. If one adds the migrants from other areas who did not go as *navétanes* to Senegal one can assume that some 30,000 seasonal workers went to Senegal (see V. Paques, op. cit., p. 12).

50 During the dry period, some 10,000—15,000 migrants go to Bamako, particularly from the areas of Nioro, Nara, Banamba, Ségou, San, Bougouni (see Cl. Meillassoux, "The Social Structure of Modern Bamako", in: *Africa*, 2/1963, pp. 138—40). In the 1950s, Kayes absorbed some 5,000 seasonal workers during every dry period (see S. E. R. E. S. A. *Etude sur l'économie agricole du Soudan*, loc. cit., p. 84—5). However, absorbed does not mean that they actually found work there. Most of the migrant labourers found no permanent work or none whatever (see J. Diallo, *Economie urbaine*, op. cit., pp. 21—8).

51 Up to 1960 mainly the peanut-growing areas along the railway line Kayes-Bamako. Since independence, the rice areas on the upper and central arms of the Niger and the cotton centres in Sègou-Koutiala district have been added.

52 At the same time, it has a number of negative economic, political and social aspects. Firstly, it often takes the form of rural exodus and leads to a considerable shortage of labour in the less developed areas. Secondly, in the cities it leads to a growing number of unemployed who then become a source of social and political unrest.

53 For a certain time they lived independent of the extended family and the FAKOROBA and broadened their horizon. Life in the city has given them new material and mental needs and the narrowness of the traditional extended family is a direct obstacle to satisfying these needs.

54 This income is often far higher than that of the village. Because of the low level of the productive forces in agriculture and the price policy of the trade monopolies during the colonial period there was a sharp difference of income between the city and the countryside (and also, although not so sharp, between the more and the less developed areas). In 1959, the average annual income per capita in trade, services and transport was 220,000 Fr.-CFA, as against 13,000 Fr.-CFA in agriculture (see République Soudanaise. "Session budgétaire de l'Assemblée législative, 17. 11. 1959", s. l., n.d.). Even if the migratory labourers in the cities are generally the worst paid, after five to six months they have saved anything from 5,000 to 10,000 or more Fr., which is far above the average annual money income per *capita* in agriculture, and this agriculture remains largely in the hands of the FAKOROBA.

55 I.e. he is even able to pay the FURU-NA-FOLO ("bride-price") which increased as commodity-money relations developed and thus made the individual more dependent on the community and the FAKOROBA.

56 "On the contrary, the youth who go to Senegal as 'navetanes'... no longer bring all the money back that they could ... They keep some of it ... They no longer give it to the family head" (*Programme de Développement Rural*, op. cit., p. 12).

57 See M. Boyer, *Les Sociétés Indigènes de Prévoyance, de Secours et de Prêts Mutuels Agricoles en Afrique Occidentale Française*, Paris 1935, p. 30 and H. Labouret, *Les Manding et leur langue*, loc. cit., pp. 62—4.

58 This is a result of the *Enquête démographique 1960* which was published in the *Annuaire statistique 1965 de la République du Mali*, Bamako 1966, p. 10. The regional values differ around this average value. The deviations above and below are not only an expression of the degree of disintegration, but are also partly determined by ethnic differences. The figure of 15.5 persons found by Leynaud (*Les cadres sociaux*, op. cit., p. 159) in the Haute-Vallée for one average family is determined by the traditional importance of the extended family structure among the Malinké living there. As against this, the relatively low average figure of 6.1 persons and 1.4 nuclear families per family in the delta (see *Enquête démographique dans le Delta Central Nigerien*, op. cit., pp. 186–7) is conditioned less by the new economic factors than by the large number of Fulbe (47.4%, see ibid., p. 24) in this area, which traditionally have smaller extended families (see J. Gallais, *Signification du groupe ethnique*, op. cit., p. 116).
59 By farm I mean the smallest independent economic unit.
60 See *Enquête agricole 1960*, op. cit., p. 6.
61 See J. Gallais, *Signification du groupe ethnique*, op. cit., p. 116.
62 *Enquête agricole 1960*, op. cit., p. 54.
63 Bachelors, widows, divorcees.
64 In the handbook for carrying out *Enquêtes agricoles* in developing countries, the term "exploitation" is defined as follows: "The term farm [*exploitation agricole*] must be quite clear to the enquirer [*enquêteur*]: who makes the land tillable, who cultivates it, who owns the money from the harvest ... or who uses the products of the fields? By such questions, one must determine what persons belong to which farms ... The precise definitions of the farm owner [*exploitant*] and the farm are as follows: The farm owner is that person who has the initiative and responsibility for the technical and economic management of the farm. The farm includes all land which is used for agricultural production by one person alone [*exploitant*] or with the help of others" (République Francaise, Ministère de la Coopération, Institut National de la Statistique et des Etudes Economiques, Service de Coopération. *Manuel pour la formation d'agents recenseurs dans le cadre d'une étude agricole par sondage dans un pays en voie de développement*, Paris 1962, p. 15).
65 The integration of this nuclear family into the extended family is above all in the non-economic field, but also had economic aspects. Thus, while the nuclear families contributed their share of the taxes, they were paid together by the FAKOROBA. In addition, the extended family – through its possibilities of mutual aid among the actually independent nuclear families – acted as an effective protective wall against the burdens of colonial exploitation.
66 That is the result of the *Enquête démographique 1960* (for country areas). In the cities, the average was 4.6 (see *Annuaire statistique 1965*, op. cit., p. 10). The *Enquête démographique dans Delta Central Nigerien* (op. cit., p. 168) found only an average size of 4.3, while Leynaud (*Les cadres sociaux*, op. cit., p. 161) gives seven persons as the average size of a nuclear family in the Haute-Vallée du Niger. The size is due to polygamy which is relatively widespread in the economically developed area (rice irrigating system).

67 This thesis is based on the results of my investigations in Barouéli (Spring 1967). Here it was shown that the fully emancipated nuclear family is somewhat larger on an average (5.1 persons) than the nuclear family still fully integrated into the Lu (4.7).
68 With a country population of 2,884,940 persons (see *Enquête agricole 1960*, op. cit., p. 11).
69 See *Enquête agricole 1960*, op. cit., p. 6.
70 See *Enquête agricole 1964/65*, op. cit., p. 10.
71 See *Enquête agricole 1960*, op. cit., p. 54.
72 See *Enquête agricole 1964/65*, op. cit., p. 23.
73 République du Mali. *Principaux Résultats de l'Enquête agricole. Années 1967 et 1968*, Bamako 1969, p. 2.
74 The report refers to the years 1964/5, 1966/7 and 1967/8. *Principaux Résultats*, op. cit., p. 2.
75 *Enquête agricole 1960*, op. cit., p. 54; *Enquête agricole 1964/65*, op. cit., p. 23.
76 According to *Enquête agricole 1960*, op. cit., p. 54 and *Enquête agricole 1964/65*, op. cit., p. 23.
77 The corresponding figures for Mali (1960) are 55.2% and 25.6% (see above).
78 For details see appendix.
79 This means, an independent unit of production and distribution. As decisive criterium for what an economic unit actually is was seen in the production and use of a large part of the product (originally meant mainly for family subsistence). That is, in the case of an extended family farm, it could definitely be in line with the traditional extended family system for an economically secondary part of the family product to be produced on the nuclear family field (DIONFORO). Unfortunately, there was not enough time to determine the exact figures.
80 But only basically, i. e. in regard to the basic validity of the traditional system of production and distribution. As is shown further on, this variation too, is not bypassed by the general development.
81 My investigations in Barouéli (1967) confirmed this. I was told of a number of cases where the village council forbade the sale of land because, they said, it was the inalienable property of all community members.
82 See J. Suret-Canale, *Les fondéments sociaux de la vie politique africaine contemporaine*, loc. cit., p. 26.
83 The spontaneous social processes in Mali have reached this stage of maturity only in the cities and not on the flat land, even if elements of private ownership of land also exist here.
84 Bourgeois authors often give such an interpretation. The S. E. R. E. S. A. study comes to such conclusions several times (see *Etude sur l'économie agricole du Soudan*, loc. cit., p. 40, 45, 74, 87 and particularly the Etudes annexes for the various regions). Also J. Chabas ("La régime foncier coutumier en A. O. E.", in: *Annales Africaines*, Paris 1957, p. 10) has this opinion.
85 See V. V. Krylov, op. cit., p. 13.

86 This does not mean that in reality both structural elements do not exist side by side.
87 With this I wish to expressly emphasize the statements in: *Klassen und Klassenkampf in den Entwicklungsländern,* loc. cit., vol. 1, pp. 49—50.
88 For details see chapters 4.2. and 5.
89 The gradual dissolution of the extended family is not the only form of its disintegration. From page . . . onward, other forms of disintegration of the traditional community are described.
90 Bokar N'Diayé, *Les castes au Mali,* Bamako 1970.
91 Ibid., pp. 115—26.
92 Ibid., p. 122.
93 Ibid., p. 125.
94 The theories expounded in this section are essentially based on sociological investigations I made in 1964/5 in the area of San and Kita and also in 1967 in the area of Ségou-Baroueli.
95 On the socio-economic situation of the DYON in pre-colonial society see pp. 61 ff.
96 This does not exclude that the former DYON — for historical reasons — do not have the best land in the village.
97 In May 1967 I had the opportunity to examine this question (also from its quantitative aspect) in Nianzana (*Arrondissement* Barouéli, district Ségou). As far as representation is concerned, one can say that Nianzana is a typical village for the developed area of Barouéli in the framework of the traditional agrarian sector. With 395 inhabitants and 68 hectares, 5.9 ploughs and 13 oxen per 100 inhabitants it has the average figures of the Barouéli *Arrondissement* (390; 73.5; 5.2; 10; figures from the files of the Barouéli Z. E. R.) which lie considerably above those for the whole of Mali (342; 34.5; 1.5; 7.1; figures from the *Rapport définitif,* op. cit., p. 27, 14, 92 and 28).
98 This is also confirmed by Leynaud (*Les cadres sociaux,* op. cit., p. 152) for the area around the upper arm of the Niger.
99 It seems that 20% is about the average quota of former DYON for the ethnic groups of Mande (above all Bambara and Malinké in Mali). J. Gallais (op. cit., p. 149) also speaks of one-fifth of the total population among the Malinké. Leynaud even declared (*Les cadres sociaux,* p. 152) that in several Malinké villages in the Haute-Vallée (e. g. in the area of Tiguiratomo) the number of former DYON was up to 40%.
100 Here, the former DYON who are integrated into the extended family (WOLOSO) are not included.
101 See *Enquête agricole 1960,* op. cit., p. 6.
102 In 1887 the *"villages de liberté"* were introduced in Mali. They were officially founded with the alleged aim of ensuring subsistence and asylum for the DYON in the conquered areas. In reality, it had the task of supplying the military bases, near which they were set up, with labour, because the forced labour and continual requisition of the local inhabitants had caused them to flee from the areas around the bases. This was definitely part and parcel of the colonial practice of "freeing slaves": the DYON-aristocracy relation was dissolved

for those interned in the *"villages de liberté"* in such a way that their labour power was given to the monopolies and their colonial, military or administrative representatives. The most comprehensive study on the *"villages de liberté"* was done by Denise Bouche, *Les villages de liberté en Afrique Noire Française*, Paris 1968.

103 Without being able to go into detail here, it should be pointed out that during the beginning of colonial rule, the FAKOROBA of the traditionally richest and most powerful extended families forced the DYON to produce the export crops demanded from the community and sent them to the army and school in place of their own sons. This was done out of opposition to colonial rule and in order to save their immediate relatives and themselves from exploitation by monopoly capital. Although this was of temporary advantage for them, it meant that those DYON broke quickest and most intensively with the traditional economy and mentality and adapted to the new conditions.

104 In 1967 in Nianzana it was taken for granted that during celebrations the former DYON perform as entertainers (dancers, drummers, etc.) and spread the news throughout the village when there was a birth or death among his former FAKOROBA relations.

105 See S. E. R. E. S. A. *Etude sur l'économie agricole du Soudan*, loc. cit.

106 In this connection, Fournier writes: "In Hombori, the canton chief lets his personal fields be cultivated by former slaves who must work for him for a certain number of days in the week" (F. Fournier, op. cit., p. 175).

107 See further down.

108 Bokar N'Diayé, *Les castes au Mali*, Bamako 1970, p. 125.

109 This, of course, must be understood only as an abstraction because in reality — so long as the traditional system continues to function as a whole — there still exist certain ties of the producer to this primary community, even if he has essentially separated from the extended family. And these often very tenacious remnants of traditional relations are the social factors which prevent the new processes unfolding quickly. However, the dialectics of this process is that the persistence of traditional relations are, in the final analysis, only an expression of the backwardness of economic processes.

110 See further down.

111 The same tendency is confirmed for the whole of Mali by the 1968/9 *Enquête agricole*. The smaller the number of persons of working age per farm, the larger the area for each such person.
Number of persons of working age per farm
1—5   5—10   11—15   16—20   21—25   26—30   31 and over
Area per persons of working age
0.93   0.74   0.80   0.75   0.75   0.53   0.61
(See *Enquête agricole 1968/69*, op. cit., table 53).

112 Calculated according to information from the Barouéli Z. E. R. and *Rapport 1967—68* (op. cit., pp. 7—8) on the basis of the buying prices in 1966/7. Only the main crops were taken into account (millet, rice, cotton and peanuts).

113 Whether the producer acquires an interest in development of the productive forces depends, of course, not only on the good and adequate work of the development service, but also largely on the material possibilities of the producer. See further down.
114 The faster development of the productive forces (and thus commodity production, etc.) achieved in this area contributes to a faster disintegration of still existing traditional structures, i. e. the processes influence each other.
115 See Service de l'Agriculture. *Rapport Annuel 1968—69*, op. cit., pp. 12—26.
116 Unfortunately, the material on the other crops is not sufficiently differentiated.
117 The Compagnie Française pour le Développement des Fibres Textiles (C. F. D. T.) took over the development service on the basis of an agreement in the following districts (the new administrative divisions of the C. F. D. T. — the "sectors" — were never identical with the state structure): Koutiala, Yorosso (sector Koutiala); Sikasso, Kadiolo (sector Sikasso); Bougouni, Yanfolila, Kolondiéba (sector Bougouni); San, Tominian (sector San); Ségou (sector Ségou); Dioila (sector Dioila) and three Z. E. R. in the Bamako district (sector Bamako) (see C. F. D. T. *Rapport Campagne Cotonnière 1968/69*. Bamako n. d., pp. 3—5). On the character of the C. F. D. T. and its role in Malinese agriculture, see further down.
118 See ibid., p. 24.
119 Ibid.
120 Only for the garden crops was organic fertiliser used (see p. 104, footnote 28).
121 See Service de l'Agriculture. *Rapport Annuel 1968/69*, op. cit., p. 118.
122 See ibid., pp. 115—17. In Bougouni and Sikasso, the more favourable natural conditions for creating fertiliser (higher humidity) plays a big role.
123 Unfortunately, only fragmentary information is available on this. On the use of artificial fertiliser in cultivation of peanuts, rice and millet in the area on the upper arm of the Niger see ibid., p. 105.
124 See C. F. D. T. *Rapport 1965/66*, loc. cit., p. 26.
125 That is, on their heads.
126 Different types of such carts exist. The smaller (one shaft) can transport up to 500 kilogrammes, and the larger (two shafts) up to one ton.
127 See Service de l'Agriculture. *Rapport Annuel 1968/69*, op. cit., p. 19.
128 According to the *Enquête agricole 1960* (op. cit., p. 15) one can estimate the total number of carts for that year to be between 5,000 and 6,000.
129 With a rural population of 4,171,200 persons (according to *Enquête agricole 1968/69*, op. cit., table 8).
130 Calculated according to Service de l'Agriculture. *Rapport Annuel 1968/69*, op. cit., p. 19 and *Enquête Agricole 1968/69*, op. cit., table 8 and according to information from the Barouéli Z. E. R.
131 According to information from the chiefs of the N'Gara and Konodimini *Secteur de Base*.
132 See *Evolution de la Situation*, op. cit., p. 6. In an average nuclear family, the small producer has an average money income of 10.000 FM annually.

133 See C. F. D. T., *Rapport Campagne cotonnière 1968/69*, loc. cit., pp. 76—7.
134 See J. Rosaliev, "Asia and Africa: Capitalism and Problems of Socialist Orientation", in: *World Marxist Review*, 7/1970.
135 See on this pages 70 ff.
136 The extended family was able to protect the individual to a limited extent from the exploitation of trade and usury capital through its FOROBA mechanism.
137 Apart from the rural proletariat, which, however, did not play any significant role quantitatively and qualitatively under the given level of social development.
138 See on this page 96.
139 K. Marx/F. Engels, *Selected Works* in 3 vols, loc. cit., vol. 1, p. 527.
140 V. I. Lenin, *"Left-Wing" Communism — an Infantile Disorder*, loc. cit., p. 24.
141 That is, in the transition phase from the traditional community to small commodity production in which capitalist relations develop, particularly in the sphere of exchange and were an integrated part of colonial and neo-colonial exploitation and dependence of the *économie de traite* type.
142 The Malinese agrarian conception was subjectively based on the rebirth of traditional community relations and not on their inevitable disintegration (see pages 38 ff.).
143 See pages 79 ff.
144 As I cannot go into this complex any further, see VIe Congrès, loc. cit., pp. 27—9 and N. Kovrigina, "Gosudarstvennyj i častnyj sektor v ekonomike Mali", in: *Mirovaja ekonomika i meždunarodnye otnošenija*, Moscow, 1/1967, pp. 127—32.
145 For the immediate reason for the founding of the S. O. M. I. E. X. see VIe Congrès, loc. cit., p. 27. For further details on measures taken to create a state sector, but which do not immediately affect agriculture, see G. Thole, "Die Republik Mali", in: *Geographische Berichte*, Berlin, 4/1967, pp. 272—283.
146 Chambre de Commerce, d'Agriculture et d'Industrie de Bamako. *"Eléments du Bilan économique de l'Année 1960"*, Bamako 1961, p. 4 (photostat).
147 See Chambre de Commerce, d'Agriculture et d'Industrie de Bamako. *Répèrtoire des Entreprises financières, commerciales, industrielles exercant en République du Mali*, Bamako 1964, p. 23 (photostat). On other foreign trade activities of the S. O. M. I. E. X. see N. Kovrigina, op. cit., p. 128.
148 Co-operative bodies on a district level (see p. 35).
149 Apart from that, the S. O. M. I. E. X. marketed several secondary industrial crops such as kapok, rubber, etc. via the S. M. D. R.
150 For this purpose, it had retail shops in all important towns (see *Répertoire*, op. cit., p. 23).
151 Through the Loi No. 65—7 portant transformation de l'Office Agricoles du Mali (see Chambre de Commerce, d'Agriculture et d'Industrie de Bamako, *Eléments du Bilan économique 1965*, loc. cit., p. 18; see also a detailed interview with the O. P. A. M. director, in: *L'Essor*, 10. 5. 1965, p. 5).

152 The Office des Céréales was created in 1959. It received the monopoly for commercialisation, for import and export of grain crops (above all millet and rice). It passed over the function of marketing to the co-operative institutions (S. M. D. R.) and to the private merchants (see *L'Essor*, 10. 5. 1965).
153 Except cotton (see further down).
154 *Coopératives de Consommation.* They were created in all towns in 1964/5 (for details see: "Une nouvelle phase du mouvement coopératif au Mali", in: *Le Mali*, 1/1966, pp. 6—19).
155 The decline in the position of the trade monopolies through the state trading organization is clearly expressed by the fact that their turnover decreased from 12,847 million FM (1959) to 3,791 million (1964/5), while the state trading organization was able to double its turnover from 1962 to 1964/5 to reach a figure of 16,575 million FM (of this, the S. O. M. I. E. X. alone had a turnover of 15,060 million FM) or 46% of the turnover of all undertakings in the modern sector of the economy. At the same time, the trade monopolies' share was only 10.5% (see République du Mali. Service statistique, *Comptes économiques du Mali 1964/65*, Bamako 1967, p. 121).
156 VIe Congrès, loc. cit., pp. 27—8. On the general significance of the creation of a state sector in the field of distribution, see N. Kovrigina, op. cit., pp. 128—31.
157 In 1965 and 1966 Mali imported from the non-socialist world market 52.4% and 54.1% respectively, and exported to it 64.4% and 61.9% respectively. (Calculated in accordance with *Annuaire statistique 1966*, op. cit., p. 129 and 136)
158 Whereby this quality does not result in isolation out of the mere existence of the state company — state organization, control and guidance of marketing is not necessarily identical with non-capitalist conditions, it is also practised in countries with expressly capitalist development (e. g. Senegal) — but must be integrated into a whole social system, the character of which is determined by those in power.
159 The C. F. D. T. is a mixed French company where state monopoly capital has the majority of shares. It was founded on 8 February 1949 (see C. F. D. T., *10 années d'action cotonnière 1949/59*, Paris 1959, p. 4).
160 The cotton production controlled by the C. F. D. T. developed as follows (in 1,000 tons):

52/3	53/4	54/5	55/6	56/7	57/8	58/9	59/60	60/1	61/2	62/3	63/4	64/5
0.20	0.53	1.14	1.53	2.60	2.08	3.82	2.65	6.40	5.89	12.28	15.76	21.77

65/6	66/7	67/8	68/9
16.18	21.73	29.89	40.89

(see *Annuaire statistique 1966*, op. cit., p. 73 and *Service de l'Agriculture Rapport Annuel 1968/69*, op. cit., p. 125).
161 See "Convention entre la République du Mali et la Compagnie Française pour le Développement du Textile", in: *Journal Officiel de la République du Mali*, 168/1964, pp. 294/6.
162 For details see article 3 of the Convention, ibid., p. 295 and C. F. D. T.

"Rapport sur la campagne cotonniere 1965–1966", Bamako 1966, p. 2 (photostat). There, on pp. 3–8, is also described the organizational system of the Service d'Encadrement of the C. F. D. T., which does not differ from the state development service. It has altogether 280 *Secteurs de Base* and 53 Z. E. R. The Z. E. R. of the C. F. D. T., which are not necessarily the same as the total number of Z. E. R. in a district, are independent of the administrative district borders and were divided into six sectors (Koutiala, Sikasso, Ségou, San, Bougouni and Bamako) in accordance with economic aspects.

163 The other crops are marketed via the S. M. D. R.
164 On capacity and equipment of the ginneries, see "Convention entre la République du Mali et la Compagnie Française", op. cit., p. 295.
165 See pages 71 f.
166 See VIe Congrès, loc. cit., pp. 92–5.
167 In order to function as such, the merchants had to fulfill a number of conditions which I cannot go into here (see: *Marchès Tropicaux et Méditerranéens*, 894/1962, p. 2965).
168 See page 166, footnote 152.
169 See "Un point capital de notre politique économique: la commercialisation des produits agricoles", in: *Le Mali*, 5/1965, p. 5.
170 By transforming the colonial-administration S. I. P. (see p. 106 footnote 76) into S. M. D. R. an important section of the future co-operative system was created on a district level. At this time, the first G. R. P. S. M. were founded.
171 See Chambre de Commerce, d'Agriculture et d'Industrie de Bamako, *Circulaire Mensuelle d'Information*, September 1962.
172 See "Une nouvelle phase du mouvement coopératif au Mali", in: *Le Mali*, 1/1966, p. 7.
173 See "Un point capital de notre politique économique: la commercialisation des produits agricoles", in: *Le Mali*, 5/1965, p. 8.
174 As far as I know, there are no figures published on this. My information came from the Ministry for Development.
175 See "Décret du 5 nov. 1964"; Chambre de Commerce, d'Agriculture et d'Industrie de Bamako. *Circulaire Mensuelle d'Information*, December 1964.
176 For details see "Statut Général des Commerçants"; Chambre de Commerce, d'Agriculture et d'Industrie de Bamako, *Circulaire Mensuelle d'Information*, May 1965.
177 In his work on the co-operatives, Lenin always points out that their character is determined by the totality of the national economic and political conditions (see V. I. Lenin, *On Co-operation*, in: *Collected Works*, Moscow 1966, pp. 472–5).
178 Koutiala district (see M'Pésoba: "Un exemple de réussite de la coopération", in: *Le Mali*, 1/1965, pp. 10–12).
179 The bakery and dispensary were financed out of the sales' profits in 1963/4 (183,000 for the whole Fédération Primaire, which makes 3,700 FM per G. R. P. S. M.).

180 In Joliba, a millet mill was bought and the equipment for a chicken farm. In the villages of the Ségou district investigated, there were also examples for the beginnings of co-operative acquisition of means of production and transport. These were sprayers (Nianzana 1965, Kintan-B. 1964) or rice-threshing machines (Fédération Primaire Tamani).
181 On questions of the relation between traditional structures and modern forms of co-operative production, see pages 87f.
182 For the concrete yields from the collective fields, see pages 87f.
183 Such relations have also been established between producers who have emancipated themselves economically within the extended family. However, these relations were still often overlapped by traditional relations.
184 I.e. the co-operative relations were far from being exclusively relations between producers independent of the extended family, but a large number of the producers' co-operative relations — despite the fact that judicially they were individual members — were mediated by the extended family. This meant that all those traditional factors which inhibit the development of the productive forces were maintained. Therefore, Samir Amin advocates that the cooperatives should be formed only by individual producers. He writes: "Here it is a question of a co-operative which is based solely on the voluntary membership of small dynamic producers who have emancipated themselves from the traditional family and social fetters." (S. Amin, op. cit., p. 232) This idea has its positive aspects. However, in my opinion, it does not take into account that — theoretically — a co-operative can definitely act as a lever to dissolve traditional structures.
185 With an official (i.e. via co-operatives) marketed production of 1.474 billion FM and an estimated gross production of the most important crops of 13.56 billion FM and a commodity production of 2.54 billion FM (in 1964/5).
186 The size of the rural population and the number of farms in the five southern regions was the basis for this calculation, because most of the agrarian products are produced in this area. It is 3,686,000 and 301,300 (see *Enquête agricole 1964/65*, op. cit., pp. 9ff.)
187 However, one must take into account that at this time, several factors were at work (price increases, etc.) which will be described at the end of this chapter.
188 According to information from the Z. E. R. Barouéli.
189 See page 147.
190 Total figures exist only for this year.
191 See "Le Développement de notre monde rural", in: *Le Mali*, 3/1965, pp. 17—18.
192 The following survey applies only to the four first regions, as in the source given in footnote 191, the Mopti and Gao regions are not separated.
193 M. Keita in his speech for the opening of the National Assembly on 23.2.1965, in: *L'Essor*, 1. 3. 1965.
194 See "Renforcement de l'Action du Parti en Direction des Paysans", in: *L'Essor*, 21. 5. 1965.

Spontaneous decay of traditional structures

195 Here, family relations and long-term debts of the producers to the merchants played a not inconsiderable role.
196 See *Comptes économiques 1959*, op. cit., p. 90.
197 See *Comptes économiques 1964/65*, op. cit., pp. 7–8 and *Annuaire statistique 1965*, op. cit., p. 45.
198 There were obviously no serious efforts made to enforce the marketing monopoly of the co-operative state bodies in this sector.
199 Rice cannot be taken into consideration, because the *Comptes économiques 1964/65* (op. cit., pp. 105–6) does not distinguish between the O. P. A. M. (which marketed in the traditional sector) and the Office du Niger when giving the profits.
200 See ibid., The O. P. A. M. on the other hand, had a deficit of 88,4 million FM (see ibid. through marketing the same products in the fiscal year 1964/5).
201 See the table on p. 151.
202 C. F. D. T. *Rapport 1965/66*, loc. cit., p. 39.
203 With urbanization and changes in eating habits of the rural population, the demand for peanuts and peanut oil rose on the home market while the demand for cotton remained relatively stable because, on the one hand, the country population had always used cotton for making textiles – so that no new market emerged – and on the other, urbanization did not lead to higher requirements of cotton, as the city population usually bought ready-made textiles or imported cloth. Even in the countryside, industrially made textiles and cloth penetrated the market. The main market for cotton was the "parallel market" in the Sahel area where cotton could not be grown even in the small amounts needed by the people living there. For example, the cotton bought up by the merchants from the Barouéli area was sufficient to satisfy the needs of the whole Nyamina-Mourdiah-Nara area on the left side of the Niger River (Information from Z. E. R. Barouéli).
204 Programme Mil, op. cit., pp. 13–14.
205 See pages 38 ff.
206 See pages 95 ff.
207 *Comptes économiques 1959*, op. cit., p. 33 and *Annuaire statistique 1967*, op. cit., p. 158.
208 See *Evaluation de la Situation économique*, op. cit., p. 6.
209 In view of the fact that, e. g. it is relatively easy to peel and steam rice within the family, it was economically much more to the advantage of the peasant to sell this processed rice on the market for a price of 34 FM per kilogramme, than to give his unpeeled rice to the official marketing bodies for a buying price of 12.50 FM per kilo (see Riziculture, *Programme Quinquennal*, op. cit., p. 11).
210 See speech by M. Keita for the participants of the first course for trade union cadres, in: *L'Essor*, 21. 3. 1965.
211 See *Programme Mil*, op. cit., pp. 13–14.
212 150 FM per taxpayer, (divided up into 50 FM for the G. R. P. S. M., 50 FM for the G. R. A., 50 FM for the Fédération Primaire) was a lot of money for the poor rural population.

213 As the G. R. P. S. M. brought no obvious economic advantages, the dues paid to the co-operative were seen as an additional tax.
214 *L'Essor*, 4. 9. 1967, p. 3.
215 Naturally, this problem, like the question of the bureaucratic bourgeoisie in general, is much more complex. However, as there exists neither concrete and differentiated material nor a substantiated study on this, and as I had to base myself largely on my own experiences and observations in the San district (1964/5) and in the Ségou district (1967), I must limit myself to these two aspects which appear to me to be important.
216 And here the issue was not only — perhaps not even mainly — the big-time black-marketing run generally with the help of the merchants, but the problem was the officials who were "at the source" and supplied their huge numbers of friends and relatives with goods as a matter of course. It was these thousands of small illegal transactions which inevitably unbalanced the young, state-co-operative market and undermined its functioning.
217 *Programme Mil*, op. cit., p. 13.
218 It was similar in other areas. E.g. from the millet study (ibid., p. 36) it is clear that during the 1964/5 season in the Ségou district 3,178 tons of rice were marketed, while the official annual statistics for the whole of Mali in 1964/5 (see *Annuaire statistique 1965*, op. cit., p. 45) give only 2,029 tons. This means that a very large percentage of the rice marketed by the official bodies "disappeared" there.
219 See M. Keita's speech on the sixth anniversary of independence, in: *L'Essor*, 26. 9. 1966, p. 4; see also G. Julis, op. cit., pp. 7—8.
220 Modibo Keita warned about this tendency at the 5th economic conference of the Ségou region, with the following words: ". . . we, who are politically responsible, must remain on guard, very much on guard, and . . . see to it that the feudal spirit, the spirit of the chiefs, does not become widespread, the spirit which cannot bear discussion" (*L'Essor*, 6. 2. 1967, p. 4).
221 During such a campaign, a group of workers from the development service, another from the S. M. D. R. or another from the state and party apparatus would come to several villages to register the goods on behalf of the authorised buying offices. "Finally, the peasants do not know how much they should deliver and, therefore, fear that if once they make a delivery, they will be made to do so again and again, while others, who live further away from the roads, deliver nothing." (See *Programme Mil*, op. cit., p. 13).
222 Ibid., p. 14.
223 See *Annuaire statistique 1966*, op. cit., p. 69; *Comptes économiques 1959*, op. cit., pp. 32—7.
224 See *Comptes économiques 1964/65*, op. cit., pp. 154—5 and p. 188. I have deducted the 1959 export figures for each of the agricultural products on the basis of the 1959 export quantities (see *Comptes économiques 1959*, op. cit., p. 130) with the help of the 1964/5 export prices. For the 1964/5 figures for animals and fish, one must take into account that these figures are for total export. The unofficial export contained herein is considerable — cattle:

1,464.0 million FM, goats and sheep: 475.0 million FM, fish: 600. million FM (see *Comptes économiques 1964/65*, op. cit., p. 154).
225 See *Comptes économiques 1964/5*, op. cit., p. 15.
226 See *Annuaire statistique 1966*, op. cit., p. 132.
227 See *Evolution de la Situation économique*, op. cit., pp. 15—18.
228 See "Un point capital de notre politique économique. La commercialisation des produits agricoles", in: *Le Mali*, 5/1965, pp. 5—9.
229 This applies particularly to the quick growth of the Bamako population. It increased within a few years from 130,800 (1960) to 161,284 (1965/66) which is a growth of 24% within just six years (see, M. L. Viellien-Rossi, "Bamako — capitale du Mali", in: *Bulletin IFAN*, Série B, 1—2/1966, p. 264 and *Annuaire statistique 1966*, op. cit., p. 29).
230 See "La campagne de commercialisation: gage de l'édification d'une économie nationale indépendante", in: *L'Essor*, 19. 2. 1968, p. 7.
231 See *Comptes économiques 1964/65*, op. cit., p. 8 and p. 25 and *Comptes économiques 1959*, op. cit., p. 134. One must take into account that it was intended in the plan to raise the millet export alone, by 50,000 tons (see *Rapport sur le Plan Quinquennal*, op. cit., p. 15).
232 See *Annuaire statistique 1966*, op. cit., p. 140.
233 On the question of agrarian-bourgeois elements, see pages 189 ff.
234 See pages 28 f.
235 See "La mobilisation générale", in: *Le Mali*, 1/1966, pp. 1—3. After the August 1967 events, the production zones were partly reoccupied.
236 See *L'Essor*, 30. 1. 1967, p. 3 and *L'Essor*, 5. 2. 1968, p. 6. Details of the action are also described there.
237 See *L'Essor*, 19. 2. 1968, p. 7.
238 See pages 28 f.
239 See *Annuaire statistique 1966*, op. cit., p. 143 and *L'Essor*, 12. 6. 1967.
240 See *L'Essor*, 19. 2. 1968, p. 7 and 5. 2. 1968, p. 6.
241 In the Ségou region in 1966/7, the co-operatives were given an interest in the marketing and the sale of consumer goods for the first time.
242 The following means of production and transport were made available by the S. M. D. R. in 1966/7: 12,740 ploughs, 1,900 carts, 1,500 multi-purpose tools, 1,000 sprayers (see *L'Essor*, 25. 9. 1967).
243 See *L'Essor*, 12. 6. 1967.
244 For tasks and methods, see *Literacy: three pilot projects*, UNESCO 1966 MC 66/VIII. 114 x/A, p. 15—16.
245 *Annuaire statistique*, op. cit., p. 105.
246 See *L'Essor*, 22. 1. 1968.
247 In the report from the 1968 co-operative seminar, it is stated: "It must now be clear to everyone that the collective field is the nucleus of the large-scale collective production that we want to carry out. It is to be seen as a model which must be extended step by step to the disadvantage of the individual fields" (*Rapport de synthèse*, op. cit., p. 28).
248 See ibid., p. 33—4.

5. The gradual development of capitalist production

In the struggle for the non-capitalist transformation of the village, the revolutionary democratic leaders in Mali found themselves confronted with the actual existence or the gradual emergence of elements of capitalist production relations in agriculture. Their extent and character were largely determined by the fact that in the Malinese village of the 1950s and 1960s – arising out of colonial and neo-colonial exploitation, dependence and backwardness – the economic and social conditions (level of productive forces, development of market relations, concentration of money as the main preconditions for its transformation into capital, separation of producers from their means of production) for broad development of capitalist production relations were very limited. The colonial and neo-colonial deformation of the developing capitalist mode of production expressed itself in the following: The elements of capitalist production relations taking root in agriculture, did not, at first, as one could expect, lead to destruction of the traditional mode of production, to a splitting up of the community into small commodity producers and their social differentiation. Instead, capitalist elements developed on the basis of continued persistence and deformation of the traditional relation and their gradual transformation into relations of exploitation and dependence with at first a *pre*-capitalist and a tendency to *semi*-capitalist character. Apart from that, these elementary forms of capitalist production arose side by side with and largely independent of the traditional relations, and thus took on the character of a socio-economic enclave.[1]

5.1. Veiled forms of exploitation through traditional conditions

The first very characteristic form of exploitation through traditional social relations was for the Fakoroba personally to acquire the surplus product of the extended family.

While in the pre-colonial era the lack of market relations – apart from other factors[2] – set strict economic limits to the Fakoroba's opportunities of personally acquiring the extended family's surplus product, although he was legally entitled to do so as its representative, a completely new situation arose as the family became integrated into more developed exchange relations. The FAKOROBA now had the FOROBA under his control (partly in the very flexible form of money) within a system which not only offered the possibility of selling surplus products on the market, but actually stimulated it. This awakened in him the desire to personally acquire part or even the whole of the extended family's surplus product [3].

The contradiction arose, on the one hand, between the norms of the traditional system which included the FAKOROBA having a determining say and, on the other, the striving of the producers themselves to make profits from their products. To the same extent as the objective possibility for the FAKOROBA to acquire the family's products changed into a subjective desire, he also became interested in increasing the surplus product and selling it on the market — i.e. in using modern tools, in extending the arable land and in planting profitable crops. At the same time, his interest in the traditional structures, especially in preserving and concolidating the FOROBA mechanism, also increased. Apart from a large number of other traditional instruments, he made particular use of the bride-price (FURU-NA-FOLO), which was steadily increased [4] to make the young members of the extended family more dependent on the community and thereby also on the FAKOROBA. The higher the bride-price, the less did the young men have an opportunity to leave the extended family against the will of the FAKOROBA. As Seydou Badian wrote, the "... patriarchal family structures ... turned into a true system of exploitation of the young by the old ..." [5]

This tendency was strongest in areas where commodity-money relations were relatively well developed and the extended family structures were still very strong; this was so in the area on the upper arm of the Niger and also in Ségou.[6] Here were big farms with extended family structures which, apart from the means of subsistence, produced large amounts of commodities (rice, cotton, peanuts) with relatively modern means of production. The producers on these farms were fed and clothed in accordance with the traditional system of production and distribution by the FAKOROBA; the whole of the profits from commodity production remained in the hands of the extended family head.

E. Leynaud, who examined this tendency in detail at the end of the 1950s in the Haute-Vallée, came to the following conclusion: "The collective organisation of labour leads to the growth of a class of big land-owners, because the economic potential depends on the family labour power. These rich landowners, LUTIGI and FA of the extended family,[7] form interest groups in every village. It can be observed that they oppose the striving of youth — whose position is that of a type of proletariat — towards social and economic emancipation." [8]

Even if Leynaud is one of the few western social anthropologists and sociologists who recognises and emphasises the changes taking place in the internal relations of decisive institutions in the pre-colonial society, one cannot agree with his socio-economic interpretation of this phenomenon. The FAKOROBA's exploitation of the family members is definitely not yet of a capitalist nature.[9] In order to place it in its correct socio-economic context, one must see that within the traditional community, the simplest form of which is the extended family, the low level of the productive forces with its communal ownership gives rise to attitudes in the worker towards his conditions of reproduction which are rooted in his existence as a member of the community. In this existence the individual never enters into free relations to his conditions of production, never becomes the owner, but is free of all ownership, is up to a point himself owned by the community to which he belongs. His surplus product thus automatically belongs to the community.[10] By personally acquiring this surplus product, which he has the legal right merely to administer as incarnation and "official" of the primary community, the FAKOROBA makes himself independent of the community, raises himself above it and thus risks destroying the basic socio-economic relations. But it is only on the basis of these relations that the FAKOROBA is able to acquire the LU's surplus product. Personal acquisition by the family head of the family members' surplus labour means that the production and distribution within the LU must function to ensure the official role of the FAKOROBA. However, this system can function only so long as it is historically, i.e. economically, necessary. Every further development of the productive forces must deprive it of its objective basis — its economic justification — and inevitably eliminate the basis for the FAKOROBA being able to exploit the family members. This does not mean that the extended family cannot persist beyond this point due to its internal strength, due to the authority of the FAKOROBA and due to general tradition. In fact, the degree of exploitation can be highest under such circumstances. However, it is under exactly these circumstances that the contradiction between the exploiter and representative of the community, on the one hand, and the striving for emancipation of the family members and the interest of the family heads in integration, on the other, is sharpest, the basic relation is most disturbed and the complete decay of the community closest.

Thus there are *two* characteristic basic tendencies for the spontaneous decay of extended family relations in the Malinese village: one is the dissolution of relations and development of nuclear family producers [11] and the other is the *persistence* and indeed the temporary consolidation of extended family relations and their transformation into exploitative relations by the family members through the FAKOROBA.

As a result of these two tendencies in the process of decay, two types of farms arise within the community. First a relatively broad, but generally poor stratum of small producers, growing in number, which, as a result of colonial exploitation, does not possess the economic prerequisites for modernising their means of production, extends the area of its fields, and raises the volume of its production.[12] Secondly, a group of farms on the basis of extended families (with largely transformed inner structure), with more favourable conditions of accumulation caused by the mechanism of production and distribution at this primitive level of productive forces, is better able to compensate more easily for the after-effects of colonial exploitation than the small producers. Such a group is thus, far more capable of buying modern means of production and extending its area of cultivation.

Both types of farms are different, not only in internal structure (nuclear or extended family), but also in economic situation. The data given by the 1960 *Enquête agricole* make this obvious.[13] It shows that a) ploughs (an essential part of more developed productive forces) are concentrated mainly on the extended family farms and b) the cultivated land of these farms is considerably larger in hectares *per capita* and per person of working age than for the nuclear family farms. Thus during the decay and transformation of extended family relations, there arises an economic and social polarisation and differentiation between small and large farms.

And for the colonial conditions under which this process takes place, it is characteristic that the small farms are formed mainly by small producers who have freed themselves from the extended family structure, and the latter are largely extended family farms[14] where the internal relations have undergone a considerable transformation.

After independence, this social differentiation continued in most of the traditional sectors of agriculture. However, a new factor arose through the changed economic conditions in the developed areas.[15] My investigations in Barouéli — a relatively developed area — showed that seven years after independence, a new tendency was making itself felt in the social differentiation accompanying spontaneous decay of the traditional structures. The old polarisation that had taken place between extended and nuclear family farms while the traditional structures were still strong had largely disappeared.[16] In general, the individual producers possessed at least as many ploughs, oxen and thus also hectares *per capita* and labourer, as did the extended family farms.

This apparent social levelling out (compared to the polarisation at the end of colonialism) was not only the external expression of an already clearly recognisable change in the type of social differentiation taking place. It was based on the greater maturity of the commodity-money relations and the higher level of the productive forces; the economic laws of (small) commodity production were at work and traditional structures were becoming weaker. This differentiation was now no longer primarily expressed in differen-

Distribution of farms, population and means of production in accordance with size of farms in hectares

Size of Farms	Percentage of Total Farms	Percentage of Population	Percentage of Total Area	Share of Ploughs %	Persons per Farm	Active Labourer per Farm	Area per Person	Area per Active Labourer
0— 1	14.3	9.1	1.8	4.5	6.6	3.0	0.07	0.16
1— 2	18.3	13.2	6.2	5.0	7.5	4.2	0.20	0.36
2— 3	18.6	14.0	10.6	10.7	7.6	3.8	0.35	0.65
3— 4	12.5	10.7	9.8	10.3	8.7	4.7	0.40	0.74
4— 5	9.1	8.2	9.4	12.1	9.4	5.4	0.50	0.90
5— 6	6.3	6.8	7.9	9.1	14.2	8.1	0.46	0.84
6— 7	5.0	7.6	7.4	7.3	18.7	10.5	0.38	0.66
7— 8	2.6	2.9	4.5	4.1	14.7	6.8	0.34	0.61
8— 9	2.5	2.7	4.8	2.2	12.9	7.3	0.53	1.10
9—10	2.2	4.1	4.7	4.6	17.6	9.5	0.65	1.14
10—20	6.8	12.8	20.8	20.0	18.9	10.5	0.54	1.00
20—30	1.1	3.1	5.9	5.3	45.1	25.0	0.73	1.31
30 and over	0.7	4.8	6.2	4.8	70.3	34.5	0.50	0.88
Total	100	100	100	100	10.2	5.3	0.43	0.82

tiation between the various types of farms (extended and nuclear family farms), but showed itself increasingly between those producers who had freed themselves from traditional structures.

An investigation of nuclear family farms (variant IV – see chapter 4.1.) showed that these new tendencies were already very clear in the Barouéli Z. E. R. This fourth variant can be divided into three sub-groups in accordance with the size of the farms which are now no longer dependent on the number of labourers working on them:

1. A relatively large group of poor peasants owned farms of up to 2 hectares. They made up 29.3% of all the farms and 25.6% of the population in variant IV [17], but owned only 14.1% of the cultivated soil and 6.7% of all ploughs. Only 8.3% of the farms in this group owned a plough at all, 83.4% owned up to only half a hectare *per capita*, the rest were from 0.51 to 0.99 hectares in size.

2. Another large group (41.4% of all farms) owned land between 2.1 and 4 hectares. Their share of the population and cultivated land was almost equal (35.1% and 34.1%). They owned 33.3% of the ploughs and 29.4% of all these farms possessed a plough. Within this group 35.3% of the farms were up to half a hectare *per capita*, 17.6% were from 0.51 to 0.99 *per capita* and 47.1% were one and more hectares *per capita*. At the same time, the values per labourer were also in the medium figures: 70.5% of the farms had 2.1 to 3 hectares per labourer and the rest up to 2 hectares.

3. A group of larger farms made up almost a third of all farms (29.3%) with a size of 4.1 to 10 hectares. They cultivated 51.8% of the land and had 39.3% of the population. They owned 60% of all ploughs and 69.2% of these farms possessed a plough. None of the farms in this group had up to 2 hectares per labourer and half a hectare *per capita*. The number of farms with an area of one and more hectares *per capita* grew with the size of the farms. Farms with 4.1 to 6 hectares made up 42.8%, with 6.1 to 8 hectares 50% and the largest (8.1 to 10 hectares) 66.7%.

Distribution of farms in variant IV according to number of hectares and area per inhabitant (in percent)

Hectares	Hectares per Person			Percentage of total farms
	0–0.5	0.51–0.99	1 and over	
0 – 2	83.4	16.6	–	29.3
2.1– 4	35.3	17.6	47.1	41.4
4.1–10	–	50.0	50.0	29.3
Percentage of total farms	39.0	26.8	34.2	100

Distribution of farms in variant IV according to number of hectares and their share of the total farms, population, persons of working age area and ploughs (in percent)

Hectares	Farms	Population	Labourers	Area	Ploughs
0 — 2	29.3	25.6	19.7	14.1	6.7
2.1— 4	41.4	35.1	39.5	34.1	33.3
4.1—10	29.3	39.3	40.8	51.8	60.0

Distribution of farms in variant IV according to number of hectares, ploughs and size of area per ten persons and per person of working age

Hectares	per 10 Persons Ploughs	Area	per person of working age Ploughs	Area
0 — 2	0.19	3.7	0.07	1.47
4.1— 6	0.68	6.7	0.18	1.77
6.1—10	1.09	9.1	0.31	2.59
IV	0.71	6.9	0.21	2.0
I —IV	0.59	5.5	0.20	1.9

The following table gives a revealing survey on the social differentiation among the nuclear family producers.

So a new aspect of social differentiation of the individual producers emerged through the spontaneous effect of the laws of commodity production as could be seen in the Barouéli Z. E. R. This new aspect was the beginning of a new phase of spontaneous socio-economic change. After the final disintegration of the extended family, the producer within the nuclear family became a small commodity producer and took the place of the extended family. The process of social differentiation was now determined solely by those producers who had freed themselves from the traditional relations.

Doubtless, this phase — based on spontaneity — can only be an intermediate stage on the road to separation of the producer from his means of production and thus eventually to capitalism. By the end of the 1960s, the spontaneous process of socio-economic change had not by any means yet reached this stage. The main result of the spontaneous decay is — and only in relatively developed areas — that, as the outcome of a growing differentiation within the group of nuclear family farms, producers developed who possessed relatively modern means of production and cultivated a relatively large area *per capita* and person of working age, and these climb into that group of large farms which were formed during the colonial period and after independence in the more backward areas, exclusively by the extended family farms.

The economic and social differentiation among the community's peasants led to changes in the relations between them. Various forms of exploitation and dependence developed. And for the level of the economic and social processes it is characteristic that relations of exploitation unfolded at the village level mainly on the basis of traditional relations, but veiled by them. In essence, they were largely of a pre-capitalist nature, even though certain elements of capitalist exploitation became visible in an embryonic form.

Such exploiter relations developed under the cloak of the traditional institution of mutual aid (LAMA and TON) and were wrongly categorised by French bourgeois socialists as *"entr'aide"* but in fact no longer had anything to do with it.[18] They constituted themselves largely as social relations between large farms with traditional structures on the one hand, and the poor small producers on the other, and were also the expression and cause of growing social differentiation and polarisation within the community. To the same extent as the process of differentiation affected the individual producer, this aspect was also expressed in veiled exploiter relations of the LAMA and the TON. In the case study I carried out in 1967[19], those farms appeared mainly as exploiting elements which had completely freed themselves from the traditional extended family structure[20], even though this is still an exception and cannot be applied to the majority of areas.

The basis of the exploitation taking place under the cloak of traditional relations was the ownership of the most important production tool, the oxplough. Differences in the ownership of the land played a secondary role.

Large plough-owning farms also ploughed in part or in their entirety the fields of the small producers who could not afford ploughs. They did this within the framework of the "LAMA". In the developed areas, in which largely industrial crops were planted, the number of farms which allowed their fields to be ploughed was much higher than in areas growing mainly subsistence crops. This is clearly shown when comparing the rice and the millet sectors in the areas of Mopti/Macina, Djénné. In the following table[21] the peasants without ploughs are grouped according to whether they had the whole area ploughed (1) or only part of it (2), or cultivated with the *daba* only (3).

Rice-growing area			Millet-growing area		
(1)	(2)	(3)	(1)	(2)	(3)
9.1%	41.8%	49.1%	—	7.1%	92.9%

This ploughing of fields belonging to non-plough-owning peasants no longer had anything to do with the traditional mutual aid. Very little of it was done as gratis help for the needy. In Nianzana, the actual help within the framework of the LAMA was about 15%. Most of the ploughing was done in exchange for labour-service or money.[22]

The main form of payment for ploughing was labour-service. R. Cailol speaks of 72%[23], and in Nianzana I was able to calculate 61%. On an average, a producer had to work on the plough-owner's field for 3–5 days in exchange for one ploughing day.[24] So the ploughing of a hectare, which usually took 8–10 days[25], meant that he had to work for 30–40 days on the plough-owner's field, which took up 20%–25% of the time he had, for climatic reasons, to cultivate and harvest his own field. So the complete lack of mechanisation for such work on large and small farms meant for the small producer that this apparent opportunity to extent production and raise his surplus product within the framework of "mutual aid" was nothing more than more labour if he was not to neglect his own produce – labour for the benefit of the plough-owner. By ploughing 2–3 hectares outside his farm, the plough-owner gained a full labourer for his cultivation and harvest work, or the possibility of cultivating another hectare.[26]

When the ploughing was paid for in money, the effect was the same: the plough-owner acquired the surplus labour of the producer. In this form of the "LAMA", the producer without a plough had to pay 500 FM daily[27] or 4,000 to 5,000 FM for ploughing 1 hectare. This corresponded to about 40% of the value of the gross product harvested on that hectare.[28] As the small producer could not afford to lack such a large part of his rice without his own family suffering, he became forced to earn the necessary money by taking on additional wage labour.

Tied to the village during the season, he could go to the town during the period between the rains or in the season could work either on a large farm in his own village or as temporary wage labourer in his immediate vicinity. This form of *"entr'aide"* created for the large agricultural producer an additional reserve in labour power for cultivation and harvest work, either through labour or via money, so that most of the non-family labourers working on these farms came from the village itself.

Origin of temporary agricultural wage labourers
in Mopti/Macina/Djénné area (percent) [29]

Origin	Cultivation Labourers	Days Worked	Harvest Labourers	Days Worked	Total Labourers	Days Worked
Village	100	97	70	41	83	53
Subdivision	—	—	13	17	6	13
Outside of Subdivision	—	3	14[30]	36	10	31
Unknown	—	—	3	6	1	3
Total	100	100	100	100	100	100

For the owner, a plough plus a pair of oxen paid for itself after ploughing 10–12 hectares for money in the form of "mutual aid".[31] In the process of the social change within the village community, there developed large farms with relatively modern instruments of production (generally belonging to the extended family, but in more developed areas they were also individual producers) and small farms with few labourers and without modern tools (generally belonging to the nuclear family), where the former acquired part of the surplus labour of the latter. From a socio-economic viewpoint, this was a pre-capitalist form of exploitation, linked with elements of exploitation through wage labour. Here it is of lesser importance that it was veiled by traditional institutions, but it was more fundamental that, first, the small producers' lack of property forced them to sell part of their labour power to ensure subsistence for their families (although as community members they still had certain collective rights to the land and in this respect were not completely without means of production), and that, secondly, the large producers were not mainly capitalist owners but basically either large farmers with a traditional structure (extended family)[32] or individual producers whose ownership of the land moved within the framework of the community constitution and their main form of organising production was not capitalist. The exploitation of wage labourers was not the foundation for this type of farm, but a secondary factor only.

A similar functional change in social relations took place in another traditional institution, the youth organisation (TON). It was expressed by the TON doing work for payment (in natural products but usually for money). In 1960, 76% of all the TON examined by the National Statistical Institute (I.N.S.E.E.) worked for payment only.[33] My investigations showed an even stronger decline of the traditional TON activities. The ten societies investigated worked for 209 days altogether in 1966/7; of these 195 days (93.3%) were for payment. The ten societies spent only 6.7% of the working days (14) on their own TON fields. In former times, I was told, gratis labour was done for the old and needy; today this is no longer usual.

E. Leynaud had similar findings: "Once, the TON used to do their agricultural work for the old and needy; it was a type of 'social service' and this voluntary aid found its acknowledgement through symbolic presents. Today it is almost always paid labour."[34] Even if the payment demanded by the TON was fairly low – 20–35 FM per TON member and working day[35] – those community members who benefitted from the TON activities in pre-colonial times were seldom able to afford this. So the TON became an additional and very cheap source of labour for the richest and largest farms.[36] They were not only able to pay the TON for their work but, because they were generally farms belonging to extended families, they had the right to decide on the activities of the TON through the village council[37], and through the pre-colonial traditions had the necessary influence to gain the agreement of this body.[38]

R. Dumont writes quite correctly that the task of the TON became more and more "to cultivate for the big peasants to whom they delivered cheap labour . . ."[39]

An investigation into who benefitted from the TON members in the Barouéli area showed that it was generally the medium and larger farms. On an average they were 2 hectares larger than the normal medium-sized farm. And it was conspicuous that most of the TON working time went into extended family farms (50.8%). But the nuclear family farms in variant III and IV — described in chapter 4.1. — already participated in the exploitation of the TON (12.3% and 16.9% respectively). It was particularly the farms in this group benefitting from TON activity that had many more hectares *per capita* and per farm than the medium farm of the same group. These two facts prove hat the tendency to social differentiation of the individual producers affectted the structure of those benefiting from TON labour.

Structure of those benefitting from TON activities
(Barouéli 1967)

	Size of farms Normal Farm	Farm with TON activities	Area per person Normal Farm	Farm with TON activities	Share of TON activities in %
I	7.48	7.30	0.57	0.57	50.8
II	4.21	5.95	0.47	0.53	20.0
III	3.52	8.95	0.89	2.02	12.3
IV	3.62	5.58	0.67	0.75	16.9
I—IV	4.57	6.85	0.59	0.64	100.0

The large farms used the concentrated labour power of the TON mainly for the intensive work of preparing the field and looking after the cultures. This was clearly reflected in the structure of the TON activities:

Structure of the TON activities[40] (Mali 1960)

Type of Work	% of working days
Land clearing	17
Ploughing (with *daba*)	26
Sowing	8
Cultivation	36
Harvesting and Threshing	9
Laying paths and repair	4

My investigations in Barouéli confirmed the same basic structure in the second half of the 1960s.

Structure of TON activities (Barouéli 1967)

Type of Work	% of working days
Land clearing	38.3
Ploughing (with *daba*)	28.4
Sowing	1.7
Cultivation	26.3
Harvest	5.3

In his paper E. Leynaud tries to prove that the TON has turned from a "social service" into a "society of agricultural wage labourers".[41] This evaluation is correct in so far as the TON did actually develop into an institution which placed cheap labour at the disposal of a certain group of large producers. But this by no means made the TON a *society of agricultural wage labourers*[42] if one takes — as one must — the socio-economic status of its members into account. The TON members were usually the unmarried members of an extended family who — in accordance with the traditional production and reproduction mechanism — placed their labour power at the disposal of the family for five days a week and in return received their means of subsistence[43]. The other two days were devoted either to the DIONFORO or to their TON duties. Thus, in pre-colonial society the member of the extended family placed part of his labour power (on the Foroba and the DIONFORO) which was surplus to that needed for immediate subsistence and a very modest surplus product, at the disposal of the whole community to ensure subsistence for all. The change in the function of the TON is that the richest farms now acquire the labour power of the village youth for almost nothing, a labour power originally meant to contribute to the reproduction of the whole village community. The reason why the price of this labour power is so far below its actual value is because the reproduction of the labour power of the individual was ensured through his integration into the subsistence conditions of the extended family.[44] However, this meant that the labour power sold by the TON had to be limited from the beginning. According to I. N. S. E. E. figures, it was eight days a year.[45] In the Barouéli area in 1967, it was an average of 21 days a year for one TON.

So one can sum up that the relations between the young members of the extended family who were organised in the TON and the richest farms were a specific variation of acquisition of the surplus product by the FAKOROBA at village level, mixed with embryonic features of capitalism, because within this framework a small group of large farms acquired that part of the labour power of the young community members which traditionally belonged to the community as a whole, and this was done in a capitalist form (through buying labour power). And for the character of this exploitation, it is irrelevant whether the surplus product from the TON youth went to the extended family as a whole or only to the FAKOROBA personally.

A third type of exploitation veiled by traditional relations at village level was that part of the community peasants' surplus products was acquired by the village chief. This was possible already before the colonial period [46], but only under colonialism did the economic conditions for it mature. After independence, three of its aspects were noteworthy.

First, the village chief acquired part of the surplus product by turning into rent some of the people's labour and tribute to the community which he alone was originally entitled to administer. R. Dumont observed such phenomena in Macina where the community peasants had to give the former representative either goods or labour.[47]

I experienced another very typical example in 1965 in the Somo district (San). A part of this area is always flooded after the rains and is then very rich in fish. These are caught by the Bozo (the Bobo of Somo themselves are farmers) who come from various villages to the flooded area during the season. Traditionally, the Somo community has the right to a part of the catch (one-tenth to one-quarter) and originally it was distributed to all members or put into the village reserve in another form. In 1965, however, the village chief, M. T., raised himself above the community and personally acquired all the fish caught on the territory of the village.

Secondly, when looked at historically, this type of exploitation shows a certain continuity from practices of the colonial *Chefferie*. While the *chefs de canton* disappeared as a social stratum through the reform of local political structures, – the former colonial village chiefs usually remained at their posts after independence, if they came from a traditional DUGUTIGI family.[48] This was the outcome of a democratic reform of the local organs which, however, was not supplemented and consolidated by corresponding socio-economic measures, so that this democracy remained nominal. This was shown by a sociological analysis of political institutes existing in the community of the 1960s.[49]

Finally – and this is partly linked to the second aspect – the Malinese type of co-operative helped to stabilise this form of exploitation. It strengthened the social position of the traditional leaders and gave them the possibility to turn the co-operative into an instrument for exploiting the community members. The following example is typical. The village chief of Somo (already mentioned) who was also automatically chairman of the co-operative in accordance with the general rule, misused this position to enrich himself.

He sold cigarettes that had been supplied to the co-operative at S. O. M. I. E. X. prices (45 FM per packet) to the co-operative members at black market prices, i.e. for 70 FM per packet. Thus he made a profit of 25 FM per packet or 65% on the purchase price.

In the village this method of aquiring the peasants' surplus labour by the village chief did not appear in a vacuum, but was mixed with the forms of exploitation already described. So new social relations developed spontaneously in the village, in the womb of the pre-capitalist community, which assumed many forms but had one common feature. This was that a small group of community members, who were generally the former community representatives, acquired the surplus labour of the mass of community peasants. The form was still largely clothed in traditional modes of production but – while containing elements of capitalist relations – the process was very characteristic for the development of capitalist modes of production in the African village and represented nothing more or less than the original accumulation of capital. On the one hand it became possible for the potential agrarian capitalist to accumulate money and means of production, and on the other hand it accelerated the pauperisation of the mass of village producers, who became forced to sell their labour power even if there was still enough land for them.

5.2. *Navétanes, landlords, planters and "bureaucratic" agrarian bourgeoisie*

Apart from the exploitation in the village concealed by the traditional forms, relations began to develop – even though very timidly – in which the exploitation of wage labour played a considerable role. Although they were a new socio-economic quality, they still had features of the original community relations.

The *navétanat* was a relatively widespread form of embryonic capitalist production relations, mixed with pre-capitalist relations. This form of exploiting seasonal workers, which developed first (and mainly) in the peanut-growing areas of Senegal[50], corresponds in its socio-economic essence, as Marx wrote, to a "transitory form from the original form of rent to capitalist rent", and he described it as "the *métayer* system, or share-cropping under which the manager (farmer) furnishes labour (his own or another's) and also a portion of working capital, and the landlord furnishes, aside from land, another portion of working capital (e. g. cattle) and the product is divided between tenant and landlord in definite proportions which vary from country to country. On the one hand, the farmer here lacks sufficient capital required for complete capitalist management. On the other hand, the share here appropriated does not bear the pure form of rent."[51] However, there were a number of differences in the share-cropping of the *navétanat* system to the model described by Marx, which gave the *navétanes* more the character of semi-proletariat than semi-capitalist tenants.[52] The land given them was more a natural form of wages. The peanut-growing peasant (generally a FAKOROBA of an extended family farm) gave the migrant worker who comes to him at the beginning of the rainy season a piece of the extended family's land, equips him with agricultural tools and seed, feeds and accommodates him during the season. On a certain number of days laid down beforehand (usually 2–4 days), the *navétane* worked on the fields of the peanut-growing peasant (Foroba) and for the rest of the time he cultivated the land he received. After the harvest, he returned the seed (usually with 100% interest), sold the rest of his peanut harvest and returned home with the proceeds.

The geographical distribution of the share-crop type *navétanat* can be localised with relative certainty, although exact figures are missing here. There is no doubt that it is most widespread in the peanut strip along the Kayes-Bamako railway line, and centres around Kita.[53] The *navétanes* emigrated to this area especially from Yelimané-Kaarta (north of the railroad) and Sénégal-Bakoy (south-west of the railroad, stretching partly into Guinea). A few of them also came from the area west of the Niger (Bougouni).

Far less widespread, but also evident[54], was the share-crop system in irrigated rice areas, particularly on the upper arm of the Niger[55], although the migrant workers here were not called *navétanes*.

The *Enquête agricole*[56] gave some figures for the spread of the share-crop system. In 1960, 5.1%[57] of the cultivated area was rented. One can assume that these production conditions were mostly such a share-crop system.

No figures were given for the number of migrant share-croppers and landlords (*diafigui*). Taking into consideration that the rented land per *navétane* was generally not larger than one to two hectares, and the average landlord let land to two to six share-croppers, one can estimate that at the end of the fifties there were twenty to thirty thousand share-croppers and some 10,000 landlords.[58] According to my survey, this ratio must have remained constant in the sixties.

Apart from the *navétanat*, there existed a second type of farm in the 1950s on which the main (or at least a significant) part of the products were produced through wage labour: the largescale farm. R. Dumont describes a large farmer of this type who came from M'Pésoba[59] and points out that this peasant was the first of this importance whom he had encountered.[60] This peasant possessed a cultivated area of 20 hectares,[61] four ploughs and eight draught oxen, two donkeys for transport and an ox-cart with which he brought some 40–50 tons of manure on to his fields. Apart from four male labourers from his own family (including himself),[62] he employed two permanent wage labourers who were accommodated, fed and clothed by him and received a monthly wage of 600 Fr.-CFA. During peak periods (cultivating work) he employed a Ton group of 15–20 youths for five days for no other payment than their food. The total income of the farm in cash – almost all of it from the sale of export crops[63] – amounted to 70,000 Fr.-CFA.

The structure of the farm is basically that of the extended family farm and makes clear that even in these cases, where wage labourers were not only employed for short periods and were largely responsible for creating the total product, their exploitation was closely linked to pre-capitalist relations of production.

The number of farmers who employed a considerable number of wage labourers (often seasonal workers)[64] apart from their own family, is very difficult to ascertain, as no figures on this exist which are even approximately accurate.[65] However, one can presume that before 1960, it was no more than a few hundred.[66] Equally, the number of agricultural wage labourers compared to the persons of working age on farms, must have been relatively few.[67]

After independence, the tendency to exploit agricultural wage labourers increased. The very incomplete latest statistics[68] for agriculture (of 1966) shows a tenfold growth of wage labour as compared to 1956[69]. Elements of exploitation penetrated into the undeveloped areas[70] and pre-capitalist forms of exploitation were substituted in the developed areas by wage labour.[71]

On a national scale, three factors were typical of this process. First, as the capitalist modes of production developed and the economic conditions changed, so did the geographical situation of the economic centres as, for example, in the areas west of Bamako (to Kayes), which were among the main areas for spontaneous development of certain elements of capitalist exploitation before independence (*navétanat*) through the stagnation of peanut production and because the border with Senegal was closed from 1960 to 1963 which led to this area generally losing in economic significance. However, re-orientation of foreign trade via the Ivory Coast during these years meant that the Sikasso-Bamako, Sikasso-Koutiala-Ségou and Sikasso-Koutiala-San-Mopti axis gained in economic importance. Linked to this, directly or indirectly, was an increase in production of lemons, oranges and pineapples in Sikasso and the development of cotton production in Koutiala. Added was increased irrigation for rice planting at the central arm of the Niger River and its tributaries of the Office du Niger).[72]

These factors created the economic prerequisites for stronger development of capitalist elements in these areas. Here – and this is the second factor – more developed forms of capitalist exploitation through wage labour developed after 1960. The embodiment of these embryonic capitalist relations of production in this area was no longer the share-cropper, but the planter (largely in the fruit-growing areas) and the capitalist tenant (in the rice-growing areas).

The first version was particularly strong in Sikasso because there existed good cultivation conditions for very profitable crops. F. Morlet[73] visited the estate of a Berthé-Ibrahima in Sikasso in 1966. It covered an area of 35 hectares and grew organges, lemons, grapefruit, mangoes, avocado, pineapple and other fruit with the help of wage labourers.[74] Estates of this size were also to be found in other areas; however, they mainly grew the refined mango. In the area of Ségou, I visited several such privately-owned mango estates, which had approximately 200–500 mango trees and permanently employed 5–10 wage labourers on cultivation. The limited market was the decisive obstacle to extending production and thus intensifying the capitalist relationship. "One single problem, but weighty: how to ensure the efficient sale of such fruit production . . ." writes Morlet, repeating the problems of his host.[75]

The second version arose, naturally enough, almost exclusively in the irrigated rice plains. Among approximately 40 tenants (with an average of 3–5 hectares) on the plains of Konosso[76] were three capitalist tenants who cultivated areas of 20–40 hectares with the help of tractors and wage labour. On the three plains of Konodimini, 97 out of the total of 1,350 tenants in 1967 each cultivated 10–19 hectares, and 14 cultivated 20–31 hectares, while the average was 3 hectares per tenant.[77] On the plains of Kouniana, Dumont noted several capitalist tenants with up to 80 hectares of leased land at the beginning of the sixties.[78]

The origins of these large areas is interesting. Originally, the man who participated most in the digging work for the irrigation system received the most irrigated land.[79] This is why the rent was later very low.[80] As the capitalist tenant either had insufficient capital to have this work done by wage labourers or – more usually – did not want to spend so much money, their share of the leased land was very small and they often had none at all.

However, the unfavourable development of the rice prices[81] caused the mass of the tenants either – in those areas where rice was already being consumed by the local population – to limit their cultivation to an area sufficient only for their own needs, or – in areas where rice remained the only saleable crop for the tenant (e.g. on the plains of Kouniana)[82] – to give up growing rice altogether and take up the more profitable cotton as a cash crop. In this way, the irrigated plains were often unused, so that for economic reasons the administration agreed to capitalist tenants cultivating larger areas, although they had done little or none of the digging work and were able to profit from the work of the small producers.

The third feature of capitalist production relations which developed in Malinese agriculture after independence was that to a considerable extent they did not develop out of the village itself, but were carried into the village from outside.

Even if the under-developed type of capitalist exploitation which evolved from the traditional structures continued to exist after independence (even intensifying and extending geographically), there was seldom a direct road from here to the more developed form of wage labour, because there was hardly any continuity between the two — the two forms were each based on a different type of exploiter, the potential or actual agrarian bourgeoisie. These were recruited, in the new form, not from the village but from the city population. The four big capitalist tenants on the Konosso plain came from San and Ségou, and of the big tenants on the Konodimini plain one-third of those with 10–19 hectares came from Ségou and in the group with more than 20 hectares, over half came from the regional capital. This type of capitalist tenant and planter had usually accumulated his first capital in the main, not in agriculture, but in the non-productive sphere. His main profession was originally merchant, official or party functionary, and he used the financial possibilities these offered which, in the last two cases, were definitely not limited to his salary. While the merchants — despite strong state encouragement[83] — did not invest much in agriculture because trade, transport, real estate and money-lending were much more profitable in the period after independence, the agrarian bourgeoisie began to grow out of the bureaucratic bourgeoisie in Mali.

The development of a bureaucratic bourgeoisie took place against the will and intentions of the revolutionary-democratic leaders who banned all lucrative activities for officials, against a background of cut salaries and democratic (although mostly ineffective) controls by trade unions, youth organisations and other forces.[84] Although they were not able to stop them altogether, the controls did curb these activities and resulted in the bureaucratic bourgecisie being less strong in Mali than in other countries.[85]

The moral and legal limitations concerned mostly the lucrative possibilities offered by the city (taxis, renting flats, etc.). In agriculture, these opportunities did not exist because they were out of sight of party headquarters, and for ideological reasons, they were not suspected of profit-making, because the soil and its tillers were considered Sacrosanct.[86]

So, basically, every official and full-time functionary — from the president[87] to the head of an *Arrondissement* — had his own farm, even if not everyone worked it in a capitalist way: this would depend largely on his position in the party or state apparatus — in a double sense. First, a senior position brought with it a relatively high and regular income and thus a prerequisite for a capitalist farm; in addition, and this seems even more important, it brought influence, prestige and power, which were of decisive importance for the material support of a capitalist farm. The influence made it possible to obtain a good piece of land in a rice area, the prestige prevented any irrigation official from even thinking of asking a senior functionary to help with the annual digging work, and the power made possible the use of state-owned means of production and transport on his private farm, and through his official connections a profitable sale of his products was guaranteed and so on. However, the way their piece of land was cultivated depended largely on the political and ideological attitude of each functionary. Many honest revolutionary cadres rejected exploitation of wage labourers on principle. Usually they had a small piece of land which they worked with their families.[88]

A large group of older functionaries was still strongly influenced by traditionalist conceptions of a "classless" African society, and for them – at least at the beginning of the 1960s – "being a good militant" was no contradiction to exploiting wage labour. Among the mass of the functionaries, the "militant" attitudes gradually disappeared and their bourgeois attitudes won the day.[89] During the course of social differentiation they became a special part of the developing national bourgeoisie. Only very few found the road to the revolutionary forces.

The spontaneous development of elements of capitalist relations of production in agriculture had a long-term and basic significance for the non-capitalist road. During this process, bourgeois elements were formed which had an objective class interest in a capitalist road. However, in view of the immaturity of the social processes, in the 1960s these social forces were strongly interlinked with traditional structures, the objective process of their formation into a class was still at its beginnings and they did not yet act as a united social force. At that stage in the development of Mali's national-democratic revolution, they did not represent an immediate danger to non-capitalist changes in the village, because of their heterogeneousness and because they played an insignificant role in social reality. But they were potentially a group which could one day become a strong and conscious advocate for capitalism in agriculture.

In the concrete phase of non-capitalist development in which the Republic of Mali found itself in the 1960s, the various elements of capitalist production relations had a very specific and sometimes contradictory significance for the processes of change taking place.

All elements of capitalist exploitation in the village – unfolding on the basis of traditional structures[90] – like every development of capitalist production relations, naturally enough, bring about tendencies which endanger the non-capitalist road.

However, in the concrete situation of the Malinese village in the 1960s, the main political and economic significance lay not so much in the danger of capitalist development, but in that it inhibited the speedy elimination of traditional structures and the rapid economic, social and political emancipation of the peasant. The elements of capitalist modes of production cemented traditional structures altered their original content and turned them into veiled but ruthless instruments for exploiting the community peasant. These elements pushed to extremes the contradictions arising out of the traditional social relations as well as the reactionary features, and blocked the road to economic and social progress. The development of embryonic capitalist forms of exploitation within the traditional structures particularly inhibited the formation and unfolding of those social forces which, in this phase, are objectively the most important social driving power of the village for the development of productive forces and social change, and which would be the main ally of the revolutionary-democratic forces. This means that the embryonic capitalist elements become a growing obstacle for non-capitalist changes.

The more developed type of exploitation through wage labour, as described through the example of the planters and tenants (Chapter 5.2.), had hardly any direct influence on the non-capitalist road, because it took place largely independent of the village – both socially and economically – and under special conditions. In the national class and power set-up this exploitation also had no weight of its own because it was still too sporadic and limited in its possibilities of development. Apart from its potential significance, this agrarian bourgeoisie became relevant as an obstacle to the non-capitalist path when its class position made itself felt in work for the state apparatus and party. In this constellation the agrarian bourgeoisie were a part of the general process of social, political and ideological differentiation of the petty-bourgeois leaders, including the middle stratum of party cadres and state officials.[91] These bourgeois elements endangered the road to social progress on a national scale – and thus indirectly also in the village – and undermined and disturbed the functioning of the political and administrative instruments for progress in the village from the inside.[92] So the agrarian bourgeois variation of the bureaucratic bourgeoisie became a decisive hindrance for the non-capitalist development of agriculture and for consolidating the alliance with the peasantry.

The revolutionary-democratic leaders of the Sudanese Union did not at first recognise the basic and immediate dangers for non-capitalist development arising out of spontaneously emerging bourgeois elements. Although they had a basically anticapitalist conception, their Narodnik-like illusions about the African road to socialism grossly underestimated the social processes and class struggle at work.[93] Such an attitude inevitably favoured the formation of bourgeois forces. This applies especially to the agrarian bourgeois phenomena in the party and state apparatus. These were underrated in the first half of the 1960s by the leadership, but objectively encouraged by the slogan "back to the soil" issued at the October 1958 party conference.[94] This slogan was, of course, not propagated to encourage capitalist production relations in agriculture,[95] but it justified *a priori* all agricultural activity.

The first criticism of bourgeois elements forming in agriculture came as early as 1962;[96] the realisation that this process represented a genuine danger for non-capitalist development became general among the revolutionary forces only in 1967/8 when the class struggle sharpened. During the course of the "révolution active" it was increasingly realised that since independence a stronger process of social differentiation had taken place, in which more bourgeois elements had developed.[97]

At the co-operative seminar in 1968 it was stated that since independence a stratum of "new rich" had grown up.[98] The first practical conclusion to be drawn was that the party and state apparatus should be purged of agrarian bourgeois elements.[99] However, the economic positions of these forces were in no way attacked, although the transformation of Modibo Keita's private estate into a "socialist production unit"[100] created a precedent for this.

REFERENCES

1 See on this problem: *Razvivajuščciesja strany: zakonomernosti, tendencii, perspectivy*, Moscow 1974, pp. 164ff.
2 Such as the natural democracy.
3 Here we do not mean that part of the surplus product of the extended family which would go to the FAKOROBA as its "official representative anyway", although the difference between the two is often not clear.
4 At the end of the 1950s the bride-price reached the amount of 20,000 – 100,000 Fr-CFA – depending on the area – partly in money and partly in animals (mainly cattle), while in the mid-1930s some 1,000 Fr (1960 value) had to be paid (see E. Leynaud, *Les cadres sociaux*, op. cit., pp. 135–6 and S. E. R. E. S. A. *Etude sur l'économie agricole du Soudan*, loc. cit., p. 127). Although the bride-price was laid down at 20,000 FM after independence through the *Code de Mariage*, I know of cases in which it was 100,000 FM and more.
5 S. Badian, op. cit., pp. 137–8.
6 See E. Leynaud, Les cadres sociaux, op. cit., pp. 147–55 and S. E. R. E. S. A. *Etude sur l'économie agricole du Soudan*, loc. cit., pp. 143–4.
7 Synonymous for FAKOROBA.
8 E. Leynaud, *Les cadres sociaux*, op. cit., p. 153.
9 This does not exclude, first, such a type of exploitation being linked with

The gradual development of capitalist production 193

capitalist forms of acquiring another's labour power and, secondly, the wealth gained through exploitation of the extended family members becoming the prerequisite for development of capitalist relations.
10 See K. Marx, *Foundations of the Critique of Political Economy*, The Pelican Marx Library 1973, pp. 492—5.
11 See pages 117f.
12 Under colonial rule, it was possible for the producer liberating himself from the traditional structures to become a medium or larger producer only through a favourable coincidence. These could be larger means acquired outside of the village (by temporary work in the city or through a war veteran's pension) or particularly favourable conditions of production (such as existed in some of the irrigated rice-growing areas). Investigations in the inner delta showed that in the 1950s, of 23 farms with a relatively large cultivation area, only three were not the property of extended families. Each of these farms had three persons and a cultivated area of 6 hectares or more per labourer. In these three cases, the producer's age was under 35 (see R. Cailol, "Enquête agricole dans le Delta Central Nigerien, Zone inondée", Office du Niger, Paris n. d., p. 29 [photostat]).
13 Compare the following table (page 176).
14 Column 6 shows that the large farms belong to the extended families.
15 See pages 118ff.
16 See table on page 134.
17 In the following, the percentages are always of variant IV and not of the total population.
18 The undifferentiated approach of the 1960 *Enquête agricole* limits the use of their results for the analysis of socio-economic relations between the community members. See especially the questionnaire used (*Enquête agricole 1960*, op. cit., p. 64).
19 In the course of my investigations in Barouéli, I carried out this case study in Nianzana, the largest and most differentiated of the villages I examined.
20 The distribution of the whole ten farms which exploit foreign labour power in the framework of the LAMA was, according to farm types:

Type of farm	I	II	III	IV
Number of farms	1	2	3	4

(On the TON see further down.)
21 See R. Cailol, op. cit., p. 60.
22 Cailol puts it this way: "These may be persons who lend their plough to relatives, but it occurs much more often that these services are exchanged: he who borrows the plough cultivates the field of its owner . . ." (R. Cailol, op. cit., p. 18).
23 Ibid.
24 In the big *Enquête* reports mentioned here, this relationship is nowhere explicitly expressed, because it could have contradicted the theory propagated

13 Ernst

there of the reciprocal character of this *"entr'aide"* (see ibid.). However, it is implied by the price of 50 to 100 Fr daily given as being paid for one labourer without plough. All those that I asked in 1964/5 in the areas of San, Kita and Sikasso confirmed the ratio of 3—5 days' work for one days' use of the plough.

25 R. Dumont (*Economie agricole dans le Monde*, Paris 1954, p. 112) gives an average of 10 days, while R. Cailol (op. cit., p. 54) found an average of 8.7 days per hectare for the rice areas.

26 If one presumes that a labourer needs an average of 80—100 days cultivation and harvest work per hectare (for rice).

27 Price in the mid-1960s. Cailol (op. cit., p. 19) gives 250 Fr CFA and Dumont (*Economie agricole dans le Monde*, loc. cit., p. 112) gives a price of 200 Fr CFA for the area of the living delta in 1950, while the *Enquête agricole* for 1960 — 10 years later — establishes prices of between 150 and 500 Fr (op. cit., p. 26).

28 I base my statements on rice because this "mutual aid" was practised mainly in this field. In 1967, the producer had a gross income of some 12,000 FM per hectare with an average hectare yield of 8,00 kg and a selling price of 15 FM per kg (see *Rapport Définitif de l'Enquête Agricole 1967—1968*, Bamako 1969, p. 25 and *L'Essor*, 12. 6. 1967).

29 R. Cailol, op. cit., p. 19.

30 These are mainly peasants from the millet-growing area who come into the rice-growing area in order to obtain additional means of subsistence. They receive payment in kind — one-tenth of the harvest (see ibid., p. 21).

31 With a price of 30,000 to 40,000 FM per plough and oxen-pair. Here, it is basically unimportant if these 10—12 hectares are ploughed in the course of one, two or more years. For the richest of the large farms, one plough is definitely amortizable in the course of one season.

32 However, to the same extent as the FAKOROBA began to acquire the surplus product of the extended family, the surplus labour of the small producers who were exploited in this framework also went to the FAKOROBA *personally*.

33 See *Enquête agricole 1960*, op. cit., p. 31.

34 E. Leynaud, *Fraternités d'âge*, op. cit., p. 59.

35 Leynaud (ibid., p. 60) established 20 Fr for the Haute-Vallée and the 1960 *Enquête agricole* (p. 31) gives a figure of some 33 Fr while in 1967 in the Barouéli area, the sum to be paid was 25 FM per day and TON member.

36 With 20—35 Fr daily, the TON labour power is considerably cheaper than a normal farm-hand who costs at least 100 FM daily.

37 If a community member wanted the TON to do certain work for him, he needed first of all the agreement of the village council. This corresponded to the role of the TON in precolonial society as a "social service" on the one hand, and to the character of the village council as a democratic institution of the community on the other (see E. Leynaud, *Fraternités d'âge*, op. cit., p. 58).

38 See the description of the composition of the village council on p. 96.

39 R. Dumont, op. cit., p. 51.

40 *Enquête agricole 1960*, op. cit., p. 32. The relatively high proportion of ploughing is explained by the small number of ploughs available. In areas with more

The gradual development of capitalist production 195

ploughs, the participation of the TON in this labour process is smaller (see R. Cailol, op. cit., p. 17. On the organization of TON labour on the field see E. Leynaud, *Fraternités d'âge*, op. cit., p. 59).
41 Ibid., pp. 58—9.
42 Leynaud's concrete description of the TON does not make this claim. The question here is that of the term, which Leynaud uses in an equally as careless a manner as that of proletariat.
43 I abstract here from any possible exploitation by the FAKOROBA which would have taken place during these five days.
44 This fact is reflected in the use of the TON income which was very seldom spent on the means of immediate subsistence: 83% of the TON organizations spent their income to organise village festivals, 10% of them used it for mutual support, 6% did not spend it at all and 8% used it for various purposes (see *Enquête agricole 1960*, op. cit., p. 33).
45 See ibid., p. 31.
46 See pages 59 ff.
47 See R. Dumont, *Afrique Noire: Développement agricole*, loc. cit., p. 171. Julis also points to similar phenomena in the Macina and Inner Delta — see op. cit., pp. 12—13.
48 This was so in most cases, because the colonial administration tried to recruit members of DUGUTIGI families to become village chiefs in order to use their authority for their own purposes.
49 See pages 95 ff.
50 The name comes from the Wolof word *navéte* (rainy season) and expresses the fact that these are seasonal workers during the rainy season (i. e. the agricultural season). During the peanut boom in Senegal (before the Second World War) 70,000 to 100,000 *navétanes* came from Mali and Guinea to Senegal each year to remain there as share-croppers for some seven months (for the concrete conditions of exploitation of the *navétanats* in Senegal, see H. Labouret, *Les paysans d'Afrique Noire*, op. cit., pp. 75—6 and 222—6; A. Letnev, op. cit., pp. 71—2, Ph. David, "Fraternité d'hivernage (le contrat de *navétanat*)", in: *Présence Africaine*, XXXI/1960, pp. 45—7, and M. Diop, *Contribution à l'étude*, op. cit., pp. 114—18). The *métayage* economy is, however, by no means only a West African phenomenon. It was and is far more pronounced in other parts of Africa (e. g. in Madagaskar) (see R. Dumont, *Afrique Noire est mal partie*, Paris 1962, pp. 115—17).
51 K. Marx, *Capital*, vol. 3, loc. cit., p. 803.
52 The description that follows is based on information which I collected in Kita in 1964.
53 See S. E. R. E. S. A. *Etude sur l'économie agricole du Soudan*, loc. cit., pp. 79—83.
54 See E. Leynaud, *Les cadres sociaux*, op. cit., p. 217.
55 Here, the number of working days on the field of the landlord (*diatigui*) was even as high as five per week. In addition, the share-cropper was paid 50 Fr daily during the period of heavy labour (weeding, harvest).

57 These are some 62,000 hectares.
58 These 10,000 embryonic village bourgeois make up some 0.7% of the agricultural labourers. These figures are confirmed by the only regional study available to me on the farms employing wage labourers and farm-hands, which is the *Enquête démographique dans le Delta Central Nigerien*. For the areas under investigation it states 0.3% *"patrons"* (who employ wage labourers) and 2.4% farm-hands (in the terms used by the study, these are identical with share-croppers) among the agricultural labourers. Unfortunately, the groups given in the study are so unfavourable that it is very difficult to draw conclusion from.
59 See R. Dumont, *Economie agricole dans le Monde*, loc. cit., pp. 106–8.
60 Ibid., p. 107.
61 The cultivation structure was as follows: 13 hectares small millet, 3 hectares sorghum and beans, 2 hectares cotton, 1 hectare peanuts and cotton, 1 hectare maize and cotton, 1 hectare rice.
62 In addition, to the family there belonged seven women still capable of work and four old women. No information is given about the number of children.
63 Dumont gives the following figures on income:

2 tons cotton	at 20,000 Fr.-CFA	40,000 Fr.-CFA
700 metres woven cotton cloth (15 cm wide)	at 20 Fr.-CFA	14,000 Fr.-CFA
Peanuts		10,000 Fr.-CFA
Rice		6,000 Fr.-CFA
Total		70,000 Fr.-CFA

64 With Leynaud (*Les cadres sociaux*, op. cit., p. 217) one can even assume that among the agricultural wage labourers, the migrant worker was in the majority.
65 The *Enquête agricole* 1960 says nothing on this. Leynaud (Les cadres sociaux, op. cit., p. 218) states: "Unfortunately, the data from this enquiry on these particular aspects of labour organization is very vague."
66 This is probably an over-estimation if one sees that the *Comptes Economiques du Mali 1956* (Paris 1960, p. 21) gives 43 farms which employed wage labour. However, this figure still seems somewhat low to me.
67 At the same place, the *Comptes Economiques du Mali 1956* gives a figure of 600 agricultural wage labourers (migrant workers).
68 This is the enquiry *Recensement général des Salariés du 31 août 1966*. Publication provisoire, Bamako 1968. In the introduction it is expressly said that migrant workers and wage labourers employed on family farms were not recorded (see p. 1).
69 The quoted study gives a sum of 8,389 workers and employees in the agricultural field. Of these, 5,495 were unskilled, 1,429 skilled workers and employees, 647 medium employees and 62 leading employees (see ibid., pp. 30–2. On the 1956 position see footnote 67). The 1960/1 *Enquête démographique*

gives 2,800 wage labourers in agriculture (see *Annuaire statistique 1966*, op. cit., p. 33).
70 Traces of it penetrated even deep into the Bobo country. In January 1965 I interviewed in Somo M. G. T., a former adjutant of the French colonial army. He cultivated 10 hectares, had a plough and two oxen plus a modern stone house which he rented out to a French road-building firm from 1957—9 and since 1961 to the *Service Civique*. His family was composed of 11 persons. Apart from himself and a leprous brother, they were all women and children. He coped with the field work with the help of a wage labourer who lived with him from 1960 and was also entered into his family book. Apart from free board and lodging, he received 1,000 FM monthly. An interesting fact is that in 1961 M. G. T. converted to Islam because the continual tribute of sacrificial animals demanded by the extended family's head — with whom he had no further contact — "got on his nerves" and he found it "useless".
71 In May 1965, S. K., a former teacher and later *chef de canton*, pensioned off since 1965 and treasurer of the Political Bureau of the Kita sub-section, reported to me that people of his standing who still had WOLOSO in the house were more and more replacing them with migrant workers because the WOLOSO had to be fed and clothed, while a migrant worker received his wages only. In addition, through the liberalisation of social relations, the WOLOSO were making more demands for clothing, etc.
72 The areas involved here are the plains of Séguéla, Tamani, Konodimini, Kokry-Sansanding and Dioro on the central arm of the Niger above and below Ségou. San-Ouest on the Bani, a tributary of the Niger, and Kouniana-Konosso and Sinkolo on the Marigots into which the Bani flows (see also "Le Développement de notre monde rural", in: *Le Mali*, 3/1965, pp. 14—15).
73 See his report in *L'Humanité*, 24. 9. 1966.
74 I visited a similar estate in Sikasso at the beginning of 1971. It was about 50 hectares and was cultivated by eight wage labourers who lived on the estate. They received free board and lodging plus 4,500 FM monthly. Further wage labourers were employed during the harvest. The owner declared that he intended to buy a tractor, but the lack of service made him hesitate. According to a survey, in the immediate surroundings of Sikasso, there are some ten to 15 estate owners of this size.
75 P. Morlet, "Le Mali an VI", in: *L'Humanité*, 22.—29. 9. 1966.
76 In February 1965 I visited the Konosso Plain with K. C., chief of the San S. D. R. At that time it was 5,000 hectares, but only a good half of it could be cultivated because of the irregular flooding.
77 According to the files of the chiefs of the Konodimini and N'Gara *Secteurs de Base*. The data about the size of the rented land is still inexact because it was collected separately according to the three plains. However, the big leaseholders rented land generally on two of the plains and often on all three.
78 See R. Dumont, *Afrique Noire. Développement agricole*, loc. cit., p. 179.
79 On the Tamani-Konodimini Plain, the tenants received one hectare for each

square meter of earth they due during the building of the system. Information of the Ségou S. D. R.
80 This is not an interest for rent in the usual sense of the word, but a fee for irrigation. In Tamani-Konodimini it was 50 kilograms per hectare which corresponded to approximately 5% of the yield. On the Konosso Plain it was 60 kg per hectare. Information from Ségou S. D. R., San S. D. R.
81 The official buying prices for rice (outside of the Office du Niger) fell from 1958/9 to 1961/2 from 12 Fr – CFA per kg to 8 FM per kg, but slowly rose to 12.50 FM per kg (1965/6) and were finally raised to 16 (see *Comptes économiques 1959*, op. cit., p. 33 and *Annuaire statistique 1966*, op. cit., p. 143).
82 See R. Dumont, *Afrique Noire: Développement agricole*, loc. cit.
83 In connection with the efforts to curb the merchants and limit their number, they were often recommended to return "to the soil". In his opening speech for the budget meeting of the National Assembly in June 1965, President Keita even announced that those merchants who do not fulfill the conditions of the Merchant Statute and decided to go in for agriculture would receive financial help from the state (see *L'Essor*, 10. 6. 1965, p. 5).
84 See G. Julis, op. cit., pp. 9–11.
85 See R. Dumont, *Afrique Noire est mal partie*, loc. cit., pp. 63–71.
86 See ibid., p. 43.
87 President Keita had a private estate in Moribabougou, 20 km from Bamako, on which he employed several dozen wage labourers.
88 See 1967 – "An I de la Révolution", loc., cit., p. 142.
89 Thus, developments in Mali very quickly answered the question we put in 1967 (see K. Ernst, "Quelques aspects sociologiques du développement rural au Mali", in: *Etudes africaines*, Leipzig 1967, p. 237).
90 See pages 172 ff.
91 See R. Ulyanovski, "On Some Questions of Non-Capitalist Development in Afro-Asian Countries", in: *World Marxist Review* 9/1969.
92 See pages 149 ff.
93 For them, the social differentiation existed for a long time only as an ideological phenomenon which could be overcome through education.
94 See Action rurale. Conférence territorial de l'Union Soudanaise, 17–18–19/10/1958 (Edition spéciale), n.d., p. 1.
95 The intention was to stop the cities becoming flooded with unemployed and with those searching for work who were leaving the countryside. The state and party functionaries were to give a good example in this movement. "In order to overcome this scourge [rural exodus – K. E.] the party called upon its members who live in the big cities to cultivate land". (1967, "An I de la Révolution", loc. cit., p. 146).
96 At the second seminar a number of people in discussion pointed to the agrarian bourgeois tendencies among a number of state and party functionaries. (See 1967, "An I de la Révolution", loc. cit., p. 143).
97 In October 1967, the administrative secretary of the Trade Union Council (U. N. T. M.), Nama Keita, said: "After national independence ... seven

years were sufficient for the contradictions in the Mali Republic to sharpen to such an extent that they have reached all fields of our life. The exploiters have come to light step by step and have become more insolent each day. The new-rich have become richer. The class attitude of one and the other have become visible" (1967, "An I de le Révolution", loc. cit., p. 152).
98 See *Rapport de Synthèse*, op. cit., pp. 13—14.
99 See *L'Essor*, 19. 2. 1968, p. 7.
100 In October 1967 M. Keita changed his estate in Moribabougou into a "Unité Socialiste de Production" (U. S. P.) of a cooperative character (see *L'Essor*, 23. 10. and 6. 11. 1967).

6. Striking a balance

It is difficult in a few sentences to strike a balance in the complicated process, lasting almost ten years, of trying to take traditional agriculture on to a non-capitalist path. To assume that this process has been wiped out through the *coup d'état* of 1968 is greatly to simplify matters.

The non-capitalist path for Mali's agriculture has had positive results which are very difficult to rescind, but it was not able to solve a large number of problems. The objective difficulties were larger than the revolutionary democrats expected, and their conception proved not to be sufficiently in accordance with histerial needs.

6.1. Positive results and lagging behind the given tasks

As a whole the malinese experiment brought a whole number of positive results – in varying degrees – which are of great significance for the development of Mali's agriculture and for the whole society. This applies to the productive forces in both the technical and human aspects, to the socio-economic processes and to the political problems involved in the non-capitalist path.

In the 1960s, the agricultural productive forces developed further, although unevenly, in the various territories not in proportion to the effort made. The histerial significance of this, however, is not so much the quantitative aspect, but more the fact that in view of the economic and social conditions it was possible in some developed areas of the traditional sector to bring about a first break through towards overcoming the old technique and methods of production. This acts as a model for the whole traditional sector to overcome two centuries of stagnation in its productive forces caused by colonial exploitation, the slave trade and other internal factors, although at the time the progress made was not general enough to be reflected in production statistics. In other words, the first and probably most complicated step for further dynamic development of the productive forces was taken –

namely, the decisive prerequisite for increased production and exchange and for overcoming the traditional relations of production.

In the socio-economic field very complicated and often contradictory processes took place during the period investigated. Their historically positive aspects are partly the result of conscious change, but are largely objective, unintentional side-effects. A major achievement on the non-capitalist road is that the foreign trade monopolies have been largely eliminated and replaced by state organisations for buying and selling (export) agrarian products. This was a first and essential step towards overcoming colonial and neo-colonial exploitation of the peasants (the decisive cause of the backwardness and deformation of economic and social structures in the village) without it being possible to eliminate neo-colonial exploitation of the *whole* country – and the peasantry – through the mechanism of the world capitalist market. At the same time, with the S. O. M. I. E. X. and the O. P. A. M., the national democratic state created instruments which could serve to find agricultural reserves for national development and to influence agricultural development through the distributive sphere in the national interest and in a non-capitalist spirit. Apart from the problems involved in making the state buying and export organisations function, the measures taken created the preconditions for noncapitalist socio-economic relations in agriculture and for limiting the uncontrolled effects of the laws of development in pre-socialist commodity production.

Another socio-economic process important for historic progress – although more the objective result of the measures taken than consciously brought about – was the disintegration of the traditional system of production and distribution, the accelerated dissolution of the structures preserved and deformed by colonialism. This set free new and significant social motive power for the development of the productive forces and for social change, and it matured social conditions to consolidate the alliance between the revolutionary-democrats and the peasantry. The efforts to found multi-purpose agricultural co-operatives corresponded to the basic needs of these new conditions. This step – at first mainly to commercialise agrarian production and to supply the peasants with consumer goods and means of production – was the necessary non-capitalist variant to overcome the stagnation of the productive forces and deformed social development in the agrarian sector which the laws governing the processes of colonial and neo-colonial dependence and exploitation had effected. The emergence of co-operative relations in several developed areas was of focal significance for the whole process of non-capitalist transformation. These new relations pointed the way towards the integration of the producer as the freed himself from the traditional structures – who in conditions of spontaneous decay could look foward only to pauperisation and exploitation — into transitory non-capitalist relations, and presented him with new opportunities for unfolding the economic and social driving forces.

From a political viewpoint, too, important results were achieved. Through liquidation of the colonial administrative *Chefferie* and its political organisations (P. S. P., dwarf parties), the most decisive political and social pillar of colonialism and neo-colonialism in the village was eliminated. The creation of democratic communal bodies and the extension of the organisational network of the Sudanese Union and mass organisations became important instruments for consolidating the positions of leading revolutionary democrats in the village. The decay of the traditional structures and the raising of the political, ideological and cultural level — which resulted consciously or unconsciously from intensive educational and development work — led to new conditions maturing in the village for the new political structures to become effective as a consolidation of the alliance between the revolutionary democrats in the city and the peasant masses.

All these historic achievements by the revolutionary democrats in Mali in the non-capitalist transformation of agriculture were essentially either important prerequisites for solution — or part-solutions — of problems. However, they did not completely succeed in transforming these prerequisites and part-solutions into economic growth, stable co-operatives and a firm alliance.

Thus, on the debit side of the developments of 1960—8 was a stagnation of agrarian production, the unsolved problem of marketing and thus stabilisation of co-operative relations, and the unsolved alliance problem. All this helped to weaken the national democratic state to such an extent that it was unable to put up any serious resistance to the *coup d'état* of November 1968.

6.2. Objective and subjective obstacles for non-capitalist transformation

There are multifarious objective and subjective causes for the non-capitalist path lagging behind objective needs. We are interested here mainly in those factors which a direct negative influence on the non-capitalist transformation of the village.

The decisive inhibiting factor proved to be the colonial backwardness in the village and the persistence of ossified traditional community structures linked with it. The latter inevitably became an obstacle to the broad development of the productive forces to rapid development of agrarian production because of the laws governing their internal function and structures, especially their system of production and distribution. The traditional structures also hindered socio-economic progress. So long as they continued to function, the founding of cooperatives did not lead to a qualitative change in the social life of the village. On the contrary, the co-operatives became so much influenced by the traditional structures and leadership that their own laws of development did not come into effect, but the system of traditional relations, under the co-operative label, were stabilised and inhibited social progress.

In many regions, the persistence of traditional socio-economic relations was a decisive cause of weakness in the alliance between the national-democratic leadership and the mass of the peasants. The gerontocracy, an integral part of traditional relations, formed an effective barrier between the two important partners of this alliance and a strong obstacle to the new democratic political structures being able to function at village level.

Through the spontaneous development of commodity exchange, new social factors arose which hindered the non-capitalist path. With the penetration of commodity-money relations, the traditional structures of the community became a vehicle for veiled exploitation of the mass of community members by a stratum of big semi-traditional and semi-capitalist producers. This aggravated and gave a new twist to all those factors inherent in the traditional relations that hindered social progress. At the same time, a new social stratum grew in the form of the national trade and usury capitalists who strongly resisted the non-capitalist changes in agriculture, particularly on the agrarian market.

They were able to gain strength, not only because of their great experience, widespread family and business ramifications, but above all through petty-bourgeois ideology which spread owing to the growth of small commodity production. They succeeded in gaining the support of a large number of those producers who were freeing themselves from the traditional structures and were going over to commodity production, i.e. those peasants whose objective interest it was to form an alliance with the revolutionary democrats and who were their potential allies. In this way the national trade and usury capitalists were able to prevent the co-operatives from being stabilised and the alliance from becoming firm.

A third important inhibiting factor arose out of the spontaneous social processes. With the extension of the state economic and administrative organs and the party apparatus in the countryside, the social and ideological differentiation took hold of the petty-bourgeois officials. Bureaucratic and bureaucratic-bourgeois tendencies appeared increasingly, undermined the instruments for non-capitalist change from within and made it impossible to win the peasant masses for a non-capitalist path.

These facts reflect the objective class interest of traditionalist social forces or those with bourgeois tendencies. They arise independently of the will of the revolutionary democratic forces and inhibit the non-capitalist path. They lie in the interests of foreign monopoly capital which has itself strongly contributed to complicating all internal processes by exploiting the country within the framework of the world capitalist economic system. However, they do not necessarily lead to the failure of non-capitalist changes. Suitable strategy and tactics can limit their effect and finally overcome them.

The Sudanese Union's conception, while corresponding to the needs of a non-capitalist path in many ways, also contained important ideological elements which — resulting from the petty-bourgeois character of the whole movement — became a subjective hindrance to the non-capitalist changes. As a whole, these ideological weaknesses are caused by the wrong assessment of the historic character of the non-capitalist stage of development.

Until the mid-1960s, the Sudanese Union's agrarian conception was strongly influenced by Narodnik-like utopian ideas about the road to socialism. It was expressed in various ways especially in an unhistorical glorification of the traditional community, an over-estimation of the "classless" character of Malinese society and an underestimation of social differentiation and of the class struggle. Out of these ideological weaknesses resulted a number of practical measures which contributed to temporarily stabilising the traditional structures, helped the uncontrolled development of spontaneous social processes and the activities of merchants who opposed the non-capitalist path and inhibited the process of integrating the producer being freed from traditional structures into the co-operative and consolidating an alliance with him.

A number of these weaknesses were recognised and corrected in the second half of the 1960s. However, as these corrections were accompanied by ultra-left tendencies in agricultural policy, their positive effect was limited. A strong urge towards collectivisation of agrarian production did not meet existing conditions and led to greater isolation of the leadership from the masses.

Thus, due to ideological and conceptual and hence practical weaknesses in the Sudanese Union's agrarian policy, the obstacles to non-capitalist changes could not be overcome (in fact, they were even partly objectively encouraged) and the necessary driving force could not be fully released. Objective and subjective inhibiting factors — together with national and international factors — led to the circumstance that in the 1960s the historic possibility in Mali, for non-capitalist changes in traditional agriculture could not be successfully completed. However, significant results were achieved, which have created favourable prerequisites for further national development, in particular for the continuation of the non-capitalist path.

Conclusions

From the traditional community to social progress in the African village

The experience gained in the attempts to take the non-capitalist path in Mali emphatically confirm Marxist-Leninist theory on the non-capitalist path to socialism. It teaches us that success is possible only if a scientific assessment of our epoch and the historical character of the non-capitalist path is made, because such an assessment is the basis for the strategy and tactics necessary to achieve this end.

Basic social, economic and political problems of non-capitalist transformation in the village

As regards the non-capitalist transformation of the village, the Malinese experience shows that for all African countries with the same or similar starting conditions,[1] three fundamental socio-economic and political problems must be gradually solved: first, domination by monopoly trade capital, local trade and usury capital and the colonial *Chefferie*[2] over the peasant producer must be eliminated in order gradually to overcome the whole system of colonial exploitation and dependence; secondly, the colonially backward and deformed traditional community relations must be overcome via the co-operative, and thirdly, the problems arising through the spontaneous unfolding of capitalist agrarian relations must be tackled in time.

Elimination of colonial structures

Of fundamental importance in the whole process of non-capitalist transformation of agriculture is the elimination of the socio-economic and political structures created during the course of the *"économie de traite"*. In practice this means, above all, curbing and gradually excluding foreign monopoly capital from its main field of colonial activity — the agrarian market. Developments in Mali showed that overcoming this domination over the peasant producers and creating state-run export, import and wholesale organisations in the agrarian field is of decisive importance both for the whole social process of development and for introducing and continuing non-capitalist changes in agriculture.

First, substitution of foreign trade monopolies on the agrarian market by state organisations makes it possible to use agricultural resources for developing the whole nation, despite the low level of market production. Secondly, through these organisations the state creates an economic instrument by which it can actively influence — via market relations — development of the agricultural forces of production and make changes in the structure of agrarian production and in the socio-economic relations in the village to consolidate their alliance with the peasantry.

Needless to say, the creation of state foreign trade organisations does not mean that exploitation by foreign capital ceases suddenly and automatically. Because the developing countries generally remain within the world capitalist system, exploitation continues through the non-equivalent exchange rate and other economic links. This exploitation becomes steadily worse through the laws of development inherent under imperialism.[3] Therefore, the curbing of foreign capital on the agrarian market and on the home market in general can become effective on a long-term basis in the spirit of non-capitalist development only if it is an integral part of measures gradually to overcome the whole system of colonial and neo-colonial dependence and exploitation. This curbing of foreign capital is, on the one hand, necessarily supplemented by a broad struggle, waged together with other developing countries, gradually to change economic relations with the imperialist countries in order to improve the position of the developing countries on the world capitalist market. On the other hand, gradual extension of economic relations between developing countries and the socialist countries is not only a basic principle of the alliance between socialism and the national liberation movement, but a fundamental means for achieving social progress in this part of the world.[4]

However, the effectiveness and profits of the state marketing bodies are inhibited by a number of internal objective and subjective factors, particularly at the beginning.

Due to the low level of the agricultural productive forces and low labour productivity, the output available for sale is small and spread over a large territory. This means that marketing becomes very costly, especially with the undeveloped rural infrastructure.

Another important disturbing factor for a state marketing system is national trade and usury capital. Thanks to their widespread personal and family relationships, their greater experience and commercial flexibility, the private merchants are far better able to adapt to the conditions of an underdeveloped agrarian market than are the big state marketing societies. Thus the private merchants cannot be driven from the other market simply by declaring a legal marketing monopoly for one or the state body. This only becomes possible when the buying organisation and stabilised co-operatives – which have come about in the process of creating non-capitalist conditions in the village – appear as partners on the market.

Finally, the state societies usually have great initial difficulties in carrying out the investments necessary for them to function and to find suitable cadres. The latter is caused not only by a lack of cadres, but by problems arising out of the existence of a bureaucratic bourgeoisie.

These factors can put a state marketing system out of action and thus, if it is set up too quickly, lead to considerable economic and political setbacks on the non-capitalist path. Therefore, it is important to build up a state marketing system by stages, taking into account the objective limits that exist and the aspects of the multi-sector economy in this field.[5]

Thus the state marketing system should concentrate on the main products (both for export and food production). Insignificant products with small marketing quotas should be left to the local merchants. In fact, it is necessary to draw this social stratum into the marketing process for as long as the co-operatives have not made their existence superfluous.[6] Transitionally, foreign capital can continue to play a certain role on the agrarian market. Such a compromise seems especially acceptable if – as in the case of Mali with the Compagnie Française pour le Développement des Fibres Textiles (C. F. D. T.) – monopol capital cannot control the agrarian market, but operates within the framework of a state-controlled development and marketing system and contributes to developing the traditional sector of agriculture.

To the extent that the state marketing bodies become stabilised and the factors which prevent their full functioning are overcome, they will gradually assume a monopoly on the agrarian market.

The elimination of colonial political structures in the village is of fundamental significance for non-capitalist changes in agriculture. In the former French colonies there existed the system of village and canton chiefs (*Chefferie*) who were put there by the colonial power to politically oppress the peasants and who became an additional factor of exploitation.[7] The political parties and organisations in the countryside which were led by the *Chefferie* represented colonial and neo-colonial interests, objectively played the same role by splitting the peasant masses from the revolutionary-democratic forces.

Liquidation of the *Chefferie* as a social force and a political institution, elimination of the conservative political organisations in the village and extension of the revolutionary party and mass organisations' influence on the country are a vital prerequisite for the social liberation of the peasant masses, for democratisation of political life in the countryside and for consolidation of the alliance with the peasantry. But experiences in Mali have shown that liquidation of the *Chefferie* and the creation of democratic communal and local bodies, plus the extension of branches of the national-democratic party and mass organisations into the countryside, remain limited in their effects so long as the traditional socio-economic relations continue to operate. With the destruction of the colonial and political structures at local level, there was a sort of renaissance of the political influence of the traditional leadership. Through their position in the community, their prestige, religious influence and family relations, these forces were largely able to control the new political bodies despite — or perhaps because of — their democratic character. Of course, this made it impossible for these bodies to be used as an instrument for non-capitalist change and for the alliance with the peasant masses to be consolidated.

On the whole one can say that the curbing and or liquidation of monopoly capital in the agrarian field and of the colonial political structures were important measures for introducing the processes necessary for non-capitalist change in traditional agriculture. From the viewpoint of the village, they create the necessary external conditions for economic, social and political progress in the countryside, although they do not do this automatically. The dialectics of the social process is such that under certain conditions these measures lead to a temporary retrograde development in the village. In some areas of Mali at the beginning of the 1960s, after liberation from the monopolies and the *Chefferie*, the village community fell back into the subsistence economy and its traditional structures were strengthened. They were areas in which commodity-money relations had not yet become an integral part of economic relations in the villages, so that when the administrative and economic pressure to produce commodities for exchange ceased, the traditional economic and social laws again became effective.[8] This makes it clear that the far-reaching elimination of colonial economic and political structures can be only the first step towards non-capitalist changes in traditional agriculture. The logic of development demands that the traditional community relations be overcome on a non-capitalist road, and this becomes the key problem for all economic, social and political progress in the countryside.

Non-capitalist transformation of traditional community structures

The non-capitalist transformation of traditional community relations is an essential part of the whole process of overcoming the system of colonial and neo-colonial dependence and exploitation in a revolutionary way. These traditional community relations arose through the low level of the productive forces; they were preserved by colonialism, adapted to the system of colonial exploitation and reproduced by the laws inherent in this system, but in ever more crippled form. Thus they are not a just pre-colonial heritage but, above all, a product and — up to a certain point — also a functional element of the system of colonial and neo-colonial dependence and exploitation. At the same time, they are also an essential internal condition for maintaining and deepening neo-colonial dependence, because its inherent laws inevitably inhibit the development of the productive forces.[9]

So it is a historically necessary process for the community to be superseded in a non-capitalist way and this process should be seen not simply as a "liberation from colonial deformations", or as a "refunctioning" or "adaptation" to the needs of "modern developments", but as a long-term, gradual and far-reaching socio-economic, political, ideological and cultural transformation in the sense that the necessary preconditions must be created in the village for an independent and socialist development of the whole country.

The best method for this has proved to be by means of co-operatives. This necessarily includes the dissolution of traditional economic and social relations, because — as was confirmed in Mali — the attempt to build co-operatives on the basis of the traditional community, without superseding the traditional inner relations, is in contradiction to the objective social laws of development and thus doomed to failure. First, it leads to temporary stabilisation of the traditional structures and thus to preserving and not overcoming these factors which are an obstacle both to social progress and to consolidating the alliance between the revolutionary city strata and classes and the peasantry. In addition — as the disintegrating effect of trade is an objective process and cannot be stopped — it hides the spontaneous social processes and, under the veil of co-operatives usually declared to be "socialist", encourages the transformation of the traditional social relations of solidarity into relations of dependence and exploitation.

This does not mean that in various phases of the transformation, certain elements and phenomena of traditional community relations cannot be retained and used for social progress; however, they will increasingly be traditional only in form.

Thus two main aspects must be seen when trying to transform traditional relations in the non-capitalist sense: 1. dissolving community relations and 2. creation of co-operatives. These two aspects are different only in the method to be employed. In reality they are closely interwoven. Although the first task is the prerequisite for success in the second, one cannot concentrate at first only on dissolving the traditional relations, and work for co-operatives only after the last remnants have disappeared. This would be fatal and would directly encourage spontaneous capitalist relations of production, as the process of disintegration is not territorially even nor can it be stopped for a certain time. The non-capitalist essence of this path is that the necessary transformation of primitive production relations is not left to chance and spontaneity — the spontaneous processes of pre-socialist commodity production, with the accompanying development of private property in land and social differentiation, would lead directly to capitalism — but the producers are integrated into co-operatives as they free themselves from the traditional system of production and distribution.

The inter-relationship between both phases must be seen as one continuous process, so that over a longer period a multifarious over-lapping and complicated inter-weaving of differing economic and social relations take place. It is a process in which traditional village relations as a whole are gradually replaced by new economic, political and cultural relations of a non-capitalist, national-democratic type.

During the first phase, when the traditional relations and in particular the extended family as an economic unit are disintegrating, it is important that a producer arise who, when liberated from the bonds of traditional structures, acquire an objective need thus a subjective desire to raise production and develop the productive forces. On the basis of these socio-economic changes, measures to develop the material and human productive forces can become effective if they do not meet with passive resistance, as occurs if the traditional relations persist. With the socio-economic changes new conditions arise for the effective integration of the peasants into the political movement for genuine democratisation in the countryside and the penetration of revolutionary ideology into the village. And as the traditional socio-economic relations disintegrate, the social forces arise which are objectively interested in further socio-economic changes in the direction of modern co-operatives. This means that as the socio-economic chains of the traditional community are destroyed, a fundamentally new social driving power is unleashed for economic and social progress in the village.

The disintegration of the traditional community cannot be achieved within a short time by administrative means, but must be seen as a process which — usually already started by spontaneous developments — can be accelerated by a whole number of interrelated and interwoven measures. The concrete measures must be determined by the concrete conditions, although there are certain general aspects:

(1) The development of commodity-money relations necessarily leads to disintegration of the traditional community and its basis, the natural economy. This is an objective law which must not only be taken into consideration when planning the strategy and tactics of the non-capitalist path, but consciously used. This means that the commodity-money relations should be developed – perhaps through increased production of cheap varieties of industrial consumer goods, with corresponding prices for selling agricultural products to the state, etc. – in such a way that the producer, through his new material desires, develops an interest in exchange and thus strengthens his striving for socio-economic emancipation from the extended family.

(2) It must not be forgotten that the socio-economic relations of the traditional community reflect a certain level of the productive forces; in other words, as long as the productive forces remain at a low level, the need for collective subsistence also remains and the traditional community retains its economic function and justification. Thus it can only be overcome finally, through a high level of economic development. Here we see that disintegration of the traditional structures *must* be a process. For practical development policy this means that all the possibilities for developing the agricultural productive forces must be used. Because particularly at the beginning the means available to the national-democratic state for investment are very limited, it is important to use all the reserves in the village. It is in this sense that utilisation of the traditional forms of simple co-operation for agricultural projects in infrastructure is of significance. Even if at first this co-operation takes place within the framework of traditional relations, in the long run (through its economic utility) it contributes to overcoming them. Further, it must be ensured that the state measures to develop the productive forces act in favour of those who have objective interests to overcome traditional structures and cannot be misused by the traditional leaders to exploit the mass of peasants.

(3) The dissolution of traditional community relations demands a number of measures to change the political conditions in the village (*after* the political structures of colonialism have been eliminated), because the strong influence of the traditional leaders in the local political organs tends to stabilise the traditional social relations. It is important to organise firmly the dynamic, already conscious or potential forces which are interested in overcoming the traditional structures (in the national-democratic party and in youth, peasant and other organisations), and to strengthen their political influence in the village. At the same time, the traditional leaders must gradually be pushed out of the village political institutions – perhaps by administrative, but mainly with political methods.

(4) The ideological factor plays a very important role in trying to overcome traditional relations. The low level of knowledge about nature and the laws of society reflected in the forms of consciousness within the traditional community are a strong element for regulating and stabilising the material relations in the village. The concentrated measures for accelerating the replacement of traditional social relations must therefore be seen mainly in its ideological aspects. They must include general measures to raise the educational and cultural standard – from literacy and health to enlightenment on the laws of nature and society – and purposeful ideological work directed at the dynamic forces who will win over the peasant masses for the economic, social and political tasks necessary to change the village.

Only the co-ordination of such measures can accelerate disintegration of the traditional structures.

As the disintegrating process of traditional production and distribution begins and progresses, it is necassary gradually to build up co-operative relations which must be adapted in level and intensity to the concrete conditions of each phase. It is definitely a possibility that where a certain level of disintegration has been reached but social differentiation among the village population is not strong, all adults could belong to the co-operative. In every case, it is important that the small producer, freeing himself from traditional structures, becomes the basis of the co-operative and plays an important part in the leadership.

Co-operative relations, particularly at the beginning, should be developed in the field of exchange, i.e. marketing of agrarian products and supplying the peasants in return with goods not produced in the village. This stimulates agrarian production and creates preconditions for the state marketing organs being more effective. At the same time, the integration of the producer emancipated from traditional structures into the system of co-operative-state market relations is of fundamental significance for the further development of social processes. The producers, by gradually quitting the natural economy with its specific methods of production and distribution, are integrated into state controlled and state encouraged co-operative exchange relations, and are not enmeshed into the capitalist market. This could be the first step in the successful transformation – in the spirit of a non-capitalist path – of the whole socio-economic relations.

Further, co-operative relations should be built up in the field of accumulation. Co-operative accumulation should be based on the profits of the co-operative and not on obligatory dues paid by its members. In this way it would be possible to develop agricultural productive forces without binding state finances, and the co-operative means could be used, first, for giving credits to the co-operative members and, secondly, for buying means of production for the co-operative or for collectively used infrastructural projects. No doubt, during the initial phase, the first version will be applied more strongly, because it helps the small producer finally to overcome the traditional system of production and distribution — in other words it touches on his immediate interests and is important for solving the problem of alliance. However, the second version will gain in significance — for the individual producer as well as for the co-operative as a whole — to the same degree as it enables the utilisation of relatively developed and expensive means of production which are not profitable for one only. Such co-operative machines lay the material basis and prepare the road for subsequent modern collective production.

Finally, such simple co-operatives can take over a number of other functions, including those once carried out by the community, such as organisation of work in the interests of the whole village, mutual support and social help for the needy. Such forms of cooperation and support cannot be considered as reviving or preserving traditional relations because — like the whole co-operative — they are carried by completely different social forces, and this determines their content. Even if there is thus a link-up with traditional forms of social security, it still fastens the disintegration of the traditional structures by taking over, by means of modern organisation within a co-operative, functions previously carried out by the pre-capitalist community, and which this made necessary to a certain extent.

I do not consider it correct to work for the development of co-operative organisation of the production process during the initial phase. To do so ignores the real level of the productive forces, the social and ideological level of the peasant during the phase of disintegrating community relations and the beginnings of non-capitalist relations in the village; it arbitrarily ignores the given conditions. Attempts to introduce co-operative conditions too early is not only economically useless, but harms consolidation of the alliance with the peasantry. The small producers, who have just escaped from the socio-economic chains of the extended family and the tutelage of the "elders" or are in the process of doing so, must necessarily see in an accelerated collectivisation a return to the old structures and a betrayal of their interests. Under such conditions, the mass of small producers refuse to help the revolutionary leaders and spontaneously turn to those who appear to represent their interests, the private merchants.

Therefore, on this level of non-capitalist transformation, it is important to exploit fully all the possibilities contained in the lower forms of co-operation in order to develop the productive forces, to change the socio-economic relations and consolidate the alliance, and thus create all the prerequisites for the higher stage of co-operation. This does not exclude simple forms of co-operation within the production process being developed; some could be an adaptation of the traditional institutions, e.g. for mutual support among the small producers for work that needs much time and labour, such as land clearance, building and maintaining irrigation systems, etc.

The founding and in particular the first stage of stabilising the co-operatives is a very complicated phase in the non-capitalist transformation of the traditional community. It is important here that the revolutionary-democratic leaders make an exact analysis of the situation, recognise its focal points and take corresponding measures. Although, under these circumstances, it is impossible to present a prescription for how to go about this, there are certain general points which must always be taken into account.

(1) When trying to win the peasants over for the co-operatives, it is very important to use a combination of ideological work and economic incentives. Experiences in Mali have shown that co-operatives can be formed fairly quickly through ideological work, because an objective need for them exists when a certain stage in the spontaneous disintegration of the traditional community is reached. However, if the peasant does not soon see concrete results, this success can turn to failure, because in the given situation, one cannot rely very much on people's consciousness playing a positive role. Above all, one must remember that the economic consciousness of the peasant who has just become emancipated from traditional production and its undeveloped division of labour, is used to seeing an immediate, concrete result of his work. From this viewpoint, it is especially important that economic measures effectively support political and ideological work. In practice this means that the peasant should be clearly shown the usefulness of cooperative work through favourable conditions of commercialisation and credits, regular supply of industrial consumer goods, etc.

(2) It is very important for the further transformation of political conditions in the village and particularly for realising their wider potential, to found and consolidate the co-operatives. As the traditional structures disintegrate and commodity production rises, social forces appear which, consciously or otherwise, push development into the direction of free market relations. It is important at this stage to create a stable political centre made up of progressive people who must gradually gain a decisive influence in the local political and administrative bodies and on whom the revolutionary-democratic forces can rely for ideological work, the establishment and stabilisation of the co-operative, and as protagonists in the struggle against spontaneously developing embryonic capitalist forces with their accompanying petty-bourgeois ideology.

(3) As a logical consequence of the above, the management of the co-operative is a highly important question from the very beginning; it is important

that it should be taken over by progressives who will guide it in a non-capitalist direction. On this management the economic stabilisation of the co-operative largely depends.

As there will at first be very few suitable cadres in the village, it will probably be necessary for central cadres — development officers, party functionaries, administration employees — to take over this management for some time. An important factor in the ideological processes for establishing and stabilising the co-operatives is to send factory workers out into the countryside. However, in view of the small scale of industry existing at the beginning, this could have only a limited application.

The management problems could be solved by drawing in the progressive, dynamic forces of the village as much and as broadly as possible. They would have to be systematically and quickly trained for their functions, ideologically and technically. For the speedy consolidation of the co-operatives and their non-capitalist character it is essential that, on the one hand, the traditional leaders are excluded from management as far as possible and, on the other, that the developing agrarian bourgeoisie are prevented from penetrating the co-operatives, so that they cannot determine their character and direction.

(4) An important aspect of co-operative transformation is the speedy development of the productive forces within the framework of the co-operatives. This creates the basic material prerequisites for their economic consolidation and for further socio-economic transformation.

These co-operatives should be seen as transitional and in steady dynamic development. The transitional character corresponds to its fundamental socio-economic relationship, the relationship to the soil. But its form of communal ownership remains. However, while this ownership is now no longer an expression of the powerlessness of the isolated individual (traditional aspect), it is still not yet an expression of the socialisation of the means of production (objective socialist aspect) inevitable when the productive forces have reached a higher stage. It is a transitional stage between these two.

To the same extent as the productive forces and commodity production develop, co-operative relations are stabilised and gradually extended to production; socialisation of the means of production gains in significance, and the objective prerequisites for a socialist transformation of the village mature.

The non-capitalist co-operative relations can be a necessary link between the traditional community and the socialist agricultural co-operative. However, the exact degree to which this non-capitalist co-operative transformation, fulfills its task and grows into socialist transformation depends on whether the necessary prerequisites for a transition to socialism have been created nationally.[10]

Spontaneous development of capitalism in agriculture

An important problem in the non-capitalist transformation of agriculture is the spontaneous development of small commodity production with its tendency to capitalist production relations. Most recent trends in African countries have shown that this process is strengthened after independence. It arises from the development of the productive forces and the new commodity-money relations and the disintegration of the traditional structures. Experiences in Mali show that countries which have taken a non-capitalist path are not spared these developments. The reasons are (1) that under pre-socialist conditions, the objective prerequisites for controlling the social processes do not exist – particularly concerning the character of production and power relations and (2) that the national-democratic leadership is ideologically heterogeneous, which leads to subjective errors in the way it is attempted to push through the non-capitalist path.

In African social reality, two variants can be observed: (1) semi-capitalist elements penetrate the traditional structures in the form of exploitation of the mass of peasants in a community by their former representatives, and (2) a group of relatively rich commodity producers develops, comparable to the large farmers in Europe who also exploit wage labourers, usually migrant workers. The position of these embryonic and semi-capitalist elements in the process of non-capitalist development is a problem of great theoretical and practical significance.

The first and most frequent variant, with its colonial-reactionary links to outdated, ossified traditional structures and elements of capitalist exploitation, is a particularly powerful hindrance to economic and social progress and to the consolidation of the alliance with the peasant masses. It must therefore be radically eliminated during the process of overcoming the traditional structures.

In trying to solve the problems linked to the second version, two aspects should, in my opinion, be considered. First, these farms can help to solve economic problems arising in the transformation of agriculture, i.e. to develop the productive forces, increase agrarian production, etc. Secondly, the laws determining its internal development are socially, economically and politically quite contrary to the non-capitalist path – which gives rise to a certain contradiction between the economic and the political-socio-economic interests of non-capitalist development.[11]

It is useful here for the developing countries to study the experiences of the Soviet Union during the New Economic Policy (N. E. P.) period, although the political prerequisites were very different.[12] Under the N. E. P., socialist power used the initiative of private capital and the peasants to solve problems which were very similar to those facing the developing countries today: developing the productive forces, reconstructing the economy and gradually raising the living standards of the working masses.[13]

When applying the lessons of the N.E.P. to actual conditions in Africa, the task cannot be to liquidate private capital immediately. It is important to use the initiative and economic interests of capitalist elements to solve a number of economic problems. At the same time it must be ensured that small elementary capitalist production must not become the main factor in the traditional sector of agriculture. Therefore, the determining variant in overcoming traditional structures must be the co-operative path. During the first phase of non-capitalist development it is, above all, necessary to neutralise the capitalist elements[14] because, so long as the power of the revolutionary democrats is not yet stabilised, they cannot afford to challenge these elements in open struggle, nor can they be integrated into the political structures of the village, without risking that the capitalist elements take over the political institutions of the village.

Only to the extent that the co-operatives have been consolidated and the political positions of the revolutionary democrats in the village strengthened, will it be possible gradually to draw the potential agrarian bourgeoisie into the co-operatives. In doing so, however, one should also take heed of Lenin's warning: "The proletarian state must effect the transition to collective farming with extreme caution and only very gradually, by the force of example, without any coercion of the middle peasant."[15]

The role of the state and peasantry in the non-capitalist transformation of agriculture

The close relationship between controls by the central institutions and a broad unfolding of mass initiative is a basic problem of the non-capitalist path. It arises out of the essence of this phase which is the preparation for socialism, and out of the alliance between the revolutionary (at first revolutionary-democratic and later proletarian) leadership and the peasant masses. On the one hand, it corresponds to the character of this alliance and the non-capitalist transformation as such that the state, as the instrument of power of the revolutionary forces, keeps control over the planning and leadership of social transformation in its own hands; on the other hand, a revolutionary movement and transformation can be successful only to the extent that the masses take a conscious and active part. And in each phase of non-capitalist development, the concrete relationship between them will be determined by the level of economic, social, political and ideological development. The cen-

tral role played by the national democratic state in changing agriculture arises from the following facts:
(1) The traditional community, for as long as it still functions, has the tendency, through its inner laws of development, to reproduce itself economically, socially, ideologically, etc., on the same level, i.e. it has only very limited internal driving power which would bring about social changes.
(2) At all levels of non-capitalist transformation — where the community has reached the stage when its main social relations are disintegrating — the danger exists of a development of capitalist tendencies in material and non-material social relations because of the spontaneity of the laws governing the development of pre-socialist commodity production. These processes in the non-capitalist transformation of agriculture mean that it can only succeed to the extent that it is introduced, pushed forward, controlled and guided in all its phases by the revolutionary party and the state.

Non-capitalist changes in the village demand the use of a number of instruments of power and development which can be grouped according to type and function, as follows:
(1) It is the function of the national-democratic party and the mass organisations more or less attached to it to mobilise and organise the peasants politically and educate them ideologically.
(2) The instruments of state power (administration, police, army) have the task mainly of suppressing counter-revolutionary forces, administrating development measures and doing ideological and educational work.
(3) State co-operative economic instruments, such as the marketing and credit-giving institutions or stations for hiring out machines and vehicles, have as their main task the purposeful use of economic stimuli (prices, supply of industrial goods, credits, means of production and transport etc.) in order to introduce and guide the socio-economic processes and develop the productive forces in agriculture.
(4) A special state development service has the principal function of mediating technical and methodological knowledge, demonstrating the advantages of modern methods of production, and influencing the founding and management of village co-operatives (depending on the degree of development achieved).
(5) General educational and socio-political instruments (schools, literacy, medical centres, etc.) and the mass media (radio and film).

The concrete form and use of the various instruments will depend greatly on the concrete conditions in each country, but it is most important that in every case politics, economy and ideology are treated as one entity. Should the relationship between these three main components be in any way disturbed. There would sooner or later be setbacks in transforming the village, which would have a nation-wide effect in view of the role played by agriculture.

Particularly during the first phase of non-capitalist change, there exist a number of limitations and obstacles to effective leadership and planning of the economic and social processes by the state and revolutionary party, which one must not overlook. They result mainly from the character of state power and the political leaders, from the multi-sector economy and the generally unfavourable economic starting points, which are characteristic of non-capitalist development.

The existence of several different forms of property, relative weakness in the state sector, the significant influence of foreign monopoly capital and a dominant subsistence economy in agriculture are factors which hinder the effective planning and leadership of non-capitalist processes by the state, and help to bring about spontaneous changes. The lack of local opportunities for accumulation and a heavy dependence on the conditions of anarchy reigning on the world capitalist market impose strict economic and material limits on the ability of the state to push forward the transformation of agriculture. This applies both to the construction of a system of instruments for development — which in many countries costs far more than the national income is able to afford — and to the use of economic stimuli for developing the productive forces, commodity production, etc. The obstacles in the way of the state trying to plan and guide transformation of the village are no less strong: through the social and ideological heterogeneity of the party and state leaders ideological differences often exist in the leading bodies on basic questions of planning and development. The differing social interests come into sharper relief when the planned measures are to be put into practice. In this process, the bureaucratic bourgeoisie that develops out of the petty-bourgeois officialdom becomes a growing hindrance to making state development instruments effective.

From this it becomes clear that if the state plays a leading role in transforming agriculture, it will become stabilised as an instrument of power of the revolutionary forces. This means that on a national scale the successful non-capitalist transformation of traditional agriculture requires the following:
(1) Continual consolidation of revolutionary political power. This demands above all the growing consolidation of the alliance, during the initial phase, between the revolutionary-democratic intelligentsia and all democratic classes and strata, so that the national-democratic mass party becomes an effective organ of leadership by the revolutionary forces, and state power is strengthened in all fields. Here it is essential that the political role of the working class grows steadily, that its alliance with the peasantry develops and grows firm, and finally that the working class becomes the decisive force in the alliance of the revolutionary and democratic forces.
(2) Ideological development of the leading revolutionary forces in the

general direction of overcoming nationalist, traditionalist and left-radical tendencies, and turning to scientific socialism on the basis of which the necessary scientific (i.e. Marxist-Leninist) conception of non-capitalist agrarian development can be worked out.

(3) economic growth of the national-democratic state which means, above all, strengthening the state sector and making it profitable; developing a national industrial sector; limiting the influence of foreign and national private capital through effective controls; and opening up all internal sources of accumulation.

(4) increasing the effectiveness of state and national-democratic party bodies to transform agriculture by overcoming bureaucratic methods of work, corruption and nepotism, by training cadres particularly the leaders technically. and politically, and creating effective structures for leadership and organisation

The emphasis on the decisive role of the state during the planned non-capitalist transformation of the village which necessarily arose from the intermal laws governing this process in no way underestimates the active role of the peasant masses.[16] On the contrary, it is important to guide and organise the process of transformation – its speed and intensity during the stages of development in such a way that it leads to growing mobilization and active participation of the peasant masses; so that, as Lenin wrote even in 1923, the "really large masses of the population actually take port."[17] According this thesis, non-capitalist transformation of the village is in the objective interests of the peasant masses, and without their conscious participation it cannot be carried out.

The experiences of the Mali Republic have shown, however, that particularly at the early stages it is difficult to draw the mass of peasants actively and consciously into the tasks of non-capitalist transformation in agriculture. Undeveloped economic conditions, archaic social structures, a low level of education and small political experience and organisation prevent the peasants from playing an active role in this process. So there is a contradiction between the necessity for democratic mass initiative and the actual possibilities for mobilising the peasants. This contradiction can really only be resolved when the objective factors preventing a solution – the low level of the productive forces, back ward economic and social structures – have been overcome. However, as these barriers can only be overcome together with the peasants, ways and means must be found gradually to resolve this contradiction.

In this process, the subjective factor is of the utmost importance. The peasants must be put into a position to participate in the non-capitalist transformation by intensive political and ideological work and by a greater degree of organisation. One the one hand, it is necessary for the political and other organisations in the village – the party and youth organisation, cultural and co-operative organisations — to be not simply an executive offshoot of the central organisations and institutions, but they should lead a life of their own to some extent. On the other hand, they should be developed into real peasants organisations. They should not be allowed to come under the influence of the traditional leaders and preserve or revive traditional structures, or become instruments for capitalist development under the influence of agrarian bourgeois elements. Through these organisations, and in the framework of the whole work of development, the peasants must be made capable of participating actively in the transformation of the village. This is a fundamental question of non-capitalist development in agriculture. Unfortunately, it is often underestimated in African countries because the petty-bourgeois leaders — especially the medium-ranking cadres — have a certain feeling of arrogance towards the peasants, arising from differences in their social positions. This leads in practice, to bureaucratic and administrative behaviour which makes mobilisation of the peasants even more difficult. Therefore, to draw the peasants into solving the problems of agriculture, a large number of ideological changes are needed. On these foundations changes in the methods of work and leadership in the central bodies for agricultural development must be made.

Only the correct relationship between the leading role of the party and state, and the democratic, active participation of the peasant masses — i.e. an economically and politically effective alliance between the revolutionary leaders and the working peasantry — can guarantee maximum speed and success in solving the problems of non-capitalist transformation of agriculture.

REFERENCES

1 That is, for all those countries in which the agrarian question was not influenced in a particular way by a large number of European settlers or through an already existing national agrarian bourgeoisie.
2 In the former British colonies of West and Central Africa, the same applies to the semi-feudal, traditional aristocracy which was preserved by the colonial power.
3 See B. Ponomarev, "Aktuelle Probleme der Theorie des revolutionären Weltprozesses", in: *Der XXIV. Parteitag der KPdSU und die Entwicklung der marxistisch-leninistischen Theorie*, Berlin 1971, pp. 112ff.
4 See V. Shelepin, "The World of Socialism and the Developing Countries", in: *New Times*, 9/1970.
5 At the international symposium "Lenin's Teaching on the National Liberation Revolutions and the Current Phase of Social Progress in the Developing Countries" which was held in October 1969 in Alma-Ata attended by scientists and prominent figures from 51 including above all, developing countries, many of the speakers emphasized that Lenin's theory on the multi-sector

economy is the key to understanding many problems and tendencies of the young independent states. The speakers at the symposium summarized: "In the light of this theory, the socio-economic essence of non-capitalist development can be only a certain relation between and the interaction of various sectors and classes and of the social groups arising out of these sectors" (S. Khamiz/J. Rosaliev, "V. I. Lenin and the Current Problems of the National Liberation Movement", in: *World Marxist Review*, 12/1969; see *Problemy nacional'no-osvoboditel'nogo dviženija. Materialy meždunarodnogo simpoziuma*, Alma-Ata 1969, Moscow 1970).

6 Ulyanovski reaches the same conclusions with respect to the sector of private small and medium trade capital: "The nationalization of the private trade sector and especially of private retail and wholesale trade has a negative effect, as experience in several countries has shown; it disturbs normal economic life, the economic links between city and countryside may even cause dissatisfaction among the people. Experiences in the Soviet Union in 1921–30, in the U. A. R., Syria, Algeria and other countries in the recent past have shown that it is necessary to allow the existence of small and medium private trade (under strict state control) so long as the state and co-operatives are not yet able to completely take over the organization of goods distribution and of exchange." (R. Ulyanovski, "Leninism, Soviet Experiences and the Liberated Countries", in: *New Times*, 2/1971).

7 See J. Suret-Canale, "Tribes, Classes and Nations in Tropical Africa", in: *World Marxist Review*, 11/1969.

8 This could, of course, only occur for a limited period on a limited territory. In areas where the commodity-money relations had already become an essential part of the system of production and exchange, the objective result of the same measures was an acceleration of the spontaneous disintegration of the traditional community.

9 See above.

10 Co-operatives can grow in both a capitalist and a socialist state. The character they take on are determined by the political and economic relations of power existing on a national level (see V. I. Lenin, *On Co-operation*, in: *Collected Works*, vol. 33, Moscow 1966, p. 472).

11 See R. A. Ulyanovski, *Besonderheiten und Schwierigkeiten der national-demokratischen Revolution auf dem nichtkapitalistischen Entwicklungsweg*, loc. cit., p. 793.

12 The N. E. P. was carried out under the dictatorship of the proletariat.

13 See R. A. Ulyanovski, *Leninism, Soviet Experiences and the Liberated Countries*, loc., cit.

14 Here one should use the principle recommended by Lenin for the European middle peasants: "The revolutionary proletariat cannot set itself the task — at least not in the immediate future or in the initial period of the dictatorship of the proletariat — of winning over this stratum, but must confine itself to the task of neutralising it i. e., rendering it neutral in the struggle between proletariat and bourgeoisie. This stratum inevitably vacillates between these

two forces; in the beginning of the new epoch and in the developed capitalist countries it will, in the main, incline towards the bourgeoisie. That is because the world outlook and the sentiments of the property owners are prevalent among this stratum, which has a direct interest in profiteering, in 'freedom' of trade and in property, and stands in direct antagonism to the wage workers" (V. I. Lenin, *Preliminary Draft Theses on the Agrarian Question*, in: *Collected Works*, vol. 31, Moscow 1966, pp. 156—7).
15 Ibid. p. 157.
16 As the bourgeois authors generally imply with their talk of an "authoritarian state socialism" which allegedly prevents the development of mass initiative, and cannot therefore be regarded as exemplary for the developing countries (see R. F. Behrendt, op. cit., pp. 36ff., 200ff. and 387ff.).
17 V. I. Lenin, *On Co-operation*, loc. cit., p. 469.

APPENDIX

Appendix 227

Administrative Structure and Population in Republic of Mali 1969

Region	District	Estimated Population	Territory (sq.km.)	Population density (inhabitants per sq.km)
Kayes	Kayes	151,830	22,188	6.8
	Bafoulabé	94,520	20.125	4.5
	Kéniéba	83.360	14.000	6.0
	Kita	142.900	35.250	4.1
	Nioro	203.930	22.500	9.1
	Yélimané	67.730	5.750	11.8
Kayes		744.270	119.813	6.2
Bamako	Bamako	377.720	16.300	23.2
	Banamba	74.260	7.700	9.6
	Dioila	119.180	13.000	9.2
	Kangaba	44.000	4.700	9.4
	Kolokani	107.270	11.700	9.2
	Koulikoro	80.680	6.000	13.4
	Nara	113.680	30.700	3.7
Bamako		916.790	90.100	10.2
Sikasso	Sikasso	232.530	15.375	15.1
	Bougouni	162.310	19.100	8.5
	Kadiolo	74.770	5.375	13.9
	Kolondiéba	85.720	9.200	9.3
	Koutiala	215.200	13.430	16.0
	Yanfolila	79.330	8.800	9.0
	Yorosso	62.010	5.200	11.9
Sikasso		911.870	76.480	11.9
Ségou	Ségou	304.390	12.750	23.9
	San	178.380	7.188	24.8
	Ké-Macina	103.230	6.563	15.7
	Niono	74.390	23.063	3.2
	Tominian	98.680	6.563	15.0
Ségou		759.070	56.127	13.5

15*

Region	District	Estimated Population	Territory (sq.km.)	Population density (inhabitants per sq.km)
Mopti	Mopti	147.620	9.340	15.8
	Bandiagara	127.800	7.250	17.6
	Bankass	114.930	6.875	16.7
	Djénné	95.110	4.563	20.8
	Douentza	123.840	23.312	5.3
	Koro	124.840	10.937	11.4
	Niafunké	171.400	15.375	11.2
	Ténenkou	85.200	11.100	7.7
Mopti		990.740	88.752	11.2
Gao	Gao	93.370	26.875	3.5
	Ansongo	64.260	22.813	2.8
	Bourem	100.030	41.068	2.4
	Diré	66.080	1.750	37.8
	Goundam	101.850	92.688	1.1
	Kidal	23.040	151.430	0.2
	G. Rharous	69.720	45.000	1.5
	Ménaka	35.770	79.813	0.4
	Tombouctou	52.140	347.438	0.2
Gao		606.260	808.870	0.7
Mali		4,929.000	1,240.142	4.0

Source: *Annuaire statistique 1969*, op. cit., p. 27.

Appendix

Illustration 1 – Republic Mali. Administrative structure
Copied from: Ministaire Plan. Direction de la Statistique. Annuaire Statistique 1967 de la Republique du Mali.
Bamako 1968, p. 9

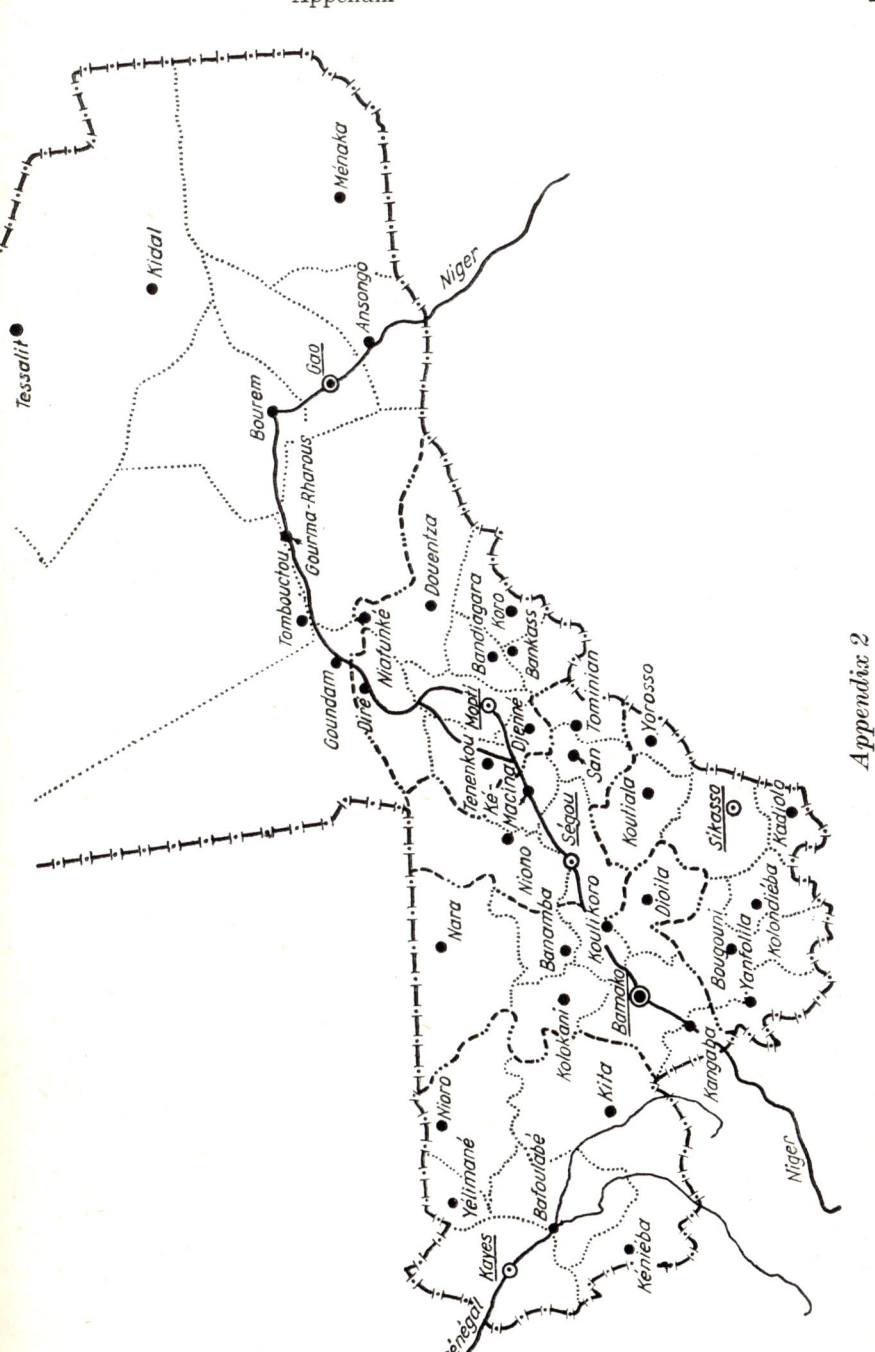

Appendix 2

Illustration 2 — Republic of Mali. Territories inhabited by the largest ethnic groups. Copied from: Ministaire Plan. Direction de la Statistique. Annuaire Statistique 1967 de la Republique du Mali. Bamako 1968, p. 9 (The author entered the ethnic groups – publisher).

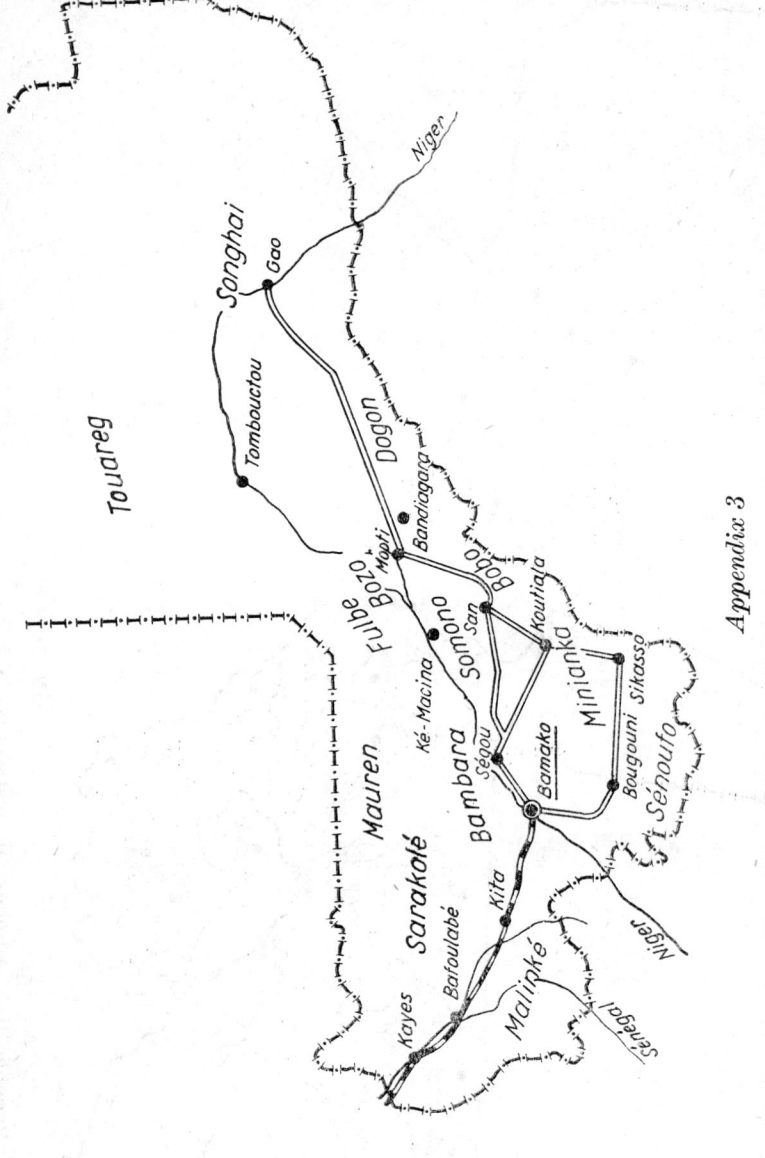

Appendix: 3

Appendix

Table 1: *Arrondissement* Barouéli – Population

No.	Basic Sector	Number of Villages	Total Population	Medium Village	Male active population Absolute	Male active population % of Total Population	Number of Families	Medium Family
1	Barouéli	4	5856	1464	1390	23.7	629	9.4
2	Kalaké	10	4446	445	695	15.6	380	11.7
3	Tafalan	8	2391	299	428	17.9	219	10.9
4	Nianzana	8	3437	417	592	17.2	335	11.2
5	N'Dyeni	9	2486	276	525	21.1	258	10.8
6	Soliko	9	2253	250	439	19.5	188	12.5
7	Sougou	9	2744	305	434	15.9	278	9.9
8	Tigui	8	1723	215	445	25.8	175	9.8
	Total	65	25336	390	4948	19.5	2462	10.3

Table 2: *Arrondissement* Barouéli – Level of Agricultural Productive Forces 1966–7

No.	Basic Sector	Ploughs	Carts	Sprayers	Multi-Purpose Instruments	Scuffler	Plough-oxen	Dung Heap exis-tent	Dung Heap func-tioning	Compost Heap exis-tent	Compost Heap func-tioning
1	Barouéli	306	153	55	9	3	602	122	107	109	90
2	Kalaké	269	103	79	8	89	544	101	75	50	50
3	Tafalan	109	43	16	3	—	212	23	13	48	18
4	Nianzana	188	53	33	1	—	372	96	67	175	144
5	N'Dyeni	116	32	25	1	—	250	23	14	48	28
6	Soliko	113	26	23	1	8	228	80	64	61	44
7	Sougou	114	33	12	—	—	188	49	14	57	57
8	Tigui	93	35	9	—	—	142	15	15	38	38
	Total	1308	428	252	24	100	2538	509	369	586	469
	Per ten inhabitants	0.52	0.17	0.10	0.009	0.039	1.0	0.2	0.15	0.23	0.19
	Per farm	0.41	0.13	0.74	0.007	0.031	0.8	0.16	0.11	0.18	0.15

Table 3: Arrondissement Barouéli – Agrarian Production 1966–7

No.	Basic Sector	Culti-vated Area	Millet % of Total Area	Millet Gross Prod. (tons)	Culti-vated Area	Cotton % of Total Area	Cotton Gross Prod. (tons)	Culti-vated Area	Peanuts % of Total Area	Peanuts Gross Prod. (tons)	Other Food Crops[1] Culti-vated Area	Other Food Crops[1] % of Total Area	Total Culti-vated Area
1	Barouéli	3495	79.0	911	414	9.35	258	295	6.65	96.7	221	5	4425
2	Kalaké	1385	49.4	887.5	563	20.4	530	698	25.2	370.4	139	5	2785
3	Tafalan	1420	71.7	578	176	8.9	99.5	285	14.4	228	99	5	1980
4	Nianzana	1576	54.2	1718	269	9.2	152	920	31.6	465.5	146	5	2911
5	N'Dyeni	865	60.6	585.6	236	16.5	127.5	256	17.9	199.9	71.5	5	1428.5
6	Soliko	1168	67.3	448.5	180.3	10.4	160	300	17.3	243.6	86.8	5	1735.1
7	Sougou	1805	84.8	476.5	128	6.0	54.5	90	4.2	37.9	106.5	5	2129.5
8	Tigui	1065	85.4	429.5	51	4.1	26.7	69	5.5	34.2	62.5	5	1247.5
	Total	12779	68.6	6094.6	2017.3	10.8	1408.2	2913	15.6	1596.2	932.3	5	18641.6
	Per ten inhabitants	5.05	—	2.74	0.81	—	0.56	1.15	—	0.63	0.37	—	7.35
	Per farm	3.99	—	2.16	0.64	—	0.44	0.91	—	0.50	0.29	—	5.82
	Per hectare	—	—	0.48	—	—	0.70	—	—	0.55	—	—	—

[1] Unfortunately, the files of the chief of the Barouéli Z. E. R. gave only the figures for the areas cultivated with millet, cotton and peanuts. Therefore, I added together the amount of total cultivated area in the investigated villages, to arrive at a representative average for the "other crops". It is about 5% of the total cultivated land with extremes from 1.3% to 15.3%. These 5% consist of 2.15% maize, 0.66% fonio and 2.19% manioc. On the basis of these figures I was able to calculate the averages for each basic sector and the Z. E. R. as a whole.

Table 4: Arondissement Barouéli — Animal Stock 1956—7

No.	Basic Sector	Horses	Donkeys	Cattle	Sheep	Goats
1	Barouéli	94	134	1015	918	418
2	Kalaké	131	134	1605	784	615
3	Tafalan	59	21	643	483	499
4	Nianzana	108	55	1765	606	477
5	N'Dyeni	64	33	949	352	260
6	Soliko	54	59	509	266	234
7	Sougou	73	32	1153	585	404
8	Tigui	46	34	608	329	280
	Total	629	482	8247	4323	3187
	Per ten inhabitants	0.21	0.19	3.26	1.71	1.26
	Per farm	0.17	0.15	2.57	1.35	0.99

Table 5: *Arrondissement* Barouéli — Comparison of Selected Villages in 1960/1 and 1966/7[1]
I — Situation 1960/1

No.	Village	Millet Culti-vated Area	Millet Yield per Hectare	Cotton Culti-vated Area	Cotton Yield per Hectare	Peanuts Culti-vated Area	Peanuts Yield per Hectare	Total-Area[2]	Production Instrum.[3] Ploughs	Carts	Oxen
1	Werke-Bougou	79	509	12	162	38	600	129	13	7	30
2	Kalaké-Marka	208	1090	48	217	84	320	340	43	12	82
3	Kalaké-Bamana	127	673	26	249	26	318	179	25	7	37
4	Kintan-Marka	90	1050	16	397	33	512	149	17	6	34
5	Kintan-Bamana	75	980	16	229	16	410	107	13	4	24
6	Mamaricissé-Bougou	143	1000	46	165	43	560	232	28	6	44
7	Berthéla	115	1100	46	139	44	530	205	22	6	35
8	Beya	120	667	4	264	25	600	149	8	2	19
	Total	967	884	214	228	309	1481	1490	169	50	375
	Per ten inhabitants	2.64	—	0.58	—	0.84	—	4.06	0.46	0.14	1.0

[1] The basis of this comparison is the Barouéli Z. E. R. as it existed in 1960/1. At the time it consisted of only 12 villages of which four are not listed in the above for various reasons. The Bouwéré and Noukoula villages were excluded because today they belong to the *Arrondissement* and Z. E. R. Konobougou. The 1966/7 figures for Bébé were lacking. Barouéli could not be included because the figures in the 1960/1 statistics were obviously wrong.
[2] Only the total of millet, cotton, peanuts.
[3] Spraying instruments were not used at that time.

II – Situation 1966/7

No.	Village	Millet Cultivated Area	Millet Yield per Hectare	Cotton Cultivated Area	Cotton Yield per Hectare	Peanuts Cultivated Area	Peanuts Yield per Hectare[4]	Total Area	Production Instruments Ploughs	Carts	Spray-ers	Oxen[5]
1	Werke-Bougou	67	477	30	579	19	549	116	20	7	8	32
2	Kalaké-Marka	605	477	165	696	25	549	795	100	39	43	226
3	Kalaké-Bamana	250	477	60	525	18	549	328	28	12	5	69
4	Kintan-Marka	197	477	79	311	15	549	291	26	15	2	54
5	Kintan-Bamana	85	477	47.5	338	21.5	549	154	23	7	1	36
6	Mamaricissé-Bougou	88	477	50	606	8	549	146	18	4	4	80
7	Berthéla	137	477	58	565	25	549	220	23	3	6	48
8	Beya	43	477	22.5	402	6	549	71.5	10	3	1	22
	Total	1472	477	512	501	137.5	549	2121.5	248	90	70	567
	Per ten inhabitants	3.83	—	1.34	—	0.36	—	5.53	0.23	0.23	0.18	1.48

[4] As the hectare yields for millet and peanuts were not given on a village basis for 1966/7, I have included the average yield from the whole *Arrondissement*
[5] 1965/6

Table 6: Basic Data in the Investigated Villages of the Barouéli Z. E. R.

No.	Village	Basic Sector	Inhabitants	Persons of Working Age	Nuclear Families	Farms	Families	Total Area	Industr. crops	Mango	Ploughs	Oxen	Carts	Sprayers
1	Nianzana	Nianzana	395	103	82	56	38	268	58	41	22	49	8	1
2	Dyigani	Tigui	95	36	28	18	9	47	16	15	8	15	4	1
3	Bakoromb.	Tafalan	298	75	45	25	18	136	38	35	23	36	5	4
4	Niola	Soliko	156	48	32	16	13	64	16	395	8	11	3	3
5	Konimbab.	Sougou	150	61	32	18	15	96	32	18	9	44	3	—
6	Sédiola	Djeni	141	33	40	13	7	44	14	15	4	12	2	2
7	Sentébougou	Barouéli	101	28	30	17	11	72	12	6	4	22	2	2
	Total		1336	384	289	163	111	727	186	525	78	188	27	13

Table 7: Population, Farms, Means of Production and Transport, Animals according to Family Categories I–IV

	Total	I Absolute	I % of Total	II Absolute	II % of Total	III Absolute	III % of Total	IV Absolute	IV % of Total
Families	111	41	36.9	13	11.7	16	14.5	41	36.9
Population	1319	608	46.1	328	24.8	172	13.1	211	16.0
Farms	163	41	25.2	42	25.8	39	23.8	41	25.2
Nuclear Families	289	129	44.6	80	27.7	39	13.5	41	14.2
Persons of Working Age	384	172	44.8	89	23.2	52	13.5	71	18.5
Area	727	315	43.3	154	21.3	113	15.5	145	19.9
Industr. Crops.	186	82	44.3	42	26.4	27	14.5	35	19.1
Mango trees	525	395	75.2	63	12.1	34	6.4	33	6.3
Ploughs	78	36	46.1	19	24.4	8	10.3	15	19.2
Dung	162	60	37.0	31	19.1	26	16.1	45	27.8
Carts	27	14	51.9	7	25.9	2	7.4	4	14.8
Oxen	188	80	42.6	55	19.2	14	7.5	39	20.7
Cows	472	242	51.3	188	39.9	4	0.1	38	8.7
Horses	35	20	57.1	7	20.0	2	5.7	6	17.2

Appendix

Table 8: Inhabitants, Nuclear Families, Farms and Persons of Working Age per Family and Farm according to Family Categories I–IV

		Total	I	II	III	IV
Inhabitants	per family	11.9	14.9	25.4	10.8	5.1
	per farm	8.1	14.9	7.8	4.4	5.1
	per nuclear family	4.6	4.7	4.1	4.4	5.1
Nuclear Families	per family	2.7	3.2	6.2	2.4	1.0
	per farm	1.8	3.2	1.9	1.0	1.0
Farms	per family	1.5	1.0	3.2	2.4	1.0
Persons of Working Age	per family	3.4	4.2	6.8	3.3	1.7
	per farm	2.3	4.2	2.1	1.3	1.7

Table 9: Cultivated Area, Mango Trees per Farm Inhabitants, Persons of Working Age, Ploughs according to Family Categories I–IV

		Total	I	II	III	IV
Cultivated land in hectares	per farm	4.5	7.7	3.7	2.9	3.5
	per inhabitant	0.55	0.52	0.47	0.65	0.69
	per person of working age	1.9	1.8	1.7	2.2	2.0
	per plough	9.4	8.8	8.1	14.1	9.7
Industr. Crops in hectares	per farm	1.1	2.0	1.0	0.7	0.9
	per inhabitant	0.14	0.13	0.13	0.15	0.17
	per person of working age	0.5	0.5	0.5	0.5	0.5
	per plough	2.4	2.3	2.2	3.4	2.3
	percentage of total cultivated area	25.6	25.9	27.1	24.1	24.6
Mango trees	per farm	3.22	9.64	1.50	0.87	0.81
	per inhabitant	0.40	0.64	0.19	0.20	0.16

Table 10: Ploughs, Oxen, Carts, Cows and Horses per Farm
and Inhabitant according to Categories I–IV

		Total	I	II	III	IV
Ploughs	per farm	0.48	0.88	0.45	0.21	0.37
	per ten inhabitants	0.59	0.59	0.60	0.47	0.71
Draught-oxen	per farm	1.16	1.95	1.31	0.36	0.95
	per ten inhabitants	1.43	1.32	1.73	0.82	1.85
Carts	per farm	0.17	0.34	0.17	0.05	0.10
	per ten inhabitants	0.20	0.23	0.21	0.12	0.19
Cows	per farm	2.90	5.91	4.48	0.10	0.93
	per ten inhabitants	3.58	3.98	5.73	0.23	1.80
Horses	per farm	0.22	0.49	0.17	0.05	0.15
	per ten inhabitants	0.27	0.33	0.21	0.12	0.29

Table 11: Distribution of Farms (IV) according
to Size and Area per ten Inhabitants

Size in hectares	\	Hectare per ten inhabitants						
	0–5 absolute	%	5.1–9.9 absolute	%	10 and over absolute	%	total absolute	%
0 – 2	10	83.4	2	16.6	–	–	12	29.3
2.1– 4	6	35.3	3	17.6	8	47.1	17	41.4
4.1– 6	–	–	4	57.2	3	42.8	7	17.1
6.1– 8	–	–	1	50.0	1	50.0	2	4.9
8.1–10	–	–	1	33.3	2	66.7	3	7.3
Total	16	39.0	11	26.8	14	34.2	41	100

Table 12: Distribution of Farms (IV) according to Size and Area per Person of Working Age

Size in hectares	0—1 absolute	0—1 %	1.1—2 absolute	1.1—2 %	2.1—3 absolute	2.1—3 %	3.1 and over absolute	3.1 and over %	Total absolute	Total %
0 — 2	5	41.7	7	58.3	—	—	—	—	12	29.3
2.1— 4	3	17.7	2	11.8	12	70.5	—	—	17	41.4
4.1— 6	—	—	—	—	7	100.0	—	—	7	17.1
6.1— 8	—	—	—	—	—	—	2	100.0	2	4.9
8.1—10	—	—	—	—	3	100.0	—	—	3	7.3
Total	8	19.5	9	21.9	22	53.7	2	4.9	41	100.0

Table 13: Distribution of Farms (IV) according to Area per ten Inhabitants and per Person of Working Age

hectares per 10 inhabitants	0—1 absolute	0—1 %	1.1—2 absolute	1.1—2 %	2.1—3 absolute	2.1—3 %	3.1 and over absolute	3.1 and over %	Total absolute	Total %
1 — 5	7	43.7	8	50.0	1	6.3	—	—	16	39.0
5.1— 9.9	1	9.1	1	9.1	8	72.7	1	9.1	11	26.8
10 and over	—	—	—	—	13	92.9	1	7.1	14	34.2
Total	8	19.5	9	21.9	22	53.7	2	4.9	41	100.0

Table 14: Members of the Ton according to Villages, Sex per Person of Working Age and total Population

Village	Male Members	% of Ton	% of active village population (male)	Female Members	% of Ton	Total Members	Total Village Population	% of Ton Members to Village Population
Kintan-B. I [1]	25	62.5	27.5	15	37.5	40	317	12.6
Kintan-B. II	8	80.0	8.8	2	20.0	10	(317)	3.2
Beya	17	63.0	32.7	10	37.0	27	176	15.3
Dyigani	32	62.8	86.5	19	37.2	51	95	53.6
Bakorombg.	15	48.4	20.0	16	51.6	31	298	10.4
Niola	38	86.4	79.2	6	13.6	44	156	28.2
Konimbabg.	13	65.0	21.3	7	35.0	20	150	13.3
Sediola	18	53.0	54.5	16	47.0	34	141	24.1
Nianzana	30	63.9	28.8	17	36.1	47	395	11.9
Sentébougou	9	47.4	32.1	10	52.6	19	101	18.8
Total	205	63.1	38.1	120	36.9	325	1839	17.7

[1] In Kintan-Bamana there exist two Ton, together 50 members, who make up 18.8% of the total population. The 33 male members are 36.3% of the active male population.

Glossary of Bambara words

BUNYA	Village reserve
DIONFORO	Field for individual use
DONSO	Hunter
DUGU	Village
DUGUTIGI	Village head
DYELI	Griot, praise-singers who pass on legends and tradition by word of mouth
DYON	Slave
DYONGORON	Released slave
FA	Synonym for FAKOROBA
FAKOROBA	Head of extended family
FAMA	King in the Bambara kingdom
FOROBA	Possessions of the extended family
Foroba	Field belonging to an extended family
FURU-NA-FOLO	Bride-price
GARANKA	Saddler
HORON	Free community member
KAFO	Federation of villages
KAFOTIGI	Head of village federation
KOROU	The "elders", extended family council
KULE	Wood-carver
LAMA	Institution for mutual aid between several extended families within a village community
LORO	Coppersmith
LU	Extended family
LUTIGI	Synonym for FAKOROBA
NUMU	Blacksmith
NYAMAKALA (plural: NYAMAKALAU)	Member of a caste
NYANA-DUGU-DA-SIRI	Earth spirit
TON	Secular youth organisation
ULA-NO	Production from the DIONFORO
WOLOSO	A slave living in a free extended family

Bibliography

I. Subject References from Marx, Engels, Lenin and International Labour Movement

Marx, K., *Capital*, vol. 1–3, Moscow n. d.
—, *Foundations of the Critique of Political Economy*, The Pelican Marx Library, 1973.
—, *Preface to the Critique of Political Economy*, in: K. Marx/F. Engels, *Selected Works*, vol. 1, Moscow 1973.
—, *First Draft of the Reply to V. I. Zasulich's Letter*, in: K. Marx/F. Engels, *Selected Works*, vol. 3, Moscow 1973.
Engels, F., *Anti-Dühring*, Progress Publishers, Moscow 1969.
—, *Origin of the Family, Private Property and State*, in: K. Marx/F. Engels, *Selected Works*, vol. 3, Moscow 1973.
—, "On Social Relations in Russia" (Article V from *Flüchtlingsliteratur*), in: K. Marx/F. Engels, *Selected Works*, vol. 2, Moscow 1973.
Lenin, V. I., *What the "Friends of the People" are and how they Fight the Social-Democrats*, in: *Collected Works*, vol. 1, Moscow 1960.
—, *The Economic Content of Narodism and the Criticism of it in Mr. Struve's Book*, in: *Collected Works*, vol. 1, Moscow 1960.
—, *The Agrarian Programme of Social-Democracy in the First Russian Revolution, 1905–1907*, in: *Collected Works*, vol. 13, Moscow 1962.
—, *On Narodism*, in: *Collected Works*, vol. 18, Moscow 1963.
—, *Democracy and Narodism in China*, in: *Collected Works*, vol. 18, Moscow 1963.
—, *Narodism and the Class of Wage-Workers*, in: *Collected Works*, vol. 20, Moscow 1964.
—, *Imperialism, the Highest Stage of Capitalism*, in: *Collected Works*, vol. 22, Moscow 1964.
—, *Address to the 2nd All-Russia Congress of Communist Organisations of the Peoples of the East*, in: *Collected Works*, vol. 30, Moscow 1965.
—, *Preliminary Draft Theses on the Agrarian Question*, in: *Collected Works*, vol. 31, Moscow 1966.
—, *The Second Congress of the Communist International. Report of the Commission on the National and Colonial Question*, in: *Collected Works*, vol. 31, Moscow 1966.

Lenin, V. I., *"Left-Wing" Communism – an Infantile Disorder*, in: Collected Works, vol. 31, Moscow 1966.
—, *Third Congress of the Communist International. Report on the Tactics of the R. C. P.*, in: Collected Works, vol. 32, Moscow 1965.
—, *Tenth Congress of the R. C. P. (B.). Report on the Substitution of a Tax in Kind for the Surplus-Grain Appropriation System*, in: Collected Works, vol. 32, Moscow 1965.
—, *On Co-operation*, in: Collected Works, vol. 33, Moscow 1966.
Erklärung der Beratung von Vertretern der kommunistischen und Arbeiterparteien, November 1960, Berlin 1961.
Internationale Beratung der kommunistischen und Arbeiterparteien (Moscow 1969), Berlin 1969.
VIII. Parteitag der Sozialistischen Einheitspartei Deutschlands (Berlin 1971), Bericht des Zentralkomitees an den VIII. Parteitag der SED. Speaker: Genosse E. Honecker, Berlin 1971.
Rechenschaftsbericht des Zentralkomitees der KPdSU an den XXIV. Parteitag der Kommunistischen Partei der Sowjetunion. Speaker: L. I. Brezshnev, Moscow/ Berlin 1971.
Der XXIV. Parteitag der KPdSU und die Entwicklung der marxistisch-leninistischen Theorie, Berlin 1971.
Hager, K., *Die entwickelte sozialistische Gesellschaft. Aufgaben der Gesellschaftswissenschaften nach dem VIII. Parteitag der SED* (Referat auf der Tagung der Gesellschaftswissenschaftler, October 1971), Berlin 1971.

II. Documents, Statistics, Laws

"1967. An I de la Révolution", Bamako n. d.
Arreté du Lieutenant-Gouverneur p. i. portant réorganisation de l'Administration indigène dans la Colonie du Soudan Francais, *Journal Officiel du Soudan Français*, 693/1935.
Arreté Territorial N° 491 D. 1–3 du 10 avril 1958, *Journal Officiel du Soudan Français*, 1379/1958.
Badian, S. (Kouyaté), *Les dirigeants africains face à leur peuple*, Paris 1965.
Banque Centrale des Etats de l'Afrique de l'Ouest. *Comptes Economiques du Mali 1956*, Paris 1960.
(B. D. P. A.), Leynaud, E. *Les cadres sociaux de la vie rurale dans la Haute-Vallée du Niger* (2 vol.), Paris 1961 (photostat).
(B. D. P. A.). de Poncins, "Projet en vue de ruralisation de l'enseignement fondamental – Mali, Paris 1964 (photostat).
(B. D. P. A.) Woillet, "La modernisation rurale dans la Haute-Vallée du Niger. Les marchés", Paris 1961 (photostat).
Caillol, R., "Enquête agricole dans le Delta Central Nigérien. (Zone inondée – Office du Niger)", Paris n. d. (photostat).
C. F. D. T., "Rapport sur les zones d'encadrement rural dirigées par la C. F. D. T. sur le territoire de la République du Mali", Paris 1961 (photostat).

Chambre de Commerce, d'Agriculture et d'Industrie de Bamako, "Annuaire Administratif de la République du Mali", Bamako 1964 (photostat).
Chambre de Commerce, d'Agriculture et d'Industrie de Bamako. "Annuaire Administratif de la République du Mali", Bamako 1965 (photostat).
Chambre de Commerce, d'Agriculture et d'Industrie de Bamako. "Annuaire Statistique 1961 de la République du Mali", Bamako 1962 (photostat).
Chambre de Commerce, d'Agriculture et d'Industrie de Bamako, "Annuaire Statistique 1962 de la République du Mali", Bamako 1963 (photostat).
Chambre de Commerce, d'Agriculture et d'Industrie de Bamako. "Eléments du Bilan économique de l'Année 1960", Bamako 1961 (photostat).
Chambre de Commerce, d'Agriculture et d'Industrie de Bamako. "Eléments du Bilan économique 1962", Bamako 1963 (photostat).
Chambre de Commerce, d'Agriculture et d'Industrie de Bamako. "Eléments du Bilan économique 1963", Bamako 1964 (photostat).
Chambre de Commerce, d'Agriculture et d'Industrie de Bamako. "Eléments du Bilan économique 1974", Bamako 1965 (photostat).
Chambre de Commerce, d'Agriculture et d'Industrie de Bamako. "Eléments du Bilan économique 1965", Bamako 1966 (photostat).
Chambre de Commerce, d'Agriculture et d'Industrie de Bamako, *Le Mali*, Bamako 1961.
Chambre de Commerce, d'Agriculture et d'Industrie de Bamako. "Notice sur le territoire du Soudan Français, Bamako 1955" (photostat).
Chambre de Commerce, d'Agriculture et d'Industrie de Bamako. "Précis fiscal, commercial, des changes et des échanges 1964", Bamako 1964 (photostat).
Chambre de Commerce, d'Agriculture et d'Industrie de Bamako. "Répertoire des Entreprises financières, industrielles exerçant en République du Mali", Bamako 1964 (photostat).
"Collectivités rurales et action". Document du Ministère de l'Economie Rurale et du Plan de la République Soudanaise, in: *Le Mali*, December 1959.
Colloque sur les politiques de développement et les diverses voies africaines vers le socialisme, Dakar 3.–8. December 1962, Paris 1963.
Haut Commissariat de l'Afrique Occidentale Francaise: *Annuaire Statistique de L'A. O. F., 1950–1954,* Paris 1957.
Conférence territorial de l'Union Soudanaise, 17/18/19. October 1958, n. d.
Congrès constitutif du P. F. A. Dakar 1.–3. July 1959.
Congrès extraordinaire de l'U. S.–R. D. A., 22. September 1960, Le Mali continue, n. d.
Congrès des paysans du Soudan, Bamako 23.–24. January 1955. Textes adoptés.
VIe Congrès de l'Union Soudanaise–R. D. A. Bamako les 10/11/12. September 1962, Bamako 1963.
2ème Congrès de L'Union Syndicale des Travailleurs du Soudan des 25–26–27 et 28 février 1960. Règlement interieur de L'Union Syndicale des Travailleurs du Soudan. Résolution générale. Résolution sur les problèmes sociaux. Résolution sur problèmes économiques. Statuts, Bamako 1960 (photostat).
1er Congrès national de l'U. N. T. M. des 24, 25, 26, 27 et 28 juillet 1963. Inter-

vention du camarade Modibo Keita Président du Gouvernement et Secrétaire général de l'U. S.–R. D. A. Rapport d'activités et d'orientation. Résolution générale. Résolution sur L'Organisation. Statuts de L'Union Nationale des Travailleurs du Mali, Bamako 1963 (photostat).

Premier Congrès Soudanaise de Technique et Colonisation africaines, Bamako-Ségou, février 1936, vol. I: Rapport général, vol. II: Rapports particuliers.

Décret portant dissolution de l'association dénommé "Union Démocratique Ségovienne" du 5 février 1959, *Journal Officiel de la République Soudanaise*, 15/1959.

Décret portant dissolution de l'association dénommé "Union Dogon" à Bandiagara du 15 mai 1959. *Journal Officiel de la République Soudanaise*, 23/1959.

Décret portant organisation, mode de Recrutement et statut du Service civique du Mali du 21 décembre 1963, *Journal Officiel de la République du Mali*, 161/1964.

Décret portant organisation du Service civique rural du 29 octobre 1960, *Journal Officiel de la République du Mali*, 69/1960.

Diarra, I., "Mass Party and the Construction of Socialism", in: *World Marxist Review*, 1/1967.

(Ecole Supérieure du Parti). *Histoire du R. D. A.*, Bamako 1964.

(Ecole Supérieure du Parti). *Programme de l'Ecole Supérieure du Parti*, Bamako n. d.

(Ecole Supérieure du Parti). *Programme des Ecoles Régionales du Parti*, Bamako n. d.

(Ecole Supérieure du Parti). *L'Union Soudanaise–R. D. A. et la libération nationale*, Bamako n. d.

(Ecole Supérieure du Parti). *L'U. S.–R. D. A.*, Bamako n. d.

Fédération du Mali. République Soudanaise. Session Budgétaire de l'Assemblée Législative, 17. November 1959, Koulouba n. d.

Gouvernement Général de l'Afrique Occidentale Française. Colonie du Haut-Sénégal et Niger. *Rapport d'Ensemble sur la Situation Générale de la Colonie du Haut-Sénégal-Niger en 1907*, Paris 1909.

Gouvernement Générale de l'Afrique Occidentale Francaise, Soudan Français. *Recueil des instructions sur l'administration des Sociétés de Prévoyance*, Koulouba 1951.

Gouvernement du Soudan Français. *Régime Fiscal 1949*, Bamako n. d.

Gouvernement du Soudan Français. Service Agriculture. *Note sur l'évolution de la mécanisation agricole du Soudan*, Bamako 1957.

K. M., "Le Mali et la recherche d'un socialisme africain", – *Démocratie nouvelle*. Paris, numéro spécial, December 1960.

Loi N° 60–8 du 9 juin 1960 portant statuts des Société mutuelles de Développement rural dans la République Soudanaise, *Journal Officiel de la République Soudanaise*, 57/1960.

Niaré, S., "Evolution de l'Economie rurale au Soudan", Bamako 1959 (photostat).

Ordonnance N° 43 portant organisation des villages au Soudan et créant des

Conseils de village du 28 mars 1959, *Journal Officiel de la République Soudanaise*, Numéro spécial, 1. April 1959.
Outre-Mer 1958. *Tableau économique et social des Etats et Territoires d'Outre-Mer à la veille de la mise en place des nouvelles institutions*, Paris 1960.
Parti de la Fédération Africaine. "L'Union Soudanaise R. D. A. a la veille de l'Indépendance", n. d.
"Rapport de Synthese du Séminaire national sur la Coopération en Milieu rural", n. d.
République du Mali. Appel à la nation du Président Modibo Keita, Bamako 1961.
République du Mali. C. F. D. T. "Rapport sur la campagne cotonnière 1965–1966", Paris 1966 (photostat).
République du Mali. C. F. D. T. "Rapport Campagne cotonnière 1968–1969", Bamako n. d. (photostat).
République du Mali. *Code du Mariage et de la tutelle en République du Mali*, Bamako 1963.
République du Mali. "Deux Années de Gestion du Comité Militaire de Libération Nationale". Déclarations du Lieutenant Moussa Traoré, Président du Comité Militaire de Libération Nationale, Président du Gouvernement et Chef de l'Etat, Bamako n. d.
République du Mali. *Enquête Agricole au Mali 1960*, Paris 1964.
République du Mali. "Ministère du Développement. Programme Mil", Bamako 1965 (photostat).
République du Mali. Ministère du Développement. "Rapport sur l'execution par le Ministre du Développement de la deuxième tranche 62–63 du Plan Quinquennal", Bamako 1963 (photostat).
République du Mali. Ministère d'Etat chargé du Plan et de la Coordination des Affaires économiques et financières. "Direction de la Statistique 1963 de la République du Mali", Bamako 1964 (photostat).
République du Mali. Ministère d'Etat chargé du Plan et de la Coordination des Affaires économiques et financières. "Direction de la Statistique, Annuaire Statistique 1964 de la République du Mali", Bamako 1865 (photostat).
République du Mali. Ministère d'Etat chargé du Plan et de la Coordination des Affaires économiques et financières. Direction de la Statistique. "Annuaire Statistique 1966 de la République du Mali", Bamako 1967 (photostat).
République du Mali. Ministère d'Etat chargé du Plan et de la Coordination des Affaires économiques et financières. "Rapport définitif de l'Enquête agricole 1964–1965", Bamako n. d. (photostat).
République du Mali. Ministère d'Etat chargé du Plan et de la Coordination des Affaires économiques et financières. Service de la Statistique générale et de la Comptabilité économique nationale. "Bulletin annuel de conjoncture. (Situation économique du Mali au 31 décembre 1962)", Bamako 1963 (photostat).
République du Mali. Ministère d'Etat chargé du Plan et de la Coordination des Affaires économiques et financières. Service de la Statistique générale et de la

Comptabilité économique nationale. "Prix et Indices des Prix", Bamako 1965 (photostat).
République du Mali. Ministère d'Etat du Plan et de la Coordination des Affaires économiques et financières. Service de la Statistique générale et de la Comptabilité économique nationale. "Perspective de la Population du Mali 1963–1973", Bamako n. d. (photostat).
République du Mali. Ministère de la Justice et du Travail. Direction générale du Travail et de la Sécurité sociale. Office National de la Main d'Oeuvre. "Recensement général des Salariés du 31 aout 1966". Publication provisoire, Bamako 1968 (photostat).
République du Mali. Ministère du Plan et de la Coordination des Affaires économiques et financières. *Comptes Economiques de la République du Mali 1959*, Paris 1962.
République du Mali. Ministère du Plan et de l'Economie rurale. Données Economiques, Paris n. d.
République du Mali. Ministère du Plan et de l'Economie rurale. "Encadrement rural en République du Mali", *Action rurale*, Edition spéciale.
République du Mali. Ministère du Plan et de l'Economie rurale. "Organisation du monde rural en République du Mali", *Action rurale*, Edition spéciale.
République du Mali. Ministère du Plan et de l'Economie rurale. "Rapport sur le Plan Quinquennal de Développement économique et social de la République du Mali 1961–1965", Paris n. d.
République du Mali. Ministère du Plan, de l'Equipement et de l'Industrie. Service de la Statistique générale de la Comptabilité nationale et de la Mécanographie. "Comptes économiques du Mali du 1er juillet 1964 au 30 juin 1967", Bamako 1969 (photostat).
République du Mali. Ministère du Plan. Service de la Statistique générale de la Comptabilité nationale et de la Mécanographie. "Evolution de la Situation économique au Mali depuis la Dévaluation de mai 1967", Bamako 1968 (photostat).
République du Mali. Ministère du Plan. Direction de la Statistique. "Annuaire Statistique 1967 de la République du Mali", Bamako 1968 (photostat).
République du Mali. Ministère du Plan, des Finances et des Affaires économiques. Service de la Statistique générale de la Mécanographie et de la Comptabilité nationale. "La Balance malienne des Payements de juillet 1964 à juillet 1968", Bamako 1969 (photostat).
République du Mali. Ministère du Plan, de l'Equipement et de l'Industrie. Service de la Statistique générale de la Comptabilité nationale et de la Mécanographie." Rapport définitif de l'Enquête agricole 1967–1968", Bamako 1969 (photostat).
République du Mali. Ministère du Plan, des Finances et des Affaires économiques. Service de la Statistique générale de la Mécanographie et de la Comptabilité nationale. "Principaux Résultats de l'Enquête agricole. Années 1967 et 1968", Bamako 1969 (photostat).
République du Mali. Ministère du Plan, de l'Equipement et de l'Industrie.

Service de la Statistique générale de la Comptabilité nationale et de la Mécanographie. "Annuaire Statistique 1968 de la République du Mali Bamako 1969" (photostat).
République du Mali. Ministère de la Production. "Service de l'Agriculture. Rapport annuel 1968–69", Bamako n. d. (photostat).
République du Mali. Mission socio-économique. "Enquête Budgétaire dans le Delta Central Nigérien (Zone Inondée-Office du Niger)", Paris 1961 (photostat).
République du Mali. Mission socio-économique du Soudan 1956–1958. *L'Alimentation des Populations rurales du Delta vif du Niger et de l'Office du Niger*, Paris 1961.
République du Mali. Mission socio-économique 1956–1958. "Enquête Démographique dans le Delta Central Nigérien". 1er Fascicule. Résultats Sommaires, Paris n. d.
République du Mali. Mission socio-économique 1956–1968. "Enquête démographique dans le Delta-Central Nigérien". Résultats détaillés, Paris n. d.
République du Mali. Office National de la Main d'Oeuvre. "Evolution des Salaires en République du Mali depuis 1953", Bamako 1962 (photostat).
République du Mali. "Où en est le Plan Quinquennal. Première campagne 1961–1962. Résultats", Bamako 1962.
République du Mali. "Panorama. Région économique de Sikasso. Année 1970", Sikasso 1971 (photostat).
République du Mali. Présidence du Gouvernement. Direction générale Plan — Statistique. Service de la Statistique générale de la Comptabilité nationale et de la Mécanographie. "Rapport de l'Enquête agricole 1968–1969", Bamako 1970 (photostat).
République du Mali. Présidence du Gouvernement. Direction générale du Plan et de la Statistique. Service de la Statistique générale, de la Comptabilité générale et de la Mécanographie. "Annuaire Statistique 1969 de la République du Mali", Bamako 1970 (photostat).
République du Mali. Région de Ségou. Cercle de San. "Statut des Groupements Ruraux Associés", San 1964.
République du Mali. Secrétariat d'Etat à l'Agriculture à l'Elevage et aux Eaux et Forêts. "Activités du Secrétariat d'Etat à l'Agriculture à l'Elevage et aux Eaux et Forêts en 1960", Bamako 1961 (photostat).
République du Mali. Secrétariat d'Etat à l'Agriculture et aux Eaux et Forêts. "Réalisation du Secrétariat d'Etat à l'Agriculture et aux Eaux et Forêts depuis le Congrès Extraordinaire du 22 septembre 1960", Bamako 1962 (photostat).
République du Mali. Service de la Statistique. *Comptes économiques du Mali 1964–1965*, Paris 1967.
(République Soudanaise, M. E. A. N.). Cotten, (A.-M.), "Le région de Sofara", Bamako 1959 (photostat).
(République Soudanaise, M. E. A. N.). Dupeyron, (G.), "Bintagoungou, village du Faguibine. Deux Aspects humaines de la crise du Lac", Bamako 1956–1957 (photostat).

(République Soudanaise, M. E. A. N.). Forget, (M.), "Le Kounary, région soudanaise à forte densité", Bamako 1957 (photostat).
(République Soudanaise, M. E. A. N.). Gallais, (J.), "Caractère de la vie agricole dans la zone sud-sahélienne (Région des Lacs Débo, Korienzé, Korarou)", Bamako 1956–57 (photostat).
(République Soudanaise, M. E. A. N.). Gallais, (J.), "Etude géographique au Delta Intérieur. Résultats préliminaires", Bamako 1959 (photostat).
(République Soudanaise, M. E. A. N.). Gallais, (J.), "Etude géographique au Delta Intérieur. Commentaire des cartes et répertoire des populations", Bamako 1959 (photostat).
(République Soudanaise, M. E. A. N.). Gallais, (J.), "Etude préliminaire de Mopti", Bamako 1959 (photostat).
(République Soudanaise, M. E. A. N.). Gallais, (J.), "La région du Diaka", Bamako 1959 (photostat).
(République Soudanaise, M. E. A. N.). Galloy, (P.), "Nomadisation et sédentarisation dans les cercles de Goundam et de Tombouctou", Bamako 1958 (photostat).
(République Soudanaise, M. E. A. N.). Grandet, (C.), "Populations sédentaires des cercles de Goundam et Tombouctou", Bamako 1956–57 (photostat).
(République Soudanaise, M. E. A. N.). Idiart, (P.), "La boucle du Niger. Cartes de géographie humaine", Bamako 1959 (photostat).
(République Soudanaise, M. E. A. N.). Idiart, (P.), "La boucle du Niger. Synthèse provisoire", Bamako 1959 (photostat).
(République Soudanaise, M. E. A. N.). Leroy, (Yves), "La pêche et le commerce du poisson à Mopti, Bamako 1956–57" (photostat).
(République Soudanaise, M. E. A. N.). Marchand, (M.)," La région de Konna", Bamako 1957 (photostat).
(République Soudanaise, M. E. A. N.). Millot, (F.), "La Haute et Moyenne Vallée du Niger", Bamako 1959 (photostat).
(République Soudanaise, M. E. A. N.). "Projet d'aménagement des Lacs Télé et Faguibine. Rapport justificatif", Bamako 1958 (photostat).
République Soudanaise. Ministère de l'Agriculture et des Eaux et Forêts. Direction de l'Agriculture. "Arachide", Bamako 1958 (photostat).
République Soudanaise. Ministère de l'Agriculture et des Eaux et Forêts. Direction de l'Agriculture. "Les Cantres d'Encadrement Rural", Bamako 1958 (photostat).
République Soudanaise. Ministère de l'Agriculture et des Eaux et Forêts. Direction de l'Agriculture. "Consideration sur la riziculture au Soudan Français", Bamako 1958 (photostat).
République Soudanaise. Ministère de l'Agriculture et des Eaux et Forêts. Direction de l'Agriculture. "L'enseignement agricole", Bamako 1958 (photostat).
(République Soudanaise. Ministère de l'Agriculture et des Eaux et Forêts. Direction de l'Agriculture). "Note sur l'encadrement rural", Bamako 1959 (photostat).

République Soudanaise. Ministère de l'Agriculture et des Eaux et Forêts. Direction de l'Agriculture. "Le problème de la fumure au Soudan", Bamako 1958 (photostat).
(République Soudanaise. Ministère de l'Agriculture et des Eaux et Forêts. Direction de l'Agriculture). "Programme de développement rural de la Haute-Vallée du Niger", Bamako 1959 (photostat).
République Soudanaise. Session budgetaire de l'Assemblée Législative. 17. November 1959, n. d.
Séminaire du Développement, Résolution générale. "Chambre de Commerce, d'Agriculture et d'Industrie de Bamako, Circulaire Mensuelle", April 1964.
2e Séminaire de l'Union Soudanaise-R. D. A. Bamako les 5—6—7 septembre 1962, Bamako 1963.
S. E. R. E. S. A. *Etude sur l'économie agricole du Soudan.* Vol. I. "Rapport général". Vol. II. "Etude des zones homogènes", 1959.
Statut général des Commercants, Chambre de Commerce, d'Agriculture et d'Industrie de Bamako. "Circulaire mensuelle d'information", Mai 1965.
(Traoré, S. L.), "Rapport sommaire sur les activités de l'Office du Niger", Ségou 1964 (photostat).

III. Important Monographies and Articles from Journals
(selection)

Afrika. *Ekonomičeskij spravočnik,* Moscow 1974.
Agrarnyj vopros i krest'janstvo v Tropičeskoj Afrike, Moscow 1964.
Amin, S., *Trois expériences africaines de développement: le Mali, la Guinée et le Ghana,* Paris 1965.
—, *L'Afrique de l'Ouest bloquée,* Paris 1971.
Ancian, G., "La modernisation du paysannat dans les Territoires d'Outre-Mer", *La Documentation Française, Notes et Etudes Documentaires,* 2129/1956.
Andreev, I. L., "Obščina i social'nye processy v osvoboždajuščejsja Afrike. Analiz opyta Respubliki Mali", in: *Voprosy filosofii,* Moscow, 8/1965.
—, "Perežitki aziatskogo sposoba proizvodstva v sovremennom afrikanskom obščestve", in: *Obščes i osobennoe v istoričeskom razvitii stran vostoka,* Moscow 1966.
Ansprenger, F., *Politik im Schwarzen Afrika,* Köln and Opladen 1961.
Arnauld, J., *Du colonialisme au socialisme,* Paris 1966.
—, *Procès du colonialisme,* Paris 1958.
Bâ, H./Dagst, J., *L'Empire Peul du Macina (1818—1853),* Paris 1962.
Bagdache, K., "V. I. Lenin and the Struggle against Opportunism and Revisionism in the National Liberation Movement", in: *World Marxist Review,* 4/1970.

Balandier, G., *Sociologie actuelle de l'Afrique Noire (Afrique centrale)*, Paris 1961.
Barbé, R., *Les classes sociales en Afrique Noire*, Paris 1964.
Barbé, R., "Les problèmes agraires dans les ex-colonies françaises d'Afrique Noire", in: *Recherches Internationales*, 22/1961.
Behrendt, R. F., *Soziale Strategie für Entwicklungsländer. Entwurf einer Entwicklungssoziologie*, Frankfurt/M. 1968.
Bélime, E., *Les travaux du Niger*, Lille 1940.
Bénot, Y., "Développement accéléré et révolution sociale en Afrique Occidentale", in: *La Pensée*, 126/1966.
—, *Idéologies des indépendances africaines*, Paris 1969.
Beuchelt, E., *Kulturwandel bei den Bambara von Ségou*, Bonn 1962.
—, *Mali*, Bonn 1966.
Bime, A., *Ségou, vieille capitale*, Angoulême 1962.
—, "Ségou-Koro et le Biton Mamari", in: *Notes Africaines*, 75/1957.
Boissier, J., "Le Chef de la terre en pays Sénoufo", in: *Outre-Mer*, 7/1935.
von Blankenburg, P., *Afrikanische Bauernwirtschaft auf dem Weg in eine moderne Landwirtschaft*, Frankfurt/Main 1965.
Bouche, D., *Les villages de liberté en Afrique Noire Française*, Paris 1968.
Bourjol, M., "Essai sur les transformations et l'évolution dialectique de la famille africaine de la 'gens' au 'ménage'", in: *Revue juridique et politique de l'Union Française*, Paris, 1/1957.
Boyer, M., *Les Sociétés Indigènes de Prévoyance, de Secours et de Prêts Mutuels Agricoles en Afrique Occidentale Française*, Paris 1935.
Braguinski, H., *Libération de l'Afrique*, Moscow, n. d.
Brehme, G., "Einparteiensystem und nationale Demokratie in Afrika", in: *Staat und Recht*, Berlin, 3/1966.
Büttner, Th., "Probleme des Feudalismus in Afrika in der vorkolonialen Periode" in: *Zeitschrift für Geschichtswissenschaft*, Berlin, 3/1964.
Capet, M., *Traité d'économie tropicale. Les économies de l'A. O. F.*, Paris, 1961.
Charbonneau, J./Charbonneau, R., *Marchés et marchands d'Afrique Noire*, Paris 1961.
Cissé, D., *Structure des Malinké de Kita*, Bamako 1970.
Cissé, D./Diabaté, M., *La dispersion des Mandeka*, Bamako 1970.
Coleman, J. S./Rosberg, C. G., *Political Parties and National Integration in Tropical Africa*, Berkeley and Los Angeles 1964.
Connaissance de la République du Mali, Bamako, n. d.
Cornevin, R./Cornevin, M., *Histoire de l'Afrique des origines à nos jours*, Paris 1964.
Coutumiers Juridiques de l'Afrique Occidentale Française, vol. 2: *Soudan*, Paris 1939.
Cremer, D. J.. *Les Bobo (la vie sociale)*, Paris 1924.
Delafosse, M., *Haut-Sénégal Niger*, Paris 1912.
Delval, J., "Le R. D. A. au Soudan Français", in: *L'Afrique et l'Asie*, 16/1951.
Dementév, J., "Kooperatovane v malinskoi derevne", in: *Mirovaja ekonomika i meždunarodnye otnošenija*, 7/1961.

Dementév, J., "Novoe v malinskoi derevne", in: *Azija i Afrika segodnja*, 10/1961.
Deschamps, H., *Les institutions politiques de l'Afrique Noire*, Paris 1965.
Desroche, H., *Coopération et développement. Mouvements coöpératifs et stratégie du développement*, Paris 1964.
"Le Développement de notre monde rural", in: *Le Mali*, 3/1965.
Dia, M., *Contribution à l'étude du mouvement coopératif en Afrique Noire*, Paris 1952.
Diabaté, M., *Si le feu s'éteignait*, Bamako 1967.
Dieterlen, G., *Essai sur la religion Bambara*, Paris 1951.
–, "Mythe et organisation sociale au Soudan Français", in: *Journal de la Société des Africanistes*, vol. XXV/1955, vol. XXIX/1959.
Diop, Ch. A., *L'Afrique Noire pré-coloniale*, Paris 1960.
Diop, M., *Contribution à l'étude des problèmes politiques en Afrique Noire*, Paris 1959.
Doublier, R., *La propriété foncière en A.O.F. Régime en droit privé*, Saint Louis 1952.
Domeneger, R./Letnev, A., "Parties and Problems of Democracy in the Countries of Tropical Africa", in: *World Marxist Review*, 10/1970.
Dumont, R., *Afrique Noire. Reconversion de l'économie agricole: Guinée, Côte d'Ivoire, Mali*, Paris 1961.
–, *L'Afrique Noire est mal partie*, Paris 1962.
–, *Economie agricole dans le Monde*, Paris 1954.
Dumont, R./Mazoyer, M., *Développement et socialisme*, Paris 1969.
Employment, Incomes and Equality. A strategy for increasing productive employment in Kenya, ILO, Geneva, 1972.
Engelberg, E., "Probleme der gesetzmäßigen Abfolge der Gesellschaftsformationen", in: *Zeitschrift für Geschichtswissenschaft*, Berlin, 2/1974.
Fanon, F., *Les damnés de la terre*, Paris 1961.
FAO. *Trade Year Book 1969*, vol. 23, Rome, 1970.
Fournier, F., "Aspects politiques du problème des chefféries au Soudan présahélien", in: *Revue juridique et politique de l'Union Française*, Paris, 1/1955.
Friedländer, P./Schilling, H., "Probleme des nichtkapitalistischen Entwicklungsweges der vom Kolonialjoch befreiten Staaten", in: *Einheit*, Berlin, 2/1965 and 3/1965.
Gallais, J., "Signification du groupe ethnique au Mali", in: *L'Homme*, 2/1962.
–, "La signification du village en Afrique Soudanienne de l'Ouest. Forces et faiblesses de la communauté villageoise", in: *Cahiers de Sociologie économique*, 2/1965.
–, "Le paysan Dogon", in: *Les Cahiers d'Outre-Mer*, Bordeaux, 70/1965.
Galloy/Vincent/Forget, *Nomades et paysans d'Afrique Noire Occidentale*, Nancy 1963.
de Ganay, S., "Les communautés d'entr'aide des Bambara du Soudan Français", in: *Actes du 5e Congrès International des Sciences Anthropologiques et Ethnologiques*, Philadelphia 1956.

Gavrilov, N. I., *Zapadnaja Afrika pod gnetom francii (1945—1959)*, Moscow, 1961.
—, "Respublika Mali — molodoe nezavisimoe gosudarstvo Afriki", in: *Narody Asii i Afriki*, Moscow, 4/1961.
Godelier, M., "La notion de 'mode de production asiatique' et les schémas marxistes d'évolution des sociétés", in: *Les Cahiers du C. E. R. M.*, Paris n. d.
Gouilly, A., *L'Islam dans l'Afrique Occidentale Française*, Paris 1922.
Guiffan, J., *Surpopulation et malnutrtion*, Paris 1969.
Hahn, E., *Historischer Materialismus und marxistische Soziologie. Studien zu methodologischen und erkenntnistheoretischen Grundlagen der soziologischen Forschung*, Berlin 1968.
Holas, B., *Les Senoufo (y compris les Minianka)*, Paris 1957.
Hopkins, N. S., *Popular Government in an African Town. Kita, Mali*, Chicago/London 1972.
Hutschenreuter, K., "New Disciplines of Science in the System of West German Neo-Colonialist Policy", in: *Theories on Africa and Neo-Colonialism*, Leipzig 1971.
Iskenderov, A. A., *Die nationale Befreiungsbewegung. Probleme, Gesetzmäßigkeiten, Perspektiven*, Berlin 1972.
Julis, G., "L'action des masses populaires au Mali. Les possibilités de leur intervention dans la vie politique et sociale", in: *Les Cahiers du C. E. R. M.*, Paris 1967.
—, "L'expérience de la République du Mali", in: *Economie et Politique*, July—August 1962.
Kamian, B., "Le rôle de la tradition et des sources musulmanes dans l'historiographie de l'Afrique Noire", in: *Le Mali*, 3/1966.
—, "Une ville de la République du Soudan: San", in: *Les Cahiers d'Outre-Mer*, 47/1959.
Kayser, B., *Economies et sociétés rurale dans le régions tropicales*, Paris 1961.
Khamiz, S./Rosaliev, J., "V. I. Lenin and the Current Problems of the National Liberation Movement", in: *World Marxist Review*, 12/1969.
Klassen und Klassenkampf in den Entwicklungsländern, vol. 1—3, Berlin 1969—1970.
Koné, J. M., "Les sociétés de culture dans le Cercle de Bougouni", in: *L'Education africaine*, 1944—1945.
Kondratyev, G. S., "Ob institute kantonalnych i derevenskich voždej v Respublike Mali", in: *Narody Azii i Afriki*, 4/1965.
—, *Put' Mali k nezavisimosti. 1945—1960*, Moscow 1970.
Körner, H., *Kolonialpolitik und Wirtschaftsentwicklung. Das Beispiel Französisch Westafrikas*, Stuttgart 1965.
Kouassigan, G. A., *L'Homme et la terre. Droits fonciers coutumiers et droit de propriété en Afrique Occidentale*, Paris 1966.
Koubbel, L. E., *Le problème de l'apparition des structures étatiques au Soudan Occidental*, Moscow 1967.
Kovrigina, N., "Gosudarstvennyj i častnyj sektor v ėkonomike Mali", in: *Mirovaja ėkonomika i meždunarodnye otnošenija*, 1/1967.

Kress, A., "On the Function of Neo-Colonialist Industrialisation Models", in: *Theories on Africa and Neo-Colonialism*, Leipzig 1971.
Krylov, V. V., "Osnovnye tendencii razvitija agrarnych otnošenii v Tropičeskoi Afrike", in: *Narody Azii i Afriki*, 4/1965.
Kuršakov, A. D., *Sozdanie gosudarstvenno-kooperativnogo sektora chozjajstva v uslovijach nekapitalističeskogo razvitija*, Leningrad 1969.
Kuznecova, S. I., *Social'naja struktura afrikanskogo goroda*, Moscow 1972.
Labouret, H., *Les Manding et leur langue*, Paris 1934.
—, *Les paysans d'Afrique Noire*, Paris 1941.
—, "Le travail familial chez les Mandingues", in: *L'Anthropologie*, 43/1933.
Letnev, A. B., *Derevnja zapadnogo Mali*, Moscow 1964.
—, "Social'naja differencija v Mali i sopredel'nych raionach Zapadnoi Afriki", in: *Narody Azii i Afriki*, 1/1963.
—, "Novoe v malinskoi derevne", in: *Sovetskaja etnografija*, 1/1964.
—, "Agrarnye otnošenija v Zapadnoi Afrike", in: *Mirovaja ėkonomika i meždunarodnye otnošenija*, 7/1962.
—, "Problèmes de l'évolution des rapports familiaux en Afrique occidentals", in: *Revue international de science sociale*, 3/1964.
Lévi-Strauss, C., *Les structures élémentaires de la parenté*, Paris 1949.
Lewin, G., "Zu einigen Problemen der 'asiatischen Produktionsweise' in der gesellschaftlichen Entwicklung Chinas", in: G. Lewin, *Die ersten fünfzig Jahre der Song-Dynastie in China*, Berlin 1973.
Leynaud, E., "Fraternités d'âge et sociétés de culture dans la Haute-Vallée du Niger", in: *Cahiers d'Etudes Africaines*, 21/1966.
—, *Les cadres sociaux de la vie rurale dans la Haute-Vallée du Niger*, Paris 1961.
Liebig, G., *Nationale und soziale Revolution in Afrika*, Berlin 1967.
Ligers, Z., *Les Sorko*, Paris 1964.
Makings, S. M., *Agricultural Problems of Developing Countries in Africa*, Nairobi/Addis Abeba 1967.
Malgras, R. P. D., "La condition sociale du paysan minyanka dans le Cercle de San", in: *Bulletin de l'I. F. A. N.*, series B., 1—2/1960.
Le Mali — Carrefour des Civilisations, Bamako 1971.
Le Mali en marche, Bamako n. d.
Maquet, J., *Africanité traditionelle et moderne*, Paris 1967.
Markov, W., "Afrika im Jahre Zehn", in: *Horizont*, Berlin, 36/1970.
—, *Arbeiterklasse und Bourgeoisie im antikolonialen Befreiungskampf*, Leipzig 1961.
—, "Zur universalgeschichtlichen Einordnung des afrikanischen Freiheitskampfes", in: *Geschichte und Geschichtsbild Afrikas*, Leipzig 1960.
—, "Fragen der Genesis und Bedeutung des vorimperialistischen Kolonialsystems", in: *Wissenschaftliche Zeitschrift der Karl-Marx-Universität Leipzig, Gesellschafts- und Sprachwissenschaftliche Reihe*, Leipzig, 1—2/1954—1955.
—, "La nation dans l'Afrique tropicale. Notion et structure", in: *L'Homme et la Société*, 2/1966.
Meillassoux, C., "Essai d'interprétation du phénomène économique dans les

sociétés traditionelles d'autosubsistance", in: *Cahiers d'Etudes Africaines*, 4/1960.
Meillassoux, C. "Histoire et institutions du Kafo de Bamako, d'après la tradition des Niaré", in: *Cahiers d'Etudes Africaines*, 14/1963.
Meillassoux, C., "The social structure of modern Bamako", in: *Africa*, 2/1965.
Mersljakov, N. S., *Stanovlanie nacionalnoj gosudarstvenosti Respubliki Mali*, Moscow 1966.
Michalski, K.-J., *Landwirtschaftliche Genossenschaften in afro-asiatischen Entwicklungsländern*, Berlin 1974.
Milcent, E., *L'A. O. F. entre en scène*, Paris 1958.
Mirski, G., "Sozialistische Tendenzen in den national befreiten Ländern", in: *Aus der Internationalen Arbeiterbewegung*, Berlin, 22/1966.
Mohr, H., "Vorkapitalistische Klassenformationen in der Diskussion", in: *Zeitschrift für Geschichtswissenschaft*, Berlin, 3/1964.
Monteil, Ch., *Les Bambara du Ségou et du Kaarta*, Paris 1924.
— *Une cité Soudanaise: Djénné, métropole du Delta Central du Niger*, Paris 1932.
Morlet, P., "Le Mali an VI", in: *L'Humanité*, 22.–29. 9. 1966.
N'Diayé, B., *Les castes au Mali*, Bamako 1970.
— *Groupes ethniques au Mali*, Bamako 1970.
Niane, D. T., *Soundjata ou l'Epopée Mandingue*, Paris 1960.
— *Recherches sur l'Empire du Mali au Moyen Age*, Conakry 1962.
Nichtkapitalistischer Entwicklungsweg. Aktuelle Probleme in Theorie und Praxis, Berlin 1972.
"L'Office du Niger", in: *La Documentation Française, Notes et Etudes Documentaires*, 2240/1956.
Non-capitalist Way of Development in the Third World, Warsaw 1971.
Olderogge, D. A./Potechin, I. I., *Die Völker Afrikas*, vol. 1 and 2, Berlin 1961.
Ortoli, H., "Le gage des personnes au Soudan Français", in: *Bulletin de l'I.F.A.N.*, 1/1939.
Otegbeye, T., "Leninism and the Problems of Revolution in Africa", in: *World Marxist Review*, 8/1970.
Oresz, A., *Einige wichtige Probleme der Erzeugung des gesellschaftlichen Bruttoproduktes, des Wachstums der industriellen und landwirtschaftlichen Produktion der Entwicklungsländer*, Budapest 1966.
Pageard, R., *Notes sur les Bambaras de Ségou*, Clichy 1957.
Palau Marti, M., *Les Dogons*, Paris 1957.
Paques, V., *Les Bambara*, Paris 1954.
—, "Dans une village soudanais, est-il possible; est-il souhaitable d'améliorer la productivité?" in: *Productivité Française*, 19–20/1953.
Paulme, D., *Organisation sociale des Dogon*, Paris 1940.
—, "Régime fonciers traditionnels en Afrique Noire", in: *Présence Africaine*, 48/1963.
Perroux, F., *L'économie des jeunes nations*, Paris 1962.
Petit-Pont, M., *Structures traditionelles et développement*, Paris 1968.

Pfeffer, K. H., *Welt im Umbruch. Gesellschaftliche und geistige Probleme in den Entwicklungsländern*, Gütersloh 1966.

"Une nouvelle phase du mouvement coopératif au Mali", in: *Le Mali*, 1/1966.

"Un point capital de notre politique économique: la commercialisation des produits agricole", in: *Le Mali*, 5/1965.

Potechin, I. I., *Afrika blickt in die Zukunft*, Berlin 1961.

—, "Land Relations in African Countries", in: *The African Communist*, 15/1963.

—, "Über den 'afrikanischen Sozialismus'", in: *Aus der Internationalen Arbeiterbewegung*, Berlin, 7 and 8/1963.

Probleme des Aufbaus einer progressiven Landwirtschaft in den Entwicklungsländern, Leipzig 1970.

Le problème de vulgarisation agricole dans la région de Barouéli (Soudan Français), in: Bulletin mensuel de l'Agence économiques de l'A. O. F., 18/1937.

Problemy nacional'nogo-osvoboditel'nogo dviženija. Materialy meždunarodnogo simpoziuma, Alma-Ata 1969, Moscow 1970.

"Progrès notables dans le production du coton", in: *Le Mali*, 2/1965.

Radčenko, G. F., *Respublika Mali*, Moscow 1969.

Radcliffe-Brown, A. R./ Forde, D., *Systèmes familiaux et matrimoniaux en Afrique*, Paris 1953.

Rathmann, L. et al., *Grundfragen des antiimperialistischen Kampfes der Völker Asiens, Afrikas und Lateinamerikas in der Gegenwart*, part 1, Berlin 1974.

Razvivajuščiesja strany: zakonomernosti, tendencii, perspektivy, Moscow 1974.

"La République du Mali", in: *La Documentation française. Notes et Etudes documentaires*, 2739/1961.

Revolution und Tradition. Zur Rolle der Tradition im antiimperialistischen Kampf der Völker Afrikas und Asiens, Leipzig 1971.

Richard-Molard, J., *Afrique Occidentale Française*, Paris 1956.

Ringer, K., *Agrarverfassung im tropischen Afrika. Zur Lehre von der Agrarverfassung: Veränderungen zur Hebung der Agrartechnik*, Freiburg im Breisgau 1963.

Rosaliev, J., "Asia and Africa: Capitalism and Problems of Socialist Orientation", in: *World Marxist Review*, 7/1970.

Rouch, J., *Les Songhay*, Paris 1954.

Rymalov, V. V., *Die UdSSR und die wirtschaftlich schwach entwickelten Länder*, Berlin 1964.

Sarraut, A., *La mise en valeur des colonies françaises*, Paris 1923.

Schelepin, V., "The World of Socialism and the Developing Countries", in: *New Times*, 9/1970.

Schilling, H., *EWG-Schatten über Afrika*, Berlin 1963.

Seibel, D., "Struktureller und funktionaler Wandel der Familie in Afrika", in: *Afrika heute* (Special Issue), 5/1967.

Sidibé, M., "Les Gens de caste ou Nyamakala au Soudan Français", in: *Notes Africaines*, 81/1959.

Skorov, G. N., *Francuzkij imperializm v Zapadnoj Afriki*, Moscow 1596.

"So, village de culture", in: *L'Education Africaine*, 32/1956.

Sobolev, A., "National Democracy – the Path to Social Progress", in: *World Marxist Review*, 2/1963.
Solodovnikov, V. G., *Nekotorye voprosy teorii i praktiki nekapitalističeskogo puti razvitija*, Moscow 1971.
Spitz, G., *Sansanding. Les irrigations du Niger*, Paris 1949.
–, *Le Soudan Français*, Paris 1955.
Stöber, H., "Zum Problem des Feudalismus in Afrika vor der Kolonialherrschaft", in: *Ethnographisch-Archäologische Zeitschrift*, Berlin, 12/1971.
4th Summit Conference of the Non-Aligned Countries, Algiers, September 1973, Economic Declaration.
Suret-Canale, J., "Les fondéments sociaux de la vie politique africaine contemporaine", in: *Recherches Internationales*, 22/1961.
–, "Les sociétés traditionelles de l'Afrique tropicale et le concept du mode de production asiatique", in: *La Pensée*, 117/1964.
–, *Schwarzafrika. Geschichte West- und Zentralafrikas*, vol. 1, Berlin 1966.
–, "La communauté villageoise en Afrique tropicale et sa signification sociale", in: *Études Africaines*, Leipzig 1967.
–, "Tribes, Classes and Nations in Tropical Africa", in: *World Marxist Review*, 11/1969.
–, *French Colonialism in Tropical Africa, 1900–1945* (translated from the French by T. Gottheiner), London 1971.
Svanidze, I. A., *Problemy razvitija sel'skogo chozjajstva Afriki*, Moscow 1969.
– *Sel'skoje chozjajstvo tropičeskoj Afriki*, Moscow 1972.
Sy, S. M., *Recherches sur l'exercice du pouvoir politique en Afrique Noire (Côte d'Ivoire, Guinée, Mali)*, Paris 1965.
Tauxier, L., *Histoire des Bambara*, Paris 1942.
Theories on Africa and Neo-Colonialism, Leipzig 1971.
Thole, G., "Die Republik Mali", in: *Geographische Berichte*, Berlin, 4/1967.
Thomas, L. V., *Le socialisme et l'Afrique*, Paris 1966.
Thompson, V./Adloff, R., *French West Africa*, Stanford 1957.
Tökei, F., *Sur le monde de production asiatique*, Budapest 1966.
Tradition und nichtkapitalistischer Entwicklungsweg in Afrika. Probleme der Überwindung vorkapitalistischer Verhältnisse in Basis und Überbau, Berlin 1971.
Traoré, I. B., *Un héros: Koumi-Diossé. (Plutôt la mort que la honte)*, Bamako 1962.
Trappe, P., *Die Entwicklungsfunktion des Genossenschaftswesens am Beispiel ostafrikanischer Stämme*, Neuwied/Berlin 1966.
–, *Warum Genossenschaften in Entwicklungsländern?* Neuwied/Berlin 1966.
Le travail en Afrique Noire, Paris 1952.
Tricart, J., "Les échanges entre la zone forestière de la Côte d'Ivoire et les savannes soudaniennes", in: *Les Cahiers d'Outre-Mer*, 35/1956.
Tyagunenko, V., "Aktuelle Fragen des nichtkapitalistischen Entwicklungsweges", in: *Sowjetwissenschaft, Gesellschaftswissenschaftliche Beiträge*, 3/1965.
Tyulpanov, S., *Das Kolonialsystem des Imperialismus und sein Zerfall*, Berlin 1959.
–, *Politische Ökonomie und ihre Anwendung in den Entwicklungsländern*, Berlin 1972.

Uschner, M., "Der Leninismus und Probleme der antiimperialistischen Befreiungsbewegung von heute", in: *Horizont*, Berlin, 24/1970.
Ulyanovski, R., "Der Einfluß des wissenschaftlichen Sozialismus auf die nationale Befreiungsbewegung", in: *Aus der Internationalen Arbeiterbewegung*, Berlin, 13 and 14/1968.
—, "On some Questions of Non-Capitalist Development in Afro-Asian Countries", in: *World Marxist Review*, 9/1969.
—, "Besonderheiten und Schwierigkeiten der nationaldemokratischen Revolution auf dem nichtkapitalistischen Entwicklungsweg", in: *Einheit*, Berlin, 6/1970.
—, "Leninism, Soviet Experiences and the Liberated Countries, in: *New Times*, 1/1971.
—, Der Sozialismus und die befreiten Länder, Berlin 1973.
UN, ECA. *Statistical Yearbook 1973* (part 1–4), Addis Abeba 1974.
UN, ECA. *Statistical Yearbook. West Africa 1973*, Addis Abeba 1974.
UN, ECA. *Survey of Economic Conditions in Africa 1970* (part 1), New York 1971.
UN. *Statistical Yearbook 1972*, New York 1973.
Vellas, P., *Moyens sociaux du développement économiques*, Paris 1968.
Villien-Rossi, M.-L., "Bamako, capitale du Mali", in: *Bulletin de l'I. F. A. N.*, sér. B, 1–2/1966.
Viguier, P., *L'Afrique de l'Ouest vue par un agriculteur: Problèmes de base en Afrique tropicale*, Paris 1968.
Vladimirova, K. V./Zalnin, V. V., *Respublika Mali. Social'no-ėkonomičeskie problemy*, Moscow 1970.
Wibaux, F., "Le mouvement coopératif en Afrique Occidentale Française", Paris 1953 (photostat).
de Wilde, J. C., *Expériences de developpement agricole en Afrique tropicale*, Paris 1967.
Woddis, J., *Africa: The Roots of Revolt*, London 1960.
—, *Africa: The Lion Awakes*, London 1961.
—, *Africa: The Way Ahead*, London 1963.
Ziegler, J., *Sociologie de la nouvelle Afrique*, Paris 1964.

IV. Important Bibliographies, Journals and Newspapers

Bibliographies

Brasseur, P., *Bibliographie générale du Mali*, Dakar 1964.
Joucla, E., *Bibliographie de l'Afrique Occidentale Française*, Paris 1937.

Journals

Afrika Heute, Bonn.
L'Afrique et l'Asie, Paris.
Aus der Internationalen Arbeiterbewegung, Berlin.
Bulletin de l'Afrique Noire (BAN), Paris.

Bulletin de l'I. F. A. N. (BIFAN), sér. B, Dakar.
Cahiers d'Etudes Africaines, Paris.
Les Cahiers d'Outre-Mer (COM), Bordeaux.
Einheit, Berlin.
Horizont, Berlin.
Le Mali, Bamako.
Mirovaja ėkonomika i meždunarodnye otnošenija, Moscow.
Narody Azii i Afriki, Moscow.
Présence Africaine, Dakar.
World Marxist Review, Prague.
Revue juridique et politique de l'Union Française, Paris.
New Times, Moscow.

Newspapers

L'Afrique Nouvelle, Dakar.
Neues Deutschland, Berlin.
L'Essor, Bamako.
L'Humanité, Paris.
Le Monde, Paris.